KU-052-741

PROMOTING PARTNERSHIP FOR HEALTH

Effective Interprofessional Education

Argument, Assumption and Evidence

Hugh Barr
Ivan Koppel
Scott Reeves
Marilyn Hammick
Della Freeth

Series editor: Hugh Barr

b 194379.

LIBRARY

ACC. No. 366254 9 DEPT

CLASS No.

UNIVERSITY
OF CHESTER

Blackwell Publishing

CAIPE

© 2005 by Blackwell Publishing Ltd

Editorial offices:
Blackwell Publishing Ltd, 9600 Garsington Road, Oxford OX4 2DQ, UK
  Tel: +44 (0)1865 776868
Blackwell Publishing Inc., 350 Main Street, Malden, MA 02148-5020, USA
  Tel: +1 781 388 8250
Blackwell Publishing Asia Pty Ltd, 550 Swanston Street, Carlton, Victoria 3053, Australia
  Tel: +61 (0)3 8359 1011

The right of the Authors to be identified as the Authors of this Work has been asserted in accordance with the Copyright, Designs and Patents Act 1988.

All rights reserved. No part of this publication may be reproduced, stored in a retrieval system, or transmitted, in any form or by any means, electronic, mechanical, photocopying, recording or otherwise, except as permitted by the UK Copyright, Designs and Patents Act 1988, without the prior permission of the publisher.

First published 2005 by Blackwell Publishing Ltd

Library of Congress Cataloging-in-Publication Data
Effective interprofessional education : argument, assumption, and evidence / by Hugh Barr ... [et al.].
    p. ; cm. – (Promoting partnership for health)
  Includes bibliographical references and index.
  ISBN-13: 978-1-4051-1654-1 (hardback : alk. paper)
  ISBN-10: 1-4051-1654-4 (hardback : alk. paper)
  1. Medical education. 2. Social work education. 3. Interprofessional relations. 4. Interdisciplinary approach in education.
I. Barr, Hugh. II. Series.
  [DNLM: 1. Health Occupations–education. 2. Education, Professional–methods.
3. Interdisciplinary Communication. 4. Interprofessional Relations. W 18 E268 2005]
R834.E355   2005
610′.71′1–dc22

2004030717

ISBN-13: 978-1-4051-1654-1
ISBN-10: 1-4051-1654-4

A catalogue record for this title is available from the British Library

Set in 10/12.5pt Palatino
by SPI Publisher Services, Pondicherry, India
Printed and bound in India
by Replika Press Pvt, Ltd, Kundli

The publisher's policy is to use permanent paper from mills that operate a sustainable forestry policy, and which has been manufactured from pulp processed using acid-free and elementary chlorine-free practices. Furthermore, the publisher ensures that the text paper and cover board used have met acceptable environmental accreditation standards.

For further information on Blackwell Publishing, visit our website:
www.blackwellpublishing.com

Contents

List of Boxes

List of Figures

List of Tables

Appendices

Contributors

Hugh Barr is Emeritus Professor of Interprofessional Education in the School of Integrated Health at the University of Westminster, Visiting Professor in Interprofessional Education in the School of Health and Social Care at the University of Greenwich, President of the UK Centre for the Advancement of Interprofessional Education (CAIPE) and Editor-in-Chief of the *Journal of Interprofessional Education*. He was formerly an Assistant Director of the then Central Council for Education and Training in Social Work.

Ivan Koppel is senior partner in an inner-city general practice in London, whose work is based on close collaboration between different professional and occupational groups. He also holds a post of Principal Lecturer at the School of Integrated Health, University of Westminster, where he is involved in teaching on the range of interprofessional courses. His research interest is in analysis of discourses in continuing and interprofessional education.

Scott Reeves is a Research Fellow in the Health Care Education Development Unit, St Bartholomew's School of Nursing and Midwifery, City University. He is also a Senior Research Fellow at the Faculty of Health and Social Care, London South Bank University. Scott is a sociologist who collaborates with colleagues from a range of health and social care backgrounds. His work focuses on the evaluation of interprofessional education and collaboration. Scott is an Associate Editor of the *Journal of Interprofessional Care*.

Marilyn Hammick is an education and research consultant, Visiting Professor of Interprofessional Education, School of Health Care Practice, Anglia Polytechnic University; Associate Editor of *Journal of Interprofessional Care*; Vice-chair of CAIPE and Consultant to Best Evidence Medical Education. Her international work includes mentoring systematic review groups and she is external evaluator to nationally funded interprofessional education projects. Marilyn was previously a Senior Lecturer, Centre for Research in Medical and Dental Education, University of Birmingham, and Reader in Interprofessional Education, Oxford Brookes University.

Della Freeth is Reader in Education for Health Care Practice at City University, London, based in the Health Care Education Development Unit at the St Bartholomew's School of Nursing and Midwifery. She is an educationalist who works alongside a wide range of health professionals, supporting the development and evaluation of educational initiatives. Her personal research interests have two overlapping foci, interprofessional collaboration and learning through simulated professional practice. She is a Board Member of CAIPE and an Associate Editor of the *Journal of Interprofessional Care*.

The Series

Promoting Partnership for Health

Health is everybody's responsibility: individuals, families, communities, professions, businesses, charities and public services. It is more than prevention and cure of disease. It is life-fulfilling for the well-being of all. Each party has its role, but effective health improvement calls for partnership, more precisely for many partnerships, which bring them together in innovative and imaginative ways. The scope for this series is correspondingly wide.

Successive books will explore partnership for health from policy, practice and educational perspectives. All three drive change. Policy presses the pace of reform everywhere, but change is also driven by the demands of practice, triggered by economic and social trends, technological advance and rising public expectations. Education responds, but also initiates, as a change agent in its own right.

Progressive health care is client centred. The series will wholeheartedly endorse that principle, but the client is also relative, citizen, client and consumer:

- Relative sustaining, and sustained by, family
- Citizen working for, and benefiting from, community, country and comity of nations
- Client of countless professions
- Consumer of health-enhancing or health-harming services

A recurrent theme will be the roles and responsibilities of professions, individually and collectively, to promote and sustain health. The focus will be on the health and social care professions, but taking into account the capability of every profession to improve or impair health. The responsibility of the professions in contemporary society will resonate throughout the series, starting from the premise that shared values of professionalism carry an inescapable obligation to further the health and well-being of all.

Each book will compare and contrast national perspectives, from developing and so-called developed nations, set within a global appreciation of opportunities and threats to health. Each will be driven, not simply by self-evident scope for one nation to learn from another, but also by the need to respond to challenges that pay no respect to national borders and can only be addressed by concerted action.

Partnership has become so fashionable that it is tempting to assume that all reasonable men and women will unite in common cause. Experience teaches otherwise: best laid plans too often founder for lack of attention to differences which can bedevil relationships between professions and between organisations. This series will not be starry-eyed. It will alert readers to the pitfalls and to ways to avoid them.

The three books introducing the series focus on collaborative working and learning between services and between professions in health and social care. In the first, Meads & Ashcroft *et al.* (2005) find collaboration critical to effective implementation of health care reforms around the world. In the second, this book makes the case for interprofessional education as a means to promote collaborative practice, corroborated by emerging evidence from systematic searches of the literature. In the third, Freeth *et al.* (2005) marry evidence with experience, to assist teachers to develop, deliver and evaluate interprofessional education programmes. All three books transcend professional, organisational and national boundaries to share experience as widely as possible for the common good, as they set the tone for the series.

Hugh Barr
Series Editor
October 2004

List of other books in this series

Freeth, D., Hammick, M., Reeves, S., Koppel, I. & Barr, H. (2005) *Effective Interprofessional Education: Development, Delivery and Evaluation*. Blackwell Publishing, Oxford.

Meads, G. & Ashcroft, J. with Barr, H., Scott, R. & Wild, A. (2005) *The Case for Interprofessional Collaboration*. Blackwell Publishing, Oxford.

Foreword by Gerard Majoor

The quality of health care suffers everywhere from fragmentation between services and between professions. Barriers are erected, not only between public health, primary care, social care and hospital-based services but also between medical, nursing, social work, allied health, management and other professions.

Each student identifies with his or her future profession, learning from its esteemed senior members and reinforced by allegiance to its associations. Valuable though this process undoubtedly is in building mutual support and discipline, it all too easily results in rigid and protective demarcations between professions who need to work closely together to respond effectively to the needs of the same patients, families and communities.

'If education is part of the problem, it must also be part of the solution', as Hugh Barr and his co-authors assert in the opening chapter of this book. Fragile though it may be, interprofessional education is a laudable attempt to deal with the downside of the professionalisation process and, more positively, to prepare health and social care students for collaboration. The key to success lies in ensuring that future interprofessional education programmes are grounded in best practice based on the evidence. This book offers an invaluable source of such information, following an exhaustive and systematic search of the literature worldwide for the most rigorous examples of interprofessional education so far reported. At the same time, it exposes conventional wisdom about interprofessional education to critical review in the light of the evidence assembled and provides a baseline for the future development of interprofessional education before and after qualification in the classroom and the workplace.

Persuasive though the case for interprofessional education is, it is difficult to establish partnerships between different institutions educating different types of health professionals and practice agencies. It is hard to harmonise curricula, to attune time schedules for teaching in college and practice and sometimes to surmount differences between teachers. But we must. Interprofessional education is one of the much needed strategies to reduce compartmentalisation and to improve the quality of health care.

Educational institutions all over the world are now introducing interprofessional education and documenting their experience. I am convinced that this book will be of great help to all those who are ready to take up that challenge.

Gerard Majoor PhD, Chairman
The Network: Towards Unity for Health
Faculty of Medicine
Maastricht University, The Netherlands

Foreword by Madeline Schmitt

It is a privilege to write a foreword for this text, which is one of a set of three books[1] addressing the rationale for, the evidence and the approaches to interprofessional education (IPE), published by Blackwell to initiate a landmark series on IPE under the guidance of Hugh Barr. We, the readers, owe a great debt to Professor Barr for his willingness to undertake the responsibility as series editor, and to him and his colleagues for the vision, persistence and careful scholarship that has resulted in the publication of these first three books.

The interest in IPE is linked with demands justified by evidence that collaborative delivery models can be more effective and efficient than traditional ones. That evidence is developing and supports the expectation that educational programmes will prepare professionals-in-training, as well as current practitioners, for collaborative work. The question is *how best* to prepare current and future professionals for practice, recognizing that health and social care is complex and that 'one size' in IPE does not fit all. This volume is written to provide us with the best evidence to date based on eight years of systematic review work with the relevant, mostly English-language, literature. The authors also strive to place the evidence in the context of discussion of broader educational issues, based on their extensive experience in implementing IPE and familiarity with a broader literature.

Publication of this volume could not come at a better time. The global, although heavily Western, perspective adopted by these UK-based authors is consistent with increasing worldwide interest in how better teamwork and collaboration among health, social care and other professionals, working in partnership with clients and their families, may more effectively address challenges in health promotion and health care delivery. In the US, heightened nationwide interest is linked to a series of reports prepared by the Institute of Medicine (IOM)[2] on health care safety and quality. Interprofessional teamwork and collaboration are prominent among the solutions proposed for both problems.

Following the initial IOM reports, in 2003 The Committee on the Health Professions Education Summit for the Board of Health Care Services of the Institute of Medicine published a report of a national interdisciplinary invitational conference of health care leaders convened in 2002[3]. The purpose of the Summit was 'to discuss and develop strategies for restructuring clinical education across the full continuum of education' (p.3). The Report focuses on five areas of competency identified by the Committee as core to all health professions' efforts to improve the safety and quality of heath care. These were patient-centered care, interdisciplinary teams, evidence-based practice, quality improvement and informatics.

The Committee noted that these are interrelated areas and adopted the following vision reflecting that inter-relationship, which is broadly consistent with the vision for this Blackwell Publishing series:

> 'All health professionals should be educated to deliver patient-centered care as members of an interdisciplinary team, emphasizing evidence-based practice, quality improvement approaches, and informatics' (p. 3).

The Committee noted that in the US:

- there is a major disconnect between isolated professional education and increasing expectations for interdisciplinary team-based care and that interdisciplinary [interprofessional] education is not yet 'the norm';
- there is reluctance to expand interdisciplinary education related to lack of research evidence on the relationship of this type of education to interdisciplinary practice and patient care; further,
- 'there is not much [evidence] about various teaching approaches' (p. 133).

Indeed, minimal research related to IPE was cited in the Report[3]. The Committee's recommendations included the allocation of government and foundation money to support research projects linking the five core competencies, including interdisciplinary team competencies, to individual and population health outcomes, and research related to evidence-based education and the identified competencies.

It is important not to 'reinvent the wheel' as further research is undertaken, simultaneously with the development and implementation of new IPE programs, but to build on what we already know based on available evidence. Professor Barr and his co-authors provide the base on which to build. Ironically, despite the assertions about lack of evidence from the US Committee on the Health Professions Education Summit, over half of the 107 higher quality studies that are the focus of analysis for the review of evidence were conducted in the US (with most of the remaining literature emanating from the UK). This difference in perception may be related to the lack of systematic efforts to evaluate the IPE literature prior to this volume. The US Committee's efforts to cover a broad scope of issues/ literature related to *five* separate competencies in the rapid time frame typical of Institute of Medicine analyses understandably uncovered little of this evidence. A perusal of the list of higher quality studies comprising the evidence reported in this volume suggests that the relevant literature is diverse and widely scattered, and, as the authors note, needed to be gleaned from a much larger body of material, an activity that was a core part of the eight-year focused effort of the evaluation team to assess comprehensively the extant IPE literature.

The evaluation team's earliest effort to conduct an assessment took the form of a Cochrane systematic review that found no studies that met its stringent criteria. In this book the authors do a thorough job of assessing the characteristics of the methodologically strongest IPE literature available. They developed multiple classification and typological schemes for search, evaluation and presentation of the evidence. Thus, in Chapters four to seven, we are informed, for example, about whether the learners represented in the studies were mostly pre-qualifying students or post-qualifying professionals; what professions they predominately represented; what proportion of the IPE initiatives examined were college or service initiated; whether the IPE targeted development of the individual professional, the collaborative enterprise, or service improvement; what types of educational models and learning approaches were most commonly used; and what outcomes were examined with what results. The authors employ more complex typologies to show the relationship of some of these key elements to each other. Throughout the book these classifications are brought to life through liberal use of brief boxed descriptions of studies to illustrate examples of various forms of IPE. They also characterise the nature of the research designs employed and the approaches to collecting data on the IPE experience.

The classifications and typologies are extremely helpful in making the strengths and weaknesses of current evidence related to IPE apparent, enabling readers to see more clearly what we do know, as well as the opportunity areas related to striking gaps in the evidence. In addition, use of these classifications and typologies enable the reader of a new piece of IPE research to quickly classify it and evaluate its strengths and weaknesses in relation to the current evidence.

A note of caution about the possible misinterpretation of the book's content is relevant here. The focus of this book is on the evaluation of the *best research evidence about IPE and its outcomes*. There is no information provided, as the authors explain, about the characteristics of the articles that were screened out of the evaluation of evidence. Thus, the reported frequencies of studies with particular characteristics should not be misinterpreted as comments about the frequency in the IPE literature as a whole. For example, the reported preponderance of service-led (as compared to college or jointly-led) IPE in the sample of 107 studies should not lead to the conclusion that this distribution characterises the entire body of IPE literature. Indeed, it might be that the literature as a whole is dominated by college-led reports. If this were true, the conclusion would be that college-led studies were more likely to be weakly designed as fewer of them passed the methodological screening criteria established by the evaluation team.

The parts of the book that go beyond the evidence are as valuable to the reader as they systematically address some of the less explored, more fundamental aspects of IPE that lend breadth and depth to the discussion, as well as highlighting some of the greatest challenges. The authors present multiple approaches and conflicting viewpoints, which encourage readers to reflect on their own particular positions. For example, in the chapter on theories the authors note the lack of explicit content about theoretical underpinnings in the research reviewed, and they acknowledge that theory-building in IPE is 'contested territory'. For those open to the use of theory as a means of enriching the knowledge base of IPE, they offer helpfully categorised brief discussions of a wide range of theories from different disciplines that may usefully frame knowledge development. In the chapter on values, the authors identify 'competing perceptions about its [IPE] very nature and purpose', and remind the reader that it is perilous to ignore or avoid discussions of value differences. The authors do not leave readers hanging about their own position on these issues. They offer a conceptual framework for how IPE improves relationships between professions, leads to positive work outcomes, and contributes to improved client care that provides hypotheses for future research, and they propose a shared set of values that they believe have the potential to move the field of IPE forward.

In the early days of IPE there was often a large disconnect between college-based learning and the experience of practice. Although health and social care require diverse health professions to interact on a daily basis, the consequences of ignoring the quality of those interactions for processes of care and outcomes of those processes have only been acknowledged broadly in the last decade. Efforts to introduce formal IPE into practice settings in response to concerns about safety and quality are concurrent with renewed college-led IPE efforts. This encourages optimism that interprofessional attitudes, values, knowledge, skills and behavior developed in college-based training will be more valued and positively reinforced in the practice experience. Future health and social care professionals exposed to IPE during training should then be better prepared for the realities of practice, rather than disillusioned by their practice experiences.

Long-term, the success of IPE depends heavily on the continuing demonstration of its effectiveness in educating health and social care professionals and establishing the links between IPE models and practice changes that improve safety and quality. Its success, however, also depends heavily on other professional, political and, especially, financial factors. How the professions respond through their licensing, accrediting and certification processes, how government administrators respond to the idea of IPE in the development of policy, and how payors in health systems in different countries allocate health care money that support and reinforce collaborative models of care are also critical factors. These are parts of the IPE story that I hope will be told in future volumes in this series.

Madeline H. Schmitt PhD, RN, FAAN, FNAP
Professor and Independence Foundation Chair in Nursing and
Interprofessional Education, University of Rochester, School of
Nursing, Rochester, New York

Notes

1. Meads, G. & Ashcroft, J., with Barr, H., Scott, R., and Wild, A. (2005) *The Case for Interprofessional Collaboration*. Oxford: Blackwell Publishing.
   Barr, H., Koppel, I., Reeves, S., Hammick, M. & Freeth, D. (2005). *Effective Interprofessional Education: Argument, Assumption and Evidence*. Oxford: Blackwell Publishing.
   Freeth, D., Hammick, M., Reeves, S., Koppel, I. & Barr, H. (2005). *Effective Interprofessional Education: Development, Delivery and Evaluation*. Oxford: Blackwell Publishing.
2. Institute of Medicine. (L.T. Kohn, J. M. Corrigan, and M.S. Donaldson (Eds)). (2000) *To Err is Human: Building a Safer Health System*. Washington, DC: National Academies Press and Institute of Medicine. (2001) *Crossing the Quality Chasm: A New Health System for the 21st Century*. Washington, DC: National Academies Press.
3. Institute of Medicine. (A.C. Greiner & E. Knebel. (Eds)) (2003) *Health Professions Education: A Bridge to Quality*. Washington, DC: National Academies Press.

Preface

This book, as originally conceived, would have been a relatively short account of a systematic review of interprofessional education in health and social care and its findings. We were, however, encouraged by our publisher to be more ambitious, to build those findings into a wider-ranging critique of interprofessional education, grounded in our experience and informed by sources beyond the few evaluations that qualified for inclusion in the review.

Synthesising the evidence base for interprofessional education has nevertheless remained central. Claims made for interprofessional education, to the effect that it improves collaboration between professions and thereby the quality of care, are no longer taken on trust. More is expected after thirty years of experience. Sustained efforts over eight years to evaluate evidence regarding the effectiveness of interprofessional education lie at the heart of this book, based on findings from systematic reviews which we have conducted as a team drawn from five professions.

We began by adopting strictly circumscribed criteria for evidence, consistent with the conduct of a Cochrane Review for Effective Practice and the Organisation of Care (EPOC) as reported by Zwarenstein *et al.* (1999 & 2001). We revised those criteria in our subsequent review (Freeth *et al.*, 2002) to make it more inclusive, as we realised that methodologies and outcomes consistent with a Cochrane Review were excluding many relevant reports.

The scope of these other reviews leads us to believe that we have come as close as may be possible to establishing the evidence base from existing data. New evaluations will generate new findings, evaluations which, if recent trends continue, will tend to be more rigorous, more credible and more dependable, but our knowledge of work in hand counsels caution in expecting early and dramatic advances. Further progress is likely to be incremental. Meanwhile, judgements must be based upon the best available evidence.

But we do more than amass evidence; we revisit conventional wisdom about interprofessional education in the light of that evidence. In doing so we call upon examples from the more rigorous and better presented evaluations, on which we concentrate.

Acknowledging, as we do, the good in past and present interprofessional achievements, this book sets an agenda to help all the interested parties to do better. It is driven by the conviction that the more informed interprofessional educators become, the more effective they will be in helping to improve interprofessional practice for the benefit of individuals, families and communities.

Lessons learned must be applied, weaknesses remedied and efforts renewed to investigate those questions for which answers have so far proved elusive.

Evidence is presented to inform policy making, programme planning, teaching and research. We have included information for our fellow researchers about ways in which interprofessional education has been evaluated – the questions framed, the methodologies applied and the findings presented. Armed with this information, it falls to them to extend methodological range and enhance rigour in conducting future evaluations. Much of this book is a distillation of their work.

We have tried to lay a foundation upon which policy makers, programme planners, teachers and researchers can build. We offer practical help in constructing the edifice in the companion volume, *Effective Interprofessional Education: Development, Delivery and Evaluation* (Freeth *et al.*, 2005), more precisely many different edifices, to realise the full potential of interprofessional education.

Both books are written as single texts. They tie in closely with a third book in the series, again prepared in parallel and in close collaboration by Meads & Ashcroft *et al.* (2005), which grounds interprofessional practice in collaboration required to effect reforms in health and social care worldwide. Each of the three books complements the others and paves the way for future contributions to the series.

In common with its companion volumes, this book is addressed to readers in the many different countries in which interprofessional education has taken root. (Readers wishing to focus on UK developments are referred to Barr, 2002). Our own experience is primarily in the UK, albeit enjoying frequent contact with colleagues around the world, reinforced by association with the *Journal of Interprofessional Care*, which is a channel for international exchange about matters interprofessional.

We have taken into account, too, what we have learned from exchanges through the national and international networks to which we belong, observation of developments and innovations at home and abroad, and active engagement in the interprofessional field as teachers and researchers, honed during many hours of debate in the team.

Alive to the risks when authors from one country endeavour to address developments in others, we invited Professor Madeline Schmitt from the United States to be our critical reader to help ensure international relevance, to challenge UK bias and to test comprehension in the context of different cultures and different health, social care and professional education systems.

Interprofessional education and practice know no boundaries. They occur whenever and wherever professions collaborate in response to public and personal needs and expectations. Our field is collaboration between professions in health and social care, a field around which it is neither easy nor helpful to draw a rigid boundary. Different professions are involved in different configurations, in different practice settings, within and between different organisations. Such collaboration comes within our purview, provided that at least one health or social care profession is included among the professions participating.

As the field has become more diverse it has been broken down into manageable parts – child protection, mental health, learning difficulties, palliative care and primary care to name but a few – including different configurations of professions and informed by different policies and priorities for education and practice, and by different academic disciplines. We look for lessons which these traditions can learn from each other. We try to put Humpty Dumpty together again so that approaches to collaborative education and practice can be combined.

Interprofessional education is bedevilled by terminological inexactitude. Competing terms have been introduced over time as it has taken root in different fields and settings, introducing subtle nuances and not a little confusion. On closer examination, however, those terms illuminate underlying differences in values, perceptions and expectations.

While endeavouring to use terms consistently, we probe behind the words in search of intended or unintended meanings that help or hinder understanding of the phenomenon which we call 'interprofessional education'. Where possible a common set of definitions is employed applicable to both books. They can be found in the Glossary for each.

We prefer an earlier definition for interprofessional education, as follows, to that published by CAIPE (1997):

'Occasions when two or more professions learn with, from and about each other to improve collaboration and the quality of care.'

We abide by CAIPE's definition of multiprofessional education as follows:

'Occasions when two or more professions learn side by side.'

Interprofessional education is a product of the education and practice systems between which it operates, systems which are markedly different from country to country. That makes this book more complex, but potentially more enriching. The challenge has been to embrace diversity between countries and fields of practice within a coherent and unifying frame of reference.

This book is divided into ten chapters. The first three set the scene for the systematic review and its findings. Chapter one identifies some of the many challenges to which interprofessional education responds. No one programme can hope to address them all. Rather, they set an agenda for different types of interprofessional education to be addressed along a continuum. Chapter two demonstrates how interprofessional education responds to one particular challenge, namely increasing demands in practice, which exceed the capacity of any one profession to respond adequately alone. It presents such education as the vehicle through which each profession sets realistic limits on claims made on it as it learns to value the contribution of other professions and share the load. It sees responding to the needs of workers as a precondition for effective care, which responds to the needs of clients. Chapter three captures the essence of interprofessional education, distinguishing between three foci: individual preparation; cultivating group/team collaboration; and improving services and the quality of client care.

Chapter four explains how and why we came to embark upon a series of systematic reviews of evaluations of interprofessional education, the databases that we selected and why, the methodology that we employed and its modification over time. It includes a critique of the methodology that we employed and the criteria applied to select 353 studies in the first instance, from which 107 'higher quality' studies, taking into account rigour and presentation, were included in our final analysis. Key features of these studies are summarised to give a flavour of the data upon which subsequent chapters draw.

The following three chapters revisit conventional wisdom about interprofessional education in the light of the evidence that we have assembled from the review, revisit rather than reappraise, which would call for original research, for which we offer pointers later. Chapter five looks afresh at earlier work to classify interprofessional education into domains, built around two dimensions – before and after qualification and college or employment led – tested against data from our review. Taking into account joint leadership, this generates six interdependent and mutually reinforcing 'domains' for interprofessional education. Chapter six presents some of the many aims advanced for interprofessional education on their merits, illustrated with examples from the review, and built into an overall system. Outcome data from the review test arguments and assumptions against evidence. Chapter seven applies adult learning principles to interprofessional learning and teaching. Again, evidence and examples are introduced from the review.

Two further chapters go beyond the scope and findings of the review (save for some of the examples) to complete our critique of interprofessional education. Chapter eight probes the values behind the attitudes and behaviour played out during interprofessional practice and ways in which they can be addressed during interprofessional education. It sees interprofessional education as offering a forum in which to compare and contrast values held by the different professions and other stakeholders. But it also demonstrates how interprofessional education is securing its own value base, building upon the values that inspired its inception, reinforced by a distillation of those drawn from the educational, professional and service delivery systems out of which it has grown and which it reinforces. Chapter nine examines some of the many theoretical perspectives which have been introduced into interprofessional education and practice from different academic disciplines. It resists the temptation to opt for any one perspective, arguing instead that interprofessional education must work to integrate diverse theoretical perspectives just as it does diverse practice perspectives. It lays no claims to formulating a coherent and comprehensive rationale, but supplies building blocks for ongoing work.

The concluding chapter looks again at our understanding of interprofessional education in the light of the road that we have travelled together. It takes stock of progress made in securing the evidence base for interprofessional education, with findings from the reviews undertaken and highlights numerous tensions, creative tensions to be held but also harnessed.

Messages shine through, encouraging us to conclude that interprofessional education does have the capacity, under favourable conditions, to help improve collaborative practice and, directly or indirectly, to improve the quality of care. Identifying and optimising those conditions becomes critical.

Argument, assumption and evidence:

- Arguments fought out in the interprofessional education arena, which ironically, if inevitably, has itself become contested territory
- Assumptions espoused by those exponents of interprofessional education for
  whom belief in their own experience is enough
- Evidence, albeit uneven and incomplete, which informs arguments and challenges assumptions about effective interprofessional education to which all
  parties may come to subscribe.

Acknowledgements

We draw extensively throughout this book on evaluations of interprofessional education conducted by fellow researchers at home and abroad, whose contribution we readily acknowledge. We have also valued support from our institutions – City, Westminster and at various times Birmingham and Oxford Brookes Universities – and from our colleagues, especially the longsuffering librarians at Westminster, who never failed to respond to our seemingly endless requests. CAIPE officers and fellow members have also provided support and encouragement.

We owe especial thanks to Professor Madeline Schmitt for her critical review of this book in draft and for drawing our attention to many additional sources.

We are indebted also to Adam Hamilton for chasing elusive sources, and to Synnove Hofseth Almas from Alesund University College in Norway, and colleagues at the University of York (UK) for permission to quote work in progress.

The work has been much helped by pump priming funding from the West London Research Network and from the Learning and Teaching Support Network for Health Sciences and Practice, to analyse and present data for an interim report (Freeth et al., 2002).

In the tradition of systematic reviews, our searches, analysis and writing have been undertaken largely on the margins of busy workloads, encroaching on time to be with families, including new partners and children born during eight otherwise preoccupied years. A big thank you from Ivan to Vivienne and Gabriel, from Scott to Ruth, William and Ewan, from Marilyn to James and Paul, and from Della to David, Rachael and Nadine.

Glossary

Visiting the newly rebuilt St Paul's Cathedral in 1710, Queen Anne circled the great space saying not a word, accompanied by the architect Sir Christopher Wren, who was beside himself with anxiety. Finally, she said: 'You have outdone yourself Sir Christopher. The cathedral is awful, amusing and artificial!' Whereupon, Sir Christopher breathed a sigh of relief, for in the language of the time *awful* meant awesome, *amusing* meant amazing and *artificial* meant artful (cited by Sullivan, 1998, p. 6).

Alive to ways in which words change their meaning in time and place, this book eschews fashionable fads and tries, so far as possible, to employ terms simply and consistently to ease communication between countries and between professions. Key terms are defined in this Glossary. Alternative terms are respected in context, to preserve authenticity, with explanations where necessary.

Action research involves the researcher in working collaboratively with participants through cycles of evaluation and development to effect positive change in their relationships or practice.

ASSIA is the Applied Social Science Index and Abstracts, an electronic bibliographic database that primarily contains social science literature.

Before and after study (BA) is a research design in which data are collected before and after an 'intervention', for example interprofessional education.

Before, during and after study (BDA) is similar to a before and after study except this type of research also collects data at some point during the intervention. This research design is also similar to an interrupted time series study (see below).

BEI is the British Educational Index, an electronic bibliographic database that primarily contains British educational literature.

CAIPE is the UK Centre for the Advancement of Interprofessional Education.

CINAHL is the Cumulative Index to Nursing and Allied Health Literature, an electronic bibliographic database that contains literature relating to those professions.

Client is the single preferred term to cover individuals, families and communities in receipt of health and social care services rather than 'patient', which refers only to an individual and carries a narrowly medical connotation, or consumer, which carries a commercial connotation, or 'service user', which has limited currency outside the UK. Other terms are used in context.

Collaboration is an active and ongoing partnership, often between people from diverse backgrounds, who work together to solve problems or provide services.

College is used as a generic term for institutions of higher and further education including universities.

Common curricula are the same for all the professions participating in multiprofessional or interprofessional education (see curriculum below).

Common learning is a concept that has a different meaning in different contexts. Originally, and still in its pure form, it refers to multiprofessional education, but common learning is also the name given to certain initiatives in interprofessional education in the UK.

Continuing professional development (CPD) is learning undertaken after initial qualification, in order to maintain competence and develop capability.

Continuing interprofessional development is CPD between professions meeting the definition for interprofessional education.

Controlled before and after study (CBA) is like a before and after study, except that to help detect change more accurately data are also collected from a control group, that is, from the subjects who do not take part in the intervention.

Cooperation is treated in this book as synonymous with collaboration.

Critical theory assumes an oppressive relationship between the rulers and the ruled. Rejecting the notion of objectivity, critical theorists attempt to use their explanations of oppression to eliminate current inequities of power.

Curriculum is used as an overarching term for all those aspects of education that contribute to the experience of learning, including aims, content, mode of delivery and assessment.

Discipline refers either to an academic discipline, such as psychology or biology, or to subspecialties within professions, for example anaesthesia or radiology within the profession of medicine.

Ethnography is rooted in anthropology. It is a methodology that aims to understand the meanings associated with the membership of different cultures and subcultures. Ethnographers attempt to gain an 'insider's point of view', usually by collecting observational, interview and documentary data.

Evaluation refers to the systematic gathering and interpretation of evidence, enabling judgement of effectiveness and value, and promoting improvement. Many evaluations have both formative and summative strands.

Health is a state of well-being to which diverse services are directed – educational, environmental, health, housing, law and order, income security and personal social services.

Health and social care are the two services most often engaged in promoting health and well-being, without excluding others.

Health and social care professions includes the allied health professions (as designated in different countries), branches of nursing, the complementary therapies, medicine, pharmacy, psychology and social work.

Initiative (as used in many of the literature sources) refers to an interprofessional education course, project, programme or sequence.

Interpretativism is a research philosophy which asserts that social reality is constructed from individuals' interpretations of their world. It therefore rejects the notion of objectivity in research, aiming rather to obtain the researcher's subjective understanding of their empirical findings.

Interprofessional education is members (or students) of two or more professions associated with health or social care, engaged in learning with, from and about each other. Other terms, with much the same meaning, are used in context.

Interprofessional learning is learning arising from interaction between members (or students) of two or more professions either as a product of interprofessional education or happening spontaneously (see serendipitous interprofessional education).

Interrupted time series study is one when one group of participants (which may contain several strata) is followed over a period of time, which is interrupted by an event, for example interprofessional education. Data are collected at a number of times pre- and post-event.

Intervention refers to the introduction of interprofessional learning into uniprofessional or multiprofessional education or as a freestanding interprofessional education programme.

Longitudinal study is research where data is collected at regular intervals, over a number of months or years.

Medline, otherwise known as Index Medicus, is an electronic bibliographic database that primarily contains medically-orientated literature.

Multiprofessional education is when members (or students) of two or more professions learn alongside one another: in other words, parallel rather than interactive learning.

Participant is used as a generic term to cover students, workers and others engaged in interprofessional education and learning. Student is used in context.

Practice placement is used to cover clinical placement, attachment, rotation, fieldwork placement, practicum and other terms used by different professions to describe opportunities for students to apply and develop their learning in the workplace.

Profession is treated throughout as a term of self-ascription, thereby avoiding the need to apply educational and regulatory criteria which may differ for the same 'profession' between countries.

Professional education is the sum total of uniprofessional, multiprofessional and interprofessional education.

Randomised controlled trial (RCT) is a scientific test of the efficacy of an intervention, which seeks to control for intervening variables by randomly allocating subjects into either an intervention group or a control group. It may be blind, double blind or triple blind, depending upon whether subjects, researchers or treatment practitioners have knowledge of the group (intervention or control) to which a subject belongs.

Serendipitous interprofessional learning is unplanned learning between professional practitioners, or between students on uniprofessional or multiprofessional programmes, which improves interprofessional collaboration.

Teamwork is the process whereby a group of people, with a common goal, work together, often, but not necessarily, to increase the efficiency of the task in hand.

Uniprofessional education is when members (or students) of a single profession learn together.

The WHO is the World Health Organization.

1 Rising to the Challenge

In this opening chapter we present some of the many factors which challenge relations between professions and, for better or worse, affect services to clients – poor communications, proliferating professions, coping with complexities, working in teams, collaborating more widely, resolving rivalry, improving quality, reforming the workforce and reforming education.

We resist the temptation to overstate the case for interprofessional education by recourse to arguments at variance with the facts. Although we highlight obstacles to be overcome, we acknowledge countless occasions when colleagues from different professions work amicably and effectively together, providing examples on which interprofessional education relies for models of good practice.

Poor communications

If only professions communicated better, problems in collaborating with each other would not arise. This widely held sentiment gains credence from numerous reports of miscommunication or non-communication between practitioners from different professions, but the reasons may be less simple than they may at first appear. Viewed thus, each profession has developed its own language to which insiders alone are privy, justified on the grounds that only then will terms be employed with precision between colleagues within a common understanding. Different professions employ different words to convey the same meaning and, more worryingly, the same words to convey different meanings, with all the attendant risks.

For Pietroni (1992) the issue had less to do with communication using profession-specific languages than the need for each profession to be conversant with a range of languages. He identified ten employed within and between health, social care and other professions. In summary, they were the languages of:

- Classical science
- The study of the mind
- Society and culture
- Traditional healing
- Alternative medicine
- Disease prevention and health education

- Ecology and environment
- Law, morality and ethics
- Research, evaluation and audit
- Policy, management and governance

A decade later, we might well add information technology.

Discourse is a more inclusive concept than language, as we explore later (see Chapter nine). For Van Dijk (1997) discourse can be understood in two ways. The first looks at the language and embedded meanings which are usually culturally determined. The second sees it as a more active phenomenon that, amongst other things, can shape individual behaviour and organisational structures. We are interested at this stage in the first of these formulations, where the challenge is not only to understand the meaning of words within a particular discourse, but also how such a discourse reflects and moulds professional beliefs, attitudes, perceptions and values. Arguably, all health and social care professions should be aware of the key discourses, the ways they are introduced into professions and interprofessional communications, and their effect on collaboration. Tension and conflict may be generated between professions when they employ different discourses.

Learning for communication may have less to do with one profession challenging another to explain its jargon, and more to do with facility in a range of discourses resulting from the breadth and depth of the educational foundation that each profession needs to enjoy. That facility may be strengthened where more graduates are recruited into professional education, accustomed to employing different discourses from their undergraduate education, and teaching is introduced from contributory disciplines which employ their own discourses. It should also be strengthened where common curricula, including communication studies, are introduced between entrants to the health and social care professions, employing common concepts and common terminology. But effective interprofessional education goes further; it generates interprofessional discourses that shape collaborative thinking and behaviour.

Only the most naive, however, would imagine that understanding a wider repertoire of discourses can resolve all communication problems between professions. Information may be withheld from one profession by another as required by its code of confidentiality or organisational policy (Hunt & van der Arend, 2002). Practitioner to practitioner exchange may be frustrated where bureaucratic procedures require that communications are routed between organisations through channels agreed and controlled by others.

Cognitive blindness may also be a problem, where one profession filters out information which might prompt actions beyond its perception of the role or competence of the other profession. Pressures of time may deny opportunities to exchange more than essential information. Under stress, each practitioner may revert to the safety of familiar behaviour patterns consistent with the discourses of his or her own profession. Prejudice may distort the manner in which a message is given and received.

Collaboration between professions is a two-way process, grounded in mutual respect for diversity and difference. On the one hand, it presupposes readiness to listen, to value what the other has to contribute, to be receptive to new ideas and information and prepared to change attitudes, perceptions and behaviour in response. On the other hand, it calls for generosity, openness and trust in a spirit of inclusion. More than mere mechanics, communication is at the heart of inter-professional relations.

Proliferating professions

Collaboration has become more complex as the number of professions has grown, as well as the number of specialities within them. Specialties have multiplied in response to an exponential growth in clinical knowledge and technological advance. Time and energy have been absorbed in intra-professional relations between growing numbers of subdivisions within professions, at the expense of the equally pressing need to foster relations with the growing number of other health and social care professions (Barr, 1994). Furthermore, increasing emphasis on health promotion and public health (WHO, 2003) has involved professions beyond the health and social care professions as commonly understood, ranging from architects to engineers and teachers to community leaders.

The number of professions called upon, from time to time, to work with each other now exceeds the capacity of each to appreciate sufficiently what the others do, increasing the risk of miscommunication, misunderstanding and boundary disputes. Practitioners may be reluctant to entrust responsibility for 'their' clients to members of another profession about whom they know little. However compelling the case for more specialisation, something has to be done to counter fragmentation, which is one of the driving forces behind interprofessional education.

Coping with complexity

The problems which clients present have either become more complex or perceived as such by practitioners. The truth may be a combination of both. Whatever the explanation, many practitioners find themselves under increasing pressure, external or self-imposed, to respond to problems beyond their education, experience and prescribed roles, a theme that we explore in greater depth in Chapter two.

They are confronted with three options:

(1)   To work within their own limits, leaving wider problems unaddressed
(2)   To work beyond those limits, albeit without the necessary education, experi-
      ence and expertise
(3)   To collaborate with other professions qualified to address the wider prob-
      lems

Interprofessional education can help in two ways. First, it can enhance practitioners' understanding of the roles and competence of other professions, the
boundaries and overlaps with their own, and ways of working across these.
Second, and more controversially, it can extend competence beyond the precon-
ceived roles of one profession as it learns from others.

Working in teams

Teamwork is the most widely discussed and most clearly defined medium
for collaboration (West & Poulton, 1993; West & Pillinger, 1996; West & Slater,
1996; Borrill et al., 2001; Onyett, 2003). Teams differ in structure and modus
operandi depending upon the task in hand, the mix of professions and their
formal relationships (Øvretveit, 1997). In primary care, for example, the team
combines professions working in the same agency, but with marked differences
in income and occupational status and the added complication where, as in
the UK, physicians are the employers for some of the other team members.
In mental health the team may include occupational therapists, psychiatric
nurses, psychiatrists and social workers, again differing in status, employed by
one or more organisation. In learning disabilities, the team typically includes
nurses and psychologists, plus either adult educators or schoolteachers,
depending on the age group of the clients. Models of teamwork in hospitals are
even more diverse.

Regardless of the model, each profession needs to understand the other professions better as they learn how to work at close quarters as fellow team members.
Although Miller et al. (2001) held that uniprofessional education has the
potential to teach knowledge and skills for teamwork they criticised its failure
to prepare students adequately for teamwork. Nor did they find interprofessional
and multiprofessional education programmes doing so.

Collaborating more widely

Collaboration is sometimes treated as being synonymous with teamwork. We beg
to differ. All teamwork is collaboration, but all collaboration is not teamwork.

Collaboration may involve a wider range of practitioners as and when the occasion requires. Practitioners who lack loyalty to the same team may not know each other, and may work together for brief or extended periods (Meerabeau & Page, 1999; Reeves & Lewin, 2004), in which case networking seems a more apt description than teamworking.

Nor is collaboration only between professions. It is also between organisations – education, health, housing, law enforcement, social care, income maintenance and others; between practice settings – residential and community; and between sectors – statutory, voluntary and commercial.

There are calls, too, for professions and services to work in partnership with individuals, families and communities, and for services and educational institutions to work in partnership to promote and manage education and training. Collaboration is multidimensional. The task for interprofessional education is correspondingly complex. Maintaining and improving collaboration between professions nevertheless remains pivotal, the axis around which other dimensions of collaboration revolve.

Emphasis is often put on teamwork to the exclusion of these other dimensions of collaboration. It assumes, moreover, that relationships in teams are stable, which is manifestly not so in many work settings, where staff turnover is high and services under strain (Engestrom *et al.*, 1999). Students are ill served when teachers propound idealised notions of textbook teamwork at variance with everyday realities of working life.

Resolving rivalry

Collaboration may be ascendant, but residual elements of competition are deeply embedded in relationships between organisations and between professions. Rivalry between professions is exacerbated by differences in power, status and esteem, associated with differences in education, gender and class (Hugman, 1991; Walby *et al.*, 1994; Wickes, 1998). It may diminish where aspiring professions improve their lot relative to the established professions by virtue of better regulation, education and remuneration, although tension may mount in the short term. Calls for parity across the health and social care professions are, however, unrealistic. They detract from the need for each profession to learn how to collaborate with others in situations where status differences are entrenched and enduring. Interprofessional education may help participants to live in a status-ridden working world, contributing towards the reduction of status differentials in the workplace, but unable to eliminate them.

Rivalry may have less to do with individuals than with their professional institutions, which stand accused of territoriality and tribalism, guardians of vested interests, intent upon protecting their members, if and when necessary at the expense of others (Larson, 1977; Freidson, 1994; Beattie, 1995; Macdonald, 1995). The imagery is colourful; the reality is more subtle. Outright turf wars between professions are mercifully few. Tension arises more often when changes in the organisation and delivery of services redraw boundaries, redistribute power and reallocate responsibilities from one profession to another to improve service delivery, contain costs or cope with uneven supply and demand in the workforce (Hughes, 1988; Porter, 1995; Brown *et al.*, 2000). Professional institutions naturally act to safeguard the interests of their members.

Improving quality

Collaboration is widely invoked as a means to improve the quality of care. Professions who work closely together, so the argument runs, not only offer mutual support but also mutual control (Koppel, 2003). Support mitigates stress to improve care and lessens the likelihood of mistakes. Control points to shortcomings within working relationships that are robust enough to accept criticism.

Pressure to improve quality comes from all quarters. In the USA, The President's Advisory Commission on Consumer Protection and Quality in the Health Care Industry provided impetus for a series of expert reports focused on safety and quality (President's Advisory Commission, 1998, prepared by The Institute of Medicine). Errors in planning and delivering treatment had been estimated to account for between 44 000 and 98 000 deaths in the USA per annum, with an estimated annual cost of between $17 and $29 billion (Kohn *et al.*, 2000). Most occurred because of systemic failure. Preventing errors meant designing safer systems of care. Errors were more likely to occur where many individuals were involved in the care. One of the Institute's identified strategies to reduce the likelihood of errors was improved teamwork through interprofessional education of students and practising professionals based on proven methods of team training (Kohn *et al.*, 2000; Institute of Medicine Committee on Quality of Health Care in America, 2001; Greiner & Knebel, 2003).

Ingersoll & Schmitt (2004) provided an evidence-based critical analysis of the relations between health care teams and performance outcomes, as an appendix to one of the Institute for Medicine reports. Quoting Sasou & Reason (1999), they distinguished between 'mistakes' and 'lapses' which arose in the planning and thinking process, and 'slips' which occurred primarily in the execution process. Mistakes and lapses, said Sasou and Reason, were more likely to occur during team processes whereas slips were caused primarily by individuals. Teams were, however, also involved in the error recovery process as Ingersoll and Schmitt spelt out.

In the UK much of the same pressure came from the Kennedy Inquiry (Department of Health, 2001a) into the unacceptably large number of deaths during paediatric surgery in Bristol. They were attributed, in part, to lack of collaboration between professions, separation of specialties within professions and lack of management of the interprofessional process, as Meads and Ashcroft (2005) discussed.

Pressure comes, too, from rising expectations of a better-informed public less deferential towards the professions than in the past. Consumerism has arrived in health and social care. Advances in health care technology and scientific knowledge (Mackay *et al.*, 1995; Royal College of Physicians of London, 1995) raise expectations that the benefits will be available to all (Hornby & Atkins, 2000). The more the public is informed about progress in diagnosis and treatment modalities the higher its expectations become, despite awareness of cost implications and budgetary constraints.

The 'popular' media are quick to point the finger of blame for allegations of malpractice, while the 'quality' media cover health and social issues ever more frequently and more thoroughly. Websites enable members of the public to find out for themselves about the medical conditions that may be worrying them and the treatment that might be prescribed. Self-help groups multiply. Pressure groups muster evidence born of members' experiences, each engaging in special pleading for more and better services in its field.

'League tables' in some countries rank or rate hospitals and other health facilities based on scores for performance indicators which encourage critical and sometimes invidious comparisons, fuelling demands for better services which must be reconciled with cost containment. The circle must be squared. Professionals are called upon to collaborate, not only to deliver better services, but also more economical services by eliminating wasteful duplication and helping to deploy the workforce more efficiently and effectively. In the USA 'managed care', introduced to provide cost-controlled packages of care to hold spiralling insurance claims in check, has become a means to achieve closer collaboration (Dombeck & Olsan, 2002). 'Care management' (its far from identical twin) also originated in the USA, but has spread to other countries as the means to coordinate packages of care mobilised from formal and informal sources (Gorman & Postle, 2003).

Reforming the workforce

In many countries moves are afoot to remodel the health and social care workforce (Meads and Ashcroft, 2005), often associated with a shift of emphasis from hospital-based to community-based care in response to demographic trends and changing disease patterns. Discrete and hierarchical relations between professions, which may have worked well enough in hospitals, can no longer be sustained in the community, where the multiple needs of patients or clients demand more flexible responses from professions whose boundaries are more permeable. Freed from demarcations and hierarchical relations, responsibilities are reassigned, power redistributed and boundaries redrawn and crossed.

However persuasive the case for workforce reform, it can generate tensions between professions. It may fuel suspicions that the hidden agenda behind modernisation is to humble the professions – anti-professionalism masquerading as interprofessionalism. On the one hand, the managerialism driving modernisation may be seen as intent upon weakening the professions, with interprofessional education its unwitting agent, to establish a 'corporate professionalism' imposed by and accountable to the employer, making professions, as we know them, subservient and attenuating their institutions (McKinlay & Arches, 1985; Hunter, 1994; Ashburner & Fitzgerald, 1996). On the other hand, it may be seen as exercising its responsibility to further relationships between professions while preserving and protecting the identity and integrity of each. The truth may lie down the middle, given the need, on the one hand, to carry the support of professions for reform and, on the other, to redraw boundaries and reassign responsibilities.

Autonomous professional practice and modern managerialism are uneasy bedfellows. Professional values are held in tension with organisational policies, priorities and procedures. Relationships between professions and management often loom larger than between profession and profession, prompting the question whether managers should be overseers and arbiters or participants and partners in interprofessional education and practice as one of the professions.

Reforming education

The root of the problem may, however, lie more in education than in practice. Professional education is a process of socialisation, a means by which students come to identify with their intended profession, its values, culture, roles and expertise. Students entering programmes for different professions in the same college have ill-informed notions about each other's roles and responsibilities at the beginning of their courses, which may be modified little by the end. Poor stereotypes about each other reported at the outset remain unchanged (Barnes et al., 2000a). If education is part of the problem, it must also be part of the solution. That proposition, above all, drives the promotion of interprofessional education.

Exposure to other professions during pre-qualifying studies may, however, be seen at best as a distraction and at worst as contamination. These objections gain credence from arguments that students need time to find their respective identities before being exposed to other professions, that interprofessional studies are the lowest common denominator (generic studies by another name) and that pressure to increase profession-specific studies leaves no time for interprofessional studies – notwithstanding the need to collaborate with other professions from the day of qualification (Dombeck, 1997; Pirrie et al., 1998).

Implications for interprofessional education

Interprofessional education designed to develop teamwork needs to be broadened to embrace collaboration in its diverse dimensions, shedding naive and idealised notions of teams, acknowledging intractable tensions resulting from rivalry and imbalances in power, and chronic instability in many working relations. Traditions within interprofessional education associated with different client groups need to be drawn together, for example, to bridge the gap between work with disabled and elderly adults, on the one hand, and children, young people and their families on the other. In the UK emphasis on preparation for collaboration in community settings needs to be counterbalanced by equal attention to hospital settings in the light of reports on medical errors.

Traditionally, interprofessional education was conceived as exchange, based upon mutual respect for identity, territory, roles and functions, which still applies in many countries. In addition, in some countries it is now expected to be a vehicle to remodel the workforce, which may generate added stresses which it must then work to resolve. Interprofessional education has entered turbulent waters.

Interprofessional educators are expected not only to cultivate collaboration, but also to foster a more flexible workforce, where one profession can substitute for another and career progression is expedited without returning to square one. Laudable though all these objectives are, they carry quite different implications for content, teaching and learning methods.

So numerous are the challenges for interprofessional education that no one programme can hope to address them all. Rather, they comprise an agenda to be addressed by a range of interprofessional education interventions over time within a continuum of learning in college and workplace. What types of interprofessional education can deliver what outcomes, at what stage, in which location, and who defines those outcomes? Answering these questions lies at the heart of this book.

Interprofessional education has travelled hopefully, sustained by the determined efforts of its exponents and their unshakable belief in its efficacy, despite setbacks and lack of supporting evidence as expectations have multiplied. No longer: the evidence base is being secured. Consistency of findings from the growing number of evaluations reported point to ways in which interprofessional education can respond to challenges such as those addressed in this chapter.

2 Learning to Work under Pressure

In Chapter one we summarised some of the many challenges for interprofessional education. In this chapter we explore how such education responds to one of these, namely the need to support health and social care practitioners as they come under increasing pressure. This may well be the key to enabling practitioners to cope with the other issues and to improve care for clients.

Responding to the needs of the workers

Putting the needs of workers first may seem perverse. It may encourage the belief that interprofessionalisation, like professionalisation, is driven by collective self-interest. Our argument is more subtle; it starts from the premise that occupational stress is not only debilitating for professionals but also injurious to their work with clients: conversely that alleviating stress liberates professionals to work more effectively for the benefit of their clients. Interprofessional learning and working may be self-interest, but it is enlightened self-interest. However altruistic the professionals, interprofessional education and practice is unlikely to win friends unless and until interprofessional educators demonstrate that it will respond to the needs of workers as well as clients. Only then can they assuage fears that learning and working together will exacerbate rather than ease pressure.

Stress is inherent in professional life, especially in health and social care; stress which interprofessional education and practice seeks to mitigate as they limit demands made of any one profession and build mutual support. Occupational stress may result from:

- Greater complexity (actual or perceived) of problems that clients present
- Rising public expectations
- The combination of high concentrations of stressful clientele and inadequate professional resources
- Working in unfamiliar social, cultural and economic milieux
- Restructuring of health and social services in response to increased demand

It would be naive to imagine that interprofessional education alone can resolve such deep-seated problems, but it may help in part as this chapter demonstrates.

Five themes

In this chapter we explore five persistent and pervasive situations in which health and social care professionals respond under pressure:

- Ageing populations
- Children and young people
- Changing family structure
- Poverty
- Migration

They are neither exhaustive nor mutually exclusive. We are less exercised here by the incidence and nature of the pressures generated than by their implications for professional practice in general, interprofessional practice in particular, and ways in which interprofessional education can help.

Ageing populations

As the number of older people increases, notably in developed countries, so, too, does the number of people with chronic illnesses and disabilities. On the one hand, young people with disabilities live longer; on the other hand, illnesses and disabilities increase with age. Concern to improve care for elderly, and for disabled and chronically ill adults, springs from the relative failure of health care systems to deal effectively with chronic and multiple conditions compared with acute and specific conditions amenable to modern medical and surgical intervention (McCallum, 1993; Pezzin & Kasper, 2002).

Older people may maintain an active and productive life longer in developed countries than in times past, thanks to better income security, better housing, better nutrition and medical advances, but dependence on health and social care services is, at best, postponed. Chronic conditions multiply inexorably with age, exceeding the capacity of any one profession or agency.

Older, disabled and chronically ill people may benefit as much as healthier people from specific medical and surgical interventions, but only concerted action by a number of professions and agencies can respond adequately to their overall situation. In the UK a ten-year plan of action for restructuring care of the elderly was published in 2001 (Department of Health, 2001b) designed to root out discrimination against older people through integration of services across health and social care and other key stakeholders, such as local councils. Progress will be measured against set criteria, such as achievements in the field of health promotion.

Interprofessional strategies have been launched in many parts of the USA to coordinate care for older people. The Veterans Administration established Interdisciplinary Team Training in Geriatrics (ITTG) in 1979 at twelve of its centres, to provide a cadre of health practitioners with the knowledge and competencies to meet the wide spectrum of health care and service needs of the ageing veteran

(Feazel, 1990). The John Hartford Foundation supported education in geriatric medicine and more recently provided funds to support the development of academic leadership in geriatric care. Having funded programmes to train physicians to care for the elderly, the Foundation built on the experience gained to re-channel and increase funding, and also to include nurses, social workers and others in 13 sites (Hyer, 1998). It promoted and funded the Geriatric Interdisciplinary Team Training Program (GITT), driven by the belief that the unprecedented growth in the number and proportion of the elderly with complex problems required the skill of several collaborating disciplines (Siegler *et al.*, 1998; John Hartford Foundation, 2004).

Support from the W.K. Kellogg Foundation to improve care for older people is well illustrated by the following example (see Box 2.1).

Box 2.1   Community coalitions to improve care for older people
(Anderson *et al.*, 1994).

Six teams in Michigan were involved in a training programme in part funded by the W.K. Kellogg Foundation designed to promote the development of services for older people in communities with less than 50 000 population and more than 20 miles from a major referral centre. The goal was to establish a working coalition within each community that would promote and develop interprofessional services for older adults according to local needs and priorities.

Key components were: the development of a team of health care professionals trained in geriatric health care; sponsorship by a community agency to provide resources for geriatric services; and appointment of a community advisory board to ensure that the services being offered were appropriate and desirable. Programme staff included nurses, social workers, physicians and an educational consultant.

The trainers worked with each sponsoring agency to choose the interprofessional team. Each included a physician, a nurse, a social worker and an administrator. The training comprised two one-week sessions on the University of Michigan campus for all three teams, together with clinical activities completed in between, ongoing consultative support and an annual retreat. Content was both generic and profession-specific. In addition to didactic methods and case studies, the training incorporated practice with feedback to facilitate problem solving and skills development.

Each team prepared quarterly progress reports including a log of clinical activities. Members also completed questionnaires before and after the campus training and again six and eighteen months afterwards. Questions covered perceptions of project goals, team effectiveness, geriatric services offered and factors seen to be positively influencing or impeding implementation of geriatric clinical services.

Responses to the baseline questionnaire were similar across the teams. Three teams reported implementing a clinical service for older adults at eighteen months. Two of the remaining teams had experienced loss of

---

(Continues)

members. The third was struggling to define the elements of the clinical service and in conflict with the local doctors and dissatisfied with its progress. Why did some teams succeed and others fail? Two team case histories were selected to probe this question. Critical differences, it emerged, were financial support from sponsoring agencies and positive reinforcement from the community.

Further reinforcement in the USA came from curriculum recommendations from the Task Force on Resident Training in Geriatrics Interdisciplinary Team Care (Counsell *et al.*, 1999). As its title suggests, the Task Force focused on training for physicians, but to prepare them to establish teams and to work effectively in them.

Interprofessional education has also been introduced in many countries to respond to the multiple needs of people with physical and learning disabilities, and chronic illnesses such as diabetes, cardiovascular disease (Solberg *et al.*, 1998), Parkinson's disease, and survivors of the HIV pandemic, as their life expectancy improves.

For example, in the USA, the Robert Wood Johnson Foundation funded major initiatives in interprofessional management of chronic conditions. In the UK, a number of charities were active, of which we chose one to describe (see Box 2.2).

Box 2.2   Learning to respond together to the needs of chronically disabled people (Jones, 1998).

Continuing Care at Home (CONCAH) ran a series of workshops throughout the UK designed to be practical and accessible to primary care professionals. They focused on the needs of chronically disabled people with neurological diseases, such as Parkinson's disease, and epilepsy, which practitioners felt were not addressed adequately. The workshop format was based on adult learning principles in that, among other features, they were interactive and learner-centred, and challenged the teams to commit to change and audit progress. Development was based on two pilot workshops that involved seven general practice teams and one hospital-based team. Innovative features of the workshops were the involvement of the patients and their caregivers and the input from a multidisciplinary panel of local experts.

Workshops were then rolled out across the UK, 17 being completed by the time of the evaluation. In total, there were 250 participants. Feedback on the sessions was overwhelmingly positive, with only a very small number of negative reflections. The organisers concluded that it was essential to moderate carefully the degree of the input from the doctors, be they GPs or members

(Continues)

of the expert panel. Contributions from the patients and caregivers were found to be essential to gain insights into problems faced in their daily lives. An important feature of the evaluation was assessment of the extent to which plans agreed during the workshops had been implemented. In 40 out of 48 practices these plans were working. Improved collaboration, another aim of the initiative, was somewhat less successful in the participants' view, only 26 out 48 practices reporting progress in this area.

Few, if any, fields have developed a more distinctive interprofessional profile than palliative care, responding as it does to the needs of mind, body and spirit within a holistic philosophy, as our next example from the Netherlands exemplifies (Box 2.3). Noteworthy is recognition that quality of care for clients depends critically upon the quality of care for workers in an inherently stressful setting.

Box 2.3   Supporting staff and patients in hospice care
(van Staa *et al.*, 2000).

Patients came first, but plans were made from the outset to build in a social support system to ease stress and prevent burnout amongst caregivers in one of the first palliative care units to open in the Netherlands. In-house interprofessional training was arranged during the first year, complemented by a weekly support group on which we focus here. All members of the team were invited but not required to attend. Work schedules disrupted continuity. Each week the composition of the group was different. Each meeting lasted 90 minutes, facilitated by one of two therapists in turn, after a relaxation exercise. There was no fixed structure thereafter, the participants choosing topics for discussion. Participation was reportedly poor at first, but improved.

Facilitators and participants tended to hold different views regarding purpose and content. One facilitator described the meetings as 'a safe place where the team members get the opportunity to enter their personal experiences of working in palliative care – and to care for themselves' (p. 101). Her role was to guide the process of introspection, but she stressed that these were not therapeutic groups. It was her responsibility to ensure that participants could safely go home or back to work at the end of each session.

For most of the participants the focus was on solving problems which had arisen in patient care. An 'inner circle' of nurses in the unit was more dependent upon the facilitators to provide advice than was an 'outer circle' of social, homecare and psychiatric nurses, plus the physiotherapist, dietician and pastor, who looked more to each other for interprofessional support. Some of the inner circle also wanted more structure, with the facilitators volunteering ideas for discussion to break silences with which they were uneasy.

Discussions most often concerned problems in teamwork and collaboration, feelings of insecurity and frustration regarding lack of institutional support

---

(*Continues*)

and resource constraints, as well as personal feelings of exhaustion and incompetence. Issues about loss and bereavement inherent in palliative work did come up, but less often than anticipated. Experience tended to confirm the view found in the literature that stress, albeit inherent in palliative care, is lessened if recognised early and offset by positive job satisfaction with staff support built in.

Children and young people

Concern about the well-being of children and young people at risk has generated efforts to integrate services for them and their families, as reported in a survey conducted by Magrab et al. (1997) for the Organisation for Economic Cooperation and Development (OECD) in seven of its member countries. They found that few childcare professionals were trained to implement or work in an integrated service delivery system. In Italy, France and the Netherlands several 'multidisciplinary' training initiatives had been launched in response to national policies to coordinate services for children and young people at risk and their families, but most were idiosyncratic and regional or local. Similarly, said Magrab and her colleagues, the UK 1989 Children Act had 'spawned a variety of multidisciplinary training activities' (p. 101).

They argued for a 'key curriculum' comprising the following, for all professions working with children at risk:

- Knowledge of concepts of service integration at all levels
- Knowledge of the roles of the various professions who serve children at risk
- Preparation for functioning as an effective team member
- Preparation for coordinating services for the family

Tucker et al. (1999) advocated an 'interdisciplinary' framework for those working with children and young people in education, health and social care, taking into account:

- The child's personal development and growth
- The kinds and levels of support needed to foster and maintain well-being
- The range of environmental factors that will necessarily impact on life chances, hopes and aspirations for the future

Principles of intervention should be applied in a common model of intervention focusing on points of transition for the child and always keeping his or her rights central.

Based on findings from her small-scale research studies into education for people working with children and young people, Lacey (2001) called for management systems to support practitioners who strive to work together with children and young people with clear lines of communication and a common focus.

Numerous projects in the USA take the school as the focus for interprofessional collaboration. The goal for Lawson & Briar-Lawson (1997) was 'school reform' – a term which they admit has many meanings and many models including:

- School based youth services
- Coordinated services to 'fix at risk students'
- Co-located, integrated and comprehensive services for children, youth and families

Preventing child abuse has become the sharp end of childcare. Nowhere has the need for closer collaboration between professions become more painfully apparent (see Box 2.4).

Box 2.4   Facing up to child abuse (Sicher *et al.*, 2000).

Protecting children from abuse was sorely neglected in Eastern European countries before the collapse of one-party rule in 1989. Policy makers and researchers were handicapped by lack of reliable data and a legacy of policies that tended to undermine the family unity. Professional training in child abuse was non-existent, as the totalitarian ideology did not admit of existence of social ills, which were ascribed exclusively to the 'decadent' West. Furthermore, professionals dealing with children were mistrusted, as they were seen to be the agents of the oppressive state apparatus.

Dissolution of rigid societal structures and economic reverses created fertile ground for child abuse. The Open Society Institute (OPI) established by George Soros became involved in a wide range of educational initiatives in 17 former Eastern bloc countries. As teachers sent from the USA began to report on mental health problems amongst children, evidence of abuse and neglect emerged. In 1995 the OPI established the East European Child Abuse and Mental Health Project. The intention of the project founders was to enable the local teams to become independent non-governmental organisations (NGOs), locally registered and capable of forwarding the agenda for development.

Project leaders adopted a three-pronged approach:

- Prevention by supporting families, including education on child development and professional support in early childhood years
- Identification and support for families with problems, rather than removing children into care
- Recognition that child abuse is a societal issue that requires collaboration at all levels in the system, from policy makers to professionals, including the police

One of the most influential projects took as its focus the education of key professionals from all the relevant agencies and fostering interprofessional

(*Continues*)

teams who would themselves become a core political and educational force within their respective countries. The educational programme had two phases. Each participating country was required to field a team of key professionals actively involved in the care of abused children, who would be committed to attend a series of four week-long educational conferences run in different countries, involving 100 people altogether. The first three weeks were mainly content-oriented, dealing with facts of abuse recognition, the role of different agencies and diverse approaches to treatment. The last week signalled a move toward the next phase by focusing on team development. At this point, the individual teams were asked to expand their membership to include other agencies, such as police and lawyers, who would constitute the kernel for change in their respective countries. From 1998, support for this phase of development included further conferences on 'multidisciplinary' organisational skills and mentoring to individual teams. This involved site visits during which it was possible to address specific local issues and to engage in action-oriented team learning and planning.

Leaders experienced numerous challenges in implementing the project. These included lack of public awareness, rigid professional hierarchies and the need to change social policies.

The recurrent message in reports into the abuse and often death of children in the UK, especially since the early 1970s, (Department of Health and Social Security, 1974; Cleveland Report, 1988; Birchall & Hallett, 1995) is failure in communication between professionals variously responsible for the same child – general practitioners, health visitors, police officers, schoolteachers, social workers and others. All too often each professional was in possession of one or more piece of the jigsaw, but no one was able to see the whole family picture before disaster struck. Time and again it seemed as though earlier and better communication might have averted tragedy. Children were at risk, but so, too, were workers operating under unremitting stress and fear of rebuke when mistakes happened.

Official inquiries called repeatedly for 'joint training' in the belief that this would engender trust and better communication between the professions responsible for child protection (see Box 2.5).

Box 2.5   Learning how to protect children (Stanford & Yelloly, 1994).

A London-based consortium piloted proposals from the then UK Central Council for Education and Training in Social Work (CCETSW) and the then English National Board for Nursing, Midwifery and Health Visiting (ENB) for ten- and sixty-day courses for social work and nurse educators during a programme at the Tavistock Centre. Both courses aimed to determine an

(Continues)

effective model for the development of shared teaching and learning for child protection.

The shorter course was competency-based. Outcomes included ability to work with other professionals, to ask for help and refer cases on when appropriate, within a common framework of knowledge and understanding of law, policy, practice and procedures. Adult learning methods drew on the existing knowledge and skills of participants from nursing, therapy, leisure and youth services. The approach was active, experiential and facilitative. The course met one day for each of the ten weeks and comprised three modules. Assessment was formative. Evaluation focused on satisfaction with presentation and content.

The longer course, leading to a Master's in child protection, set out to enable participants to work effectively in multiprofessional networks. 'Serious intellectual fare' (p. 50) included knowledge of research methods and findings, law and a range of applied theoretical and conceptual frameworks. Again, emphasis was put on learning from experience. The pattern was day release every two weeks for two years. Participants came from social work, health visiting and nursing. Assessment was summative and included written assignments. Evaluation was based on before and after questionnaires augmented by interviews. The course had reportedly met expectations regarding inter-agency working.

Concern about child protection has become so high profile in the UK that it has, until recently, tended to overshadow the need for wider collaboration in work with other children and their families (Chief Secretary to the Treasury, 2003).

Changing family structure

The decline of the extended family as a social unit, with loss of mutual support and control, carries major implications for the provision of health and social care services and for the professions that deliver them. The nuclear family, which has replaced the extended family in many developed countries, is also in jeopardy as falling birth rates and family breakdown contribute to the growing number of one-parent families and more single people living alone. Alternative lifestyles generate alternative support systems more or less adequately, with more or less implications for the health and social care professions.

The decline of traditional notions of family is a double challenge. Although health and social care professionals may find it difficult to establish and sustain contact with an often mobile population of single people, they are nevertheless trained for the most part to work with individuals rather than families. Working pressures, which often preclude home visits, reduce the likelihood that the individual will be seen and understood as a member of a family. Workers may fail to recognise the impact of family dynamics on the individual member, or the significance of positive and negative interactions between members for the family as a unit.

Workers from different professions – doctor, nurse, probation officer, priest, schoolteacher, social worker, youth leader, and so on, may be in touch with different members of the same family unbeknown to each other. Contact, if and when established between those workers, may be inhibited by the need for each to work within agency and professional structures, policies and regulations, and to respect confidences entrusted by his or her client within the family. The need for collaboration may not always be apparent. Professionals are therefore ill placed to mobilise the resources of the whole family to support individual members in need and to respond together to the family, based upon their collective understanding.

These are some of the reasons why family systems theory has been introduced into interprofessional education and practice, as the following case study exemplifies (see Box 2.6). It draws on experience in family therapy, but is more inclusive. Systemic family work involves, at least potentially, all professions involved in working with a family and its members. Interprofessional education for family systems work is correspondingly inclusive.

Box 2.6   Learning to work together with the whole family (Larivaara & Taanila, 2004).

The School of Medicine at the University of Oulu in Finland launched an interprofessional family systems programme in 2002, to replace a family doctor programme that had run for some years. The new programme lasted two years and was based on systems theory, the biopsychosocial notion of health and illness (Engel, 1977) and social constructionism. It was built around three key concepts – client and family orientation, networking and resources utilisation. It aimed to give participants competencies for interprofessional cooperation with families and communities. It included direct teaching for two days per month and independent studies. Innovative learning methods included preparing genogrammes (about personal family backgrounds) and network charts (based on work with communities).

The teams recruited consisted of participants from different professions, 76 trainees being chosen from the following professions: careers advice, counselling, general practice, nursing, parish work, physiotherapy, psychology, health profession teaching, school teaching and social work. They were divided into four groups of 18 to 20, meeting for the most part in three municipalities, learning with fellow trainees from their own communities.

The common strand prompting enrolment was a desire to learn new ways to solve the increasingly complex problems of clients and client families and to find ways to cope at work.

Trainees became more aware of the need to approach their clients as equals, respecting their autonomy and responsibility for their own lives, building on

---

(*Continues*)

their personal resources. They also learned that it was possible to alleviate the psychic burden on individual workers by working in teams, thereby releasing their creativity. They began to work in pairs and groups more often, acquiring new ideas from each other, applying them in work with clients, as they came to appreciate that no one profession had the absolute truth, and to be more tolerant of uncertainty.

Work reportedly became more rewarding and more hopeful. Trainees said that they coped better under pressure, with less burnout. They found the courage to look at themselves, as they became more self-aware.

Poverty

The link between poverty and health has long been acknowledged. The WHO has led a concerted effort during the past 20 years, especially under the leadership of its former Director-General, Dr Brundtland, to reorient its work from concentration on specific health interventions, such as the elimination of polio and tuberculosis, to address wider economic and political concerns. At the same time, it recognised that local, national and international partnership is essential for effective change (WHO, 1999). It now monitors approaches to poverty reduction in individual countries (Dood & Hinshelwood, 2002) taking into account quality of services and ease of access to them, but also factors such as underpinning attitudes within political and health delivery systems that affect implementation of public health and primary care interventions.

In the UK, the groundbreaking report by Sir Douglas Black (Black *et al.*, 1988) established the link between economic and health status. Its raft of recommendations conflicted with the ideology of the Government of the day and was rejected. The incoming Government elected in 1997 commissioned a new report from Sir Donald Acheson (Acheson, 1998) who identified the need for a multifaceted approach to tackle health inequalities. Ministers responded with a commitment to joint working across all relevant Government departments, including education, employment and housing, as well as health (Department of Health, 1999). The impact of 'seamless working' can be seen in the introduction of health improvement programmes (HIMPs) which required commitment from both health and local authorities to implement a concerted strategy for change.

Health professionals have become more aware of the adverse effects of poverty on the health of individuals, young and old, and of families. They know all too well that dealing with the presenting health problem is not enough, without tackling underlying economic and social causes, but many are ill placed and ill equipped to engage directly with them. Social care professionals have become more aware of chronic health conditions associated with poverty and attendant unemployment, malnutrition and poor housing, and educational disadvantage, but they are neither equipped nor authorised to respond. Health and social care professions therefore need each other. Viewed thus, they are the axis around which collaboration revolves, involving a wider spectrum of professions.

Poverty has more impact on some health and social care workers than on others, given its uneven distribution between communities and between countries. Clients in inner-city or downtown areas present more frequent, more intense, more complex and more intractable problems rooted in poverty, than in the more affluent suburbs. Services under strain respond with difficulty, beset by vacancies, high turnover and low morale among the professional workforce, compounded by less cash resources, resulting from less revenue from local taxation. Nowhere is the need for mutual support between professions and between agencies, to respond to the magnitude and complexity of the problems and to share the load more compelling than in the inner city, nor professions and agencies alike more isolated where they need each other most. The following example indicates how one team reviewed the impact of poverty on its clients and effected improvements (see Box 2.7).

Box 2.7   Joint action on poverty (Bond, 1999).

Research into poverty in Nottingham, showing that about half of all inhabitants were dependent on state benefits, prompted a two-year SPIDA (Strategies for Practices in Disadvantaged Areas) action research project. The design of the project facilitated learning and evaluation. However, it became clear early on that it was not appropriate to follow the initial design, which presupposed specific outcomes. In a true action-research fashion, the project workers collaborated with the relevant stakeholders to develop a design that brought to the fore processes of change that challenged established ways of working and professional or academic hierarchies. The research was based on a single-handed inner-city practice, serving a large population of young people. A third of the patients came from non-white backgrounds.

Applying principles of collaborative enquiry, all tasks were shared, such as data collection and contributions to the writing of reports. Team learning principles propounded by Dechant et al. (1993) informed the design of the process of team interaction.

Enquiry members met fortnightly (for 30 sessions) to learn and reflect on their attitudes to poverty, to share their findings from data collection and their efforts to liaise with other agencies. Local people were involved as well, first through an open meeting to compare the progress of the project and then through focus groups. This provided a further input to the project.

Outcomes of the project were encouraging. Individual learning developed into team-based interprofessional learning. Members felt empowered to participate equally within the team and to reach out to other agencies and other primary care centres. Outreach involved the team in collaborating, for instance, with a school nurse on health education and propagating the message of the project in other localities.

(Continues)

Attitudes to poverty and understanding of the importance of consistent anti-racist approaches were cited as positive outcomes. The team created a poverty profile – a collection of statistics about their population that detailed the demographic characteristics and health impact of poverty, enhanced by the local directory of services. However, the most powerful learning occurred when individual team members began to have insight into the impact of poverty on living conditions and their ability to act empathetically on behalf of those in deprived circumstances. The organisation of the surgery was affected as well, for example by providing better information and more baby clinic sessions.

Similar problems can and do arise in rural areas where depopulation and associated loss of economic productivity and public services may exacerbate them. Here, too, there are often chronic problems in recruiting and retaining health professionals, especially doctors. These problems call for different models for collaborative practice, sustained by different models of interprofessional education.

If poverty impacts on professionals in developed countries, then how much more so in developing countries where its prevalence and severity, and lack of resources to respond, is so much greater? This makes the case for interprofessional collaboration even more compelling. Some developing countries have been constrained by demarcations between professions inherited from colonial days, but others have developed local models responsive to local needs, designed to deploy scarce resources to optimal effect.

However much health and social care professions collaborate with individuals and families they can do little more than alleviate symptoms unless and until community intervention tackles underlying economic and social causes. Here especially, developed countries have much to learn from developing countries (see Box 2.8).

Box 2.8   Learning to work with rural poverty (Lazarus *et al.*, 1998).

South African community partnerships began socially accountable models for health professions education, research and service in 1991. Most South Africans have inadequate access to basic services including health care. Between 25% and 55% live in poverty. Seventy-five percent of the poor live in rural areas. Malnutrition is common, infant mortality high and HIV illness endemic. Against this background the W.K. Kellogg Foundation initiated seven Community Partnerships in Health Professions Education.

In Boeshbuck Ridge, for example, some 200 students rotated through the project each year as part of their 'rural block'. They came from medicine,

(Continues)

occupational therapy, physiotherapy, speech and hearing therapy, and social work. The teaching and learning context was a community hospital and two community health centres (staffed by nurses and visited by doctors twice a week). In addition, a rehabilitation centre accommodated disabled children cared for by their parents, supported by health workers, community rehabilitation workers, traditional healers and faith healers.

Students stayed in the homes of community members in neighbouring villages and townships. They visited local schools to conduct health-related research projects. Much of their learning was based on problem case studies. Assessment included reports on family attachments, student diaries and examinations.

These programmes have lacked systematic evaluation, but two have reportedly generated extensive cross-discipline collaboration among traditionally discipline-specific faculties, resulting in curricular changes, including integrated modules. All three have resulted in broader-based services involving more professions. Communities accustomed to receiving only nursing care now have dentistry, occupational therapy, ophthalmology, rehabilitation and nutrition services. Students reportedly learned to refer to other professions and to improve their critical thinking through exposure to other professions and different approaches. They developed an understanding of the health care needs of their communities, while their teachers thought beyond the boundaries of their respective disciplines. Early exposure, said the report, increased the chance that students would choose to work in these communities. Not least, aspirations were raised, and options widened, for young people in the communities as they identified with students embarking on so many different careers.

Migration

Pressure on health and social care workers is further exacerbated by increased mobility of population within and between countries, which can weaken kinship ties and increase dependence upon health and social care services in both the home and host community.

Migrants tend to be drawn from the most educated and most enterprising groups, whose economic and social contribution cannot easily be replaced in their home communities. This adds greatly to the concentration of highly dependent groups left behind. Many are elderly with multiple needs, taxing limited health, social care and other services. Immigrants bring highly marketable educational skills, which inject new enterprise into the economy of the host nations. Indeed, many join the health and social care workforce.

Settling in the host community is by no means always stressful, nor unduly demanding on health and social care services. Stress is more likely when language, ethnicity and/or religion differ from the host community and especially for those who arrive as refugees or illegally; stress which can extend to those to whom they turn for help and advice. Some migrant groups bring different disease patterns, from different cultural contexts, with which health care workers may be unfamiliar, lacking the expertise to diagnose and treat. They may also present health conditions for which treatment was not available in the country of origin, made worse by neglect and sometimes by poor living conditions (Karmi, 1993). Stress in adjusting to cultural expectations, reluctance to seek help from official agencies, limited income after remitting money to relatives back home and sometimes inability to communicate in the language of the host country, may exacerbate problems (Lillie-Blanton & Hudman, 2001).

Concentration of immigrants in the inner city puts pressure on hard-pressed services, which must be ready to respond to the needs of a transient population in intermittent contact with health and social care workers, and liable to fall between the safety nets which each service seeks to provide. Problems, if and when presented, may be more advanced, less amenable to help and, in consequence, more demanding on workers. Effective action lies in working with minority groups ready and able to support new arrivals. Although agencies and professions may do so separately, more effective relations may be built collectively.

Many immigrants, their children and grandchildren establish themselves successfully in the land of their adoption. Others fail to escape the poverty trap exacerbated by poor housing, under-education and unemployment. Disadvantage passes from generation to generation. So, too, does discrimination. Customs, beliefs, life styles and dietary habits handed down may be associated with poor health. Engaging with these is difficult, if not impossible, without active support from the minority communities concerned. External intervention may be construed as insensitive at best, and discriminatory at worst, bedevilled by ethical and cultural conundrums. Few health and social care professionals feel adequately equipped to deal with these situations, although some from particular communities, or working closely with them, are well placed to build coalitions between professionals and community leaders.

One interprofessional network has made a concerted response to the combined impact of poverty, migration and multiculturalism on health. Community Campus Partnership originated in the USA and has since spread worldwide. It engages faculty and students from schools of medicine, health and social care in health-related collaborative projects with surrounding community groups to improve local services and, in doing so, to strengthen community orientation in learning and the quality and quantity of community-based practice placements (Gelmon et al., 1998). Some projects are even more ambitious. They mobilise the expertise of the university across all academic disciplines, singly and in combination, so far as necessary and practicable, to respond to wide-ranging needs identified by local people in the surrounding community to improve their quality of life (Casto et al., 1998).

The Community Campus Partnership movement has taken root in many developing countries, notably in Latin America and South Africa, supported by the W. K. Kellogg Foundation, which redirected funds previously allocated to support USA initiatives. It is closely associated with Towards Unity for Health (TUFH) launched with backing from the WHO in 1999 to improve the relevance and performance of health service delivery systems through the creation of productive and sustainable partnerships between universities and communities. It includes 23 projects in 11 Latin American countries, involving 15 health special-ties in developing experimental models of health care reform (Boelen, 2000; Goble, 2003) and became part of the worldwide Network: Community Partner-ships for Health through Innovative Education, Service and Research in 2002 which was then renamed the Network: Towards Unity for Health.

We have already included one community-campus example from South Africa (see Box 2.8). We have chosen for our second one of the many American commu-nity-campus partnership programmes, which mobilise the combined capacity of health and social care professions in hard-pressed services to respond to seem-ingly intractable poverty in communities with large numbers of immigrants and minority ethnic groups. It happens to be in a sparsely populated rural area, but might equally be in an inner city (see Box 2.9).

Box 2.9   Recruiting professionals in a deprived rural community
(Slack *et al.*, 2002).

The Nuestro Salud Project in Arizona was one of five linked interprofessional projects in the USA seeking to improve recruitment of health care workers in rural areas, providing training for 17 different professions serving disadvan-taged Hispanic, Afro-American, Amish, Native American and Anglo popula-tions. Services provided included: individual clinical care, case management, population-level interventions and collaborative research. Case conferences and local coalitions facilitated collaboration with local communities.

The Project served Santa Cruz County, bordering Mexico, with a population density of 25.7 people per square mile, of whom 78% were Hispanic. Only 32% were high school graduates, 54% did not have health insurance, 24% were unemployed and the median income was 23% of the State average. Cross-border trade was the backbone of the economy, but brought with it problems of law enforcement (including illegal migration) and environmental stress from pollution, including rivers polluted by raw sewage.

The programme provided practice training lasting between four weeks and one year for graduate and undergraduate students in nursing, pharmacy, medicine, social work, public health and nutrition, from two universities. Their first assignment was to conduct a community-based assessment using a systems model, interviewing residents to obtain their perspectives. Resi-dents then asked the programme for student involvement in community projects, from which the students made a choice. Examples included: helping to run health fairs, convening a domestic violence forum, teaching child development and producing a TV series on adolescent health. Knowledge

---

(Continues)

derived from the local community ensured that case management was responsive where 80% of clients had low income and 54% had language problems. Self-instructional modules backed up the practice learning in its early stages complemented by weekly seminars on case management and community health.

Exposure to rural practice helped rural recruitment and retention strategies. Data from one of the projects indicated that 20% of the students went on to practice in rural areas. Other benefits were a reduction in the isolation of rural practitioners, relationship building between universities and those practitioners, and networking between rural and urban service providers. Urban-based professionals meeting rural residents were thought likely to be more aware of their problems, while university faculties developed expertise in rural care.

A chain reaction?

Reviewing interprofessional education in West London, Barr *et al.* (1998) formulated a chain reaction (Figure 2.1), which we have modified below to demonstrate how such education, as it leads into interprofessional practice, holds the potential not only to reduce stress but also to improve client care. Each of the links made can be found in at least one of the examples given in this chapter.

Positive interaction

- Problem solving complemented didactic teaching in Michigan
- CONCAH workshops in the UK were interactive and learner-centred
- Participants in the Finland Study worked more in pairs and groups as their programme progressed
- Participation was problem-based and improved over time in the Netherlands

Mutual trust and support

- Workshops in Eastern Europe engendered trust, which was not possible in totalitarian days

Collaboration

- The Community Coalition in Michigan cultivated interprofessional collaboration in teams and with local communities
- The support group in the Dutch palliative care unit discussed problems in teams, but was more successful cultivating collaborative learning among senior than junior staff
- Team development was the second part of the workshops in Eastern Europe
- Students on the longer courses at the Tavistock Centre learned how to network
- Individual learning gave way to team-based learning in Nottingham
- Teachers from different disciplines collaborated more after engaging in interprofessional practice learning for their students

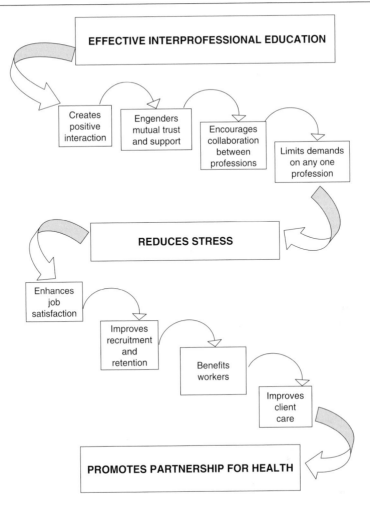

Figure 2.1 A chain reaction.

Limiting demands
- Students on the shorter Tavistock course learned to ask for help and to refer
- Participants in Finland felt less omnipotent as they learnt to value clients' resources

Reducing stress

- Participants in CONCAH workshops developed insight in the problems faced in working lives
- Stress was lessened when recognised early in the Dutch palliative care unit
- Participants in Finland became more able to tolerate uncertainty, coped better with stress and were less prone to burn out

Enhanced job satisfaction

- Participants in Nottingham were empowered

- Participants in Finland found ways to cope at work

Improved recruitment and retentions

- Interprofessional practice learning on the USA/Mexican border improved staff recruitment and retention
- Practice experience in rural areas in South Africa encouraged students to consider working in rural communities

Improved client care

- Some of the teams in the Community Coalition established new services
- Forty out of 48 practices taking part in CONCAH workshops implemented plans made
- Action research in Nottingham challenged existing ways of working
- Students on the USA/Mexican border and in South Africa initiated community projects during their placements
- Career aspirations were raised for young people in rural South African communities as a result of meeting students

Examples of interprofessional education, however carefully chosen, cannot establish conclusively each link in the above chain. Nor can interprofessional education do so alone. It paves the way for teamwork, which improves job satisfaction and reduces occupational stress and turnover as UK (Borrill *et al.*, 2001) and USA studies (Baggs & Ryan, 1990; Baggs *et al.*, 1997) have found. Effective interprofessional education does not, however, hand over to teamwork; it continues alongside and sometimes within it.

Conclusion

Many of the studies included in our systematic review (see Chapter six) reported participants' satisfaction with the learning experience, but by their very nature could not tell us about satisfaction with interprofessional working. Findings which reported impact on practice referred invariably to improvements in services and/or benefit to clients. Client and practitioner satisfaction are, however, related entities, as arguments and evidence presented in this chapter have shown. We offer an overview of interprofessional education in the next chapter before presenting the evidence from our systematic review.

3 Capturing Interprofessional Education in Essence

In this chapter we try to capture the essence of interprofessional education: its origins, rationale, semantics, definition, key variables, aims, content and learning methods, outcomes and quality indicators. Many of these themes are touched on but lightly, as a prelude to fuller discussion in Chapters five, six and seven, informed by evidence from the review.

Searching for origins

The genesis of interprofessional education is widely attributed to a seminal report from a World Health Organization working group in Geneva (WHO, 1988), but closer examination reveals that that report drew upon extant examples in no fewer than 14 countries. Earlier WHO reports (1973, 1978a) may have prompted earlier initiatives in many countries (Meads & Ashcroft, 2005), but reference to the WHO is lacking in examples of interprofessional education reported in the literature before 1988, which more often seemed to be initiated in response to local and national needs and circumstances rather than international injunctions. The significance of the 1988 WHO report therefore lies more in reinforcing than in instigating interprofessional education.

Formulating a rationale

The 1988 WHO report advocated shared learning to complement profession-specific programmes. Students should learn together during certain periods of their education, said the WHO, to acquire skills necessary for solving the priority problems of individuals and communities known to be particularly amenable to teamwork. Emphasis should be put on learning how to interact with one another and community orientation to ensure relevance to the health needs of people and team competence.

Deliberations in Geneva were informed by those of an earlier WHO working group in Copenhagen, where delegates had argued that students from health professions with complementary roles in teams should share learning to discover the value of working together, as they defined and solved problems within a common frame of reference. They held that such learning should employ partici- patory learning methods to modify reciprocal attitudes, foster team spirit, identify and value respective roles, while effecting change in both practice and the profes- sions. This approach, said the working group, would support the development of integrated health care, based on common values, knowledge and skills (d'Ivernois & Vodoratski, 1988).

The WHO gave its regions responsibility for promoting interprofessional edu- cation. Many developing countries and some smaller European nations re- sponded to this lead, but its influence in larger developed countries, which embraced interprofessional education, is less evident. We have chosen Canada as an example of a national initiative (see Box 3.1).

Box 3.1   Canada as a case study (Oandasan *et al.*, 2004).

Intent upon enhancing interprofessional collaboration between the health and social professions, the Canadian Federal Government has rolled out a number of initiatives since the early 1990s. A key one, Collaboration for Prevention, encouraged health care organizations to implement several projects demon- strating how health care teams could work together and involve patients in decision making. Building upon this work, the Federal Government agency, Health Canada, announced in 2000 that $800m would be distributed through provincial and territorial agreements to support primary care pro- viders to help foster collaborative approaches to meeting patients' health care needs.

More recently, the First Minister's accord on health care renewal (Health Canada, 2003) identified new routes in education for health care professionals. Interprofessional Education for Collaborative Patient-centred Practice (IECPCP) became a central component for the future education of the health professions, to ensure that they have the knowledge, skills and attitudes to practice in a patient-centred way. A research team was assigned the task of examining the development and implementation of IECPCP. It reviewed national and international trends in interprofessional education and practice, informed by successful and unsuccessful examples found in a nationwide survey and a literature review. Core elements were analysed first for collaborative practice and then for interprofessional educa- tion. A key recommendation from this study was the need for theoretically based interprofessional education which is patient-centred and undertaken in a non-threatening and reflective learning environment in small interprofes- sional groups.

Sinking in the semantics

Successive initiatives in different countries have introduced their own termin-ology, so much so that the field has become a semantic 'quagmire' (Leathard, 1994, p. 5). Prefixes (inter-, multi- and cross-) precede adjectives (professional, disciplinary and agency) which precede nouns (education, training, studies and learning) in seemingly endless permutations. *Joint training* and *shared learning* offer more prosaic alternatives, but the field is bedevilled by competing terms. Some lack definition; others are given precise but restricted definitions which lack general currency.

Consistent with its name, CAIPE uses *interprofessional education* to describe its field of activity, as does the wider movement worldwide of which it is part. *Multiprofessional education* is, however, more often used in those countries and movements which follow the lead given by the WHO.

Adopting definitions

The following WHO (1988) definition of multiprofessional education wears well and accords closely with that of interprofessional education used in this book:

> 'The process by which a group of students or workers from health related occupations with different educational backgrounds learn together during certain periods of their education, with interaction as an important goal to collaborate in providing promotive, preventive, curative, rehabilitative and other health related services.' (p. 5)

Helpful though this definition is, we find the one for interprofessional education from CAIPE (1997, p. 19), as modified in the Preface, simpler and more manage-able: 'Occasions when two or more professions learn with, from and about each other to improve collaboration and the quality of care.' We also found it helpful to adopt the CAIPE distinction between interprofessional education and multipro-fessional education defined as: 'Occasions when two or more professions learn side by side for whatever reason.'

Identifying interprofessional education

If defining interprofessional education is difficult, identifying it is doubly so. Numerous examples can be found in the literature, as our review demonstrates in the next chapter, but much interprofessional learning is serendipitous, happening by chance in unplanned and perhaps unacknowledged ways (Freeth *et al.*, 2005, Chapter one). It occurs during interactions between different professions in the course of everyday work. Background information may, for example, be provided by one profession about a case that contributes to the learning of a colleague from another profession (Barr, 2003a).

Learning that informs collaboration may also occur during uniprofessional and multiprofessional education when, for example, a topic is considered from different professional perspectives or a case study introduces different professions and prompts discussion about their roles and relationships. Such learning is not dependent upon the physical presence of the parties to the collaborative practice. Teachers and participants may introduce other professions, for example, in case studies or role-play.

Conceptually, the boundary between interprofessional, multiprofessional and uniprofessional education may be clear, but operationally it is blurred and permeable. Interprofessional learning can and does develop within uni-professional and especially multiprofessional education. This is an opportunity, not a problem. Conversely, interprofessional education may become multiprofessional education for lack of understanding of its principles and methods, or failure to invest the necessary resources to deliver them.

Arguably, interprofessional learning is more effective when it ceases to be serendipitous, that is, when it is planned, recognised and so becomes accessible to the application of those principles and methods, although we have no evidence to that effect. Much, perhaps most, interprofessional learning will, however, always remain casual, incidental and sometimes hidden from view. Indeed, that may be seen as one of the fruits of interprofessional education as its values, perspectives and approaches permeate the wider culture of learning and practice.

Formulating principles for interprofessional learning

Interprofessional education is collaborative, egalitarian, group directed, experiential, reflective and applied. We describe each of these as follows, pending fuller discussion later of the characteristics of interprofessional education.

Collaborative learning is both end and means. Interprofessional education is a microcosm of collaborative practice, a demonstration of the art of the possible. Much though teachers may encourage collaborative learning, competition is never wholly absent from professional and interprofessional education. Rivalry may also be played out between the professions participating, rivalry introduced from relationships in the world of work to be examined as part of the learning experience.

Egalitarian learning minimises status differences between participant and teacher, and between participant and participant. Every effort is made to set aside differences between professions in income, social class, educational background and public esteem, so that participants may learn as equals.

Group directed learning goes beyond self-directed learning as understood in adult learning. It comes into play when participants carry collective responsibility for group assignments. On the one hand, these expose attitudes and habits that impede collaborative practice to critical review and revision. On the other hand, they enable participants to test and develop collaborative competencies. Group directed learning is reinforced when it leads to group assessment.

Experiential learning is a powerful medium in interprofessional education to modify entrenched attitudes and to develop collaborative skills. Participants experience, and reflect upon, interprofessional encounters during group discussion and work as a team in a practice setting. Each participant contributes his or her experience for the benefit of fellow participants and of the group as a whole. Conversely, he or she benefits from the experience of the other participants. Exchange is not, however, limited to personal experience. A well planned curriculum, skilfully facilitated, enables participants to introduce the corporate experience of their agencies.

Reflective learning puts much emphasis on Schön's (1983, 1987 & 1991) writing about reflective practice. He distinguished between reflection-in-action, where the professional had to make quick decisions, and reflection-on-action, where he or she had time, opportunity and encouragement to learn from experience. Both contribute to the store of personal knowledge that models professional practice.

Interprofessional reflection exposes perspectives, values and modes of action by one profession to scrutiny by one or more other, scrutiny that allows questioning, clarification and sometimes challenge. This co-reflection, by which we understand ways in which participants reflect one to another, has been likened to the double mirror used by the hairdresser, one in which the customer sees for themself, the other held behind by the hairdresser to see things that personal reflection cannot reveal (Wee, 1997). Pressing the analogy, one participant may not like what fellow participants expose to view through the second mirror and may need the support of the group to cope with personal or professional traits about which he/she had hitherto been blind. Time and opportunity may be more readily available in college-based learning, although work-based learning may have more immediate call upon practice experience.

Applied learning relates the content and experience of interprofessional education to collaborative practice, identifying the barriers that may impede it and ways in which they can be surmounted, and the strategies that can enhance it. Indeed, these principles are consonant with adult learning theories that emphasise a need for group interaction and the understanding of how revisiting and reflecting on learning is essential for it to become embedded (Jarvis *et al.*, 2003).

One or more foci of purpose

Earlier work suggested that it might be helpful to classify interprofessional education initiatives in the current review according to their focus on one or more of three purposes:

(1) Preparing individuals for collaboration
(2) Cultivating collaboration in groups or teams
(3) Improving services and the quality of care

The first of these focuses on establishing knowledge bases, acquisition of skills and the modification of attitudes and perceptions by individuals to pave the way for collaborative practice between professions, within and between organisations and with clients, their caregivers and communities. The second focuses on learning how to collaborate as a group or team-based activity, either directly between the parties (practitioners in the workplace) or by proxy (students during courses). The third focuses on purposeful collective action to effect change and improve the quality of services and care for clients, which becomes interprofessional education if and when learning is built in between the participant professions. All three overlap (see Figure 3.1).

Focus one may stand alone in college-based interprofessional education, but it may also feed into the second within the same programme or subsequently. The second may be a precondition for the third, the machinery through which professions collaborate to effect change. Conversely, engagement in such joint action may strengthen the knowledge and skills of individual participants, reinforce collaborative practice and ultimately contribute to an improvement of services.

Preparing individuals for collaborative practice is generally a responsibility of college-led interprofessional education, whereas improving care is primarily service-led interprofessional education. Figure 3.1 shows how cultivating collaboration may be a shared endeavour, with overlap of purpose possible whatever the focus primarily selected, and the potential for all three purposes to operate. These are propositions to which we return in the light of findings from our review (see Chapter four).

Suffice it to say, meanwhile, that each focus has different implications for the content, learning methods and location of interprofessional education, and its

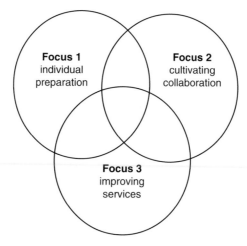

Figure 3.1   Three foci of interprofessional education.

stage in professional learning, all of which call for scrutiny in the light of the evidence we present in the next chapter.

Integrated or freestanding

Interprofessional education in the early years was typically freestanding, initiatives being outside the mainstream of uniprofessional education (e.g. Jones, 1986; Spratley & Pietroni, 1994). That may account for the clarity and coherence of their message, but also for their marginality and insecurity. Few outlasted initial funding or the enthusiasm of their champions. Increasingly, interprofessional education is built into uniprofessional or multiprofessional education programmes as dimensions, options or emphases. This provides a measure of security and continuity.

Interprofessional educators may find much in the accumulated experience of freestanding programmes to consider for inclusion in integrated programmes. Doing this depends, on the one hand, upon making examples of such programmes accessible and, on the other hand, upon the readiness of educators to recognise and value lessons from the past, which is difficult where they are under the mistaken impression that they are the pioneers.

Before or after qualification

Interprofessional education may be delivered before or after qualification. Conventional wisdom long held that it should be left until some time after qualification when practitioners had found their respective identities and had experience under their belts to share (Dombeck, 1997; Pirrie et al., 1998). This is no longer the case. The need for practitioners to engage in collaborative practice from 'day one' makes the case for pre-qualifying interprofessional education, especially in the UK.

If interprofessional education is to be before qualification at what stage should it be introduced? Opinions differ between those who believe that it should begin as soon as practicable (e.g. Areskog 1994, 1995a,b) and those (echoing the preceding argument) who believe that it should be left until the final year, when students have begun to find their feet in their respective professions (e.g. Wahlström et al., 1997).

Many now argue for a continuum of interprofessional education interwoven with uniprofessional and multiprofessional education at every stage in pre-qualifying programmes and throughout lifelong continuing interprofessional development (see Freeth et al., 2005, Chapter one).

In college or the workplace

College and workplace offer different but complementary opportunities for interprofessional learning. Each can reinforce the other. The distinction between the two is, however, less clear than it may at first appear. Work-based learning may be college-led, for example student placements, or employment-led, for example staff development, with different implications for its focus, aims, content and learning methods. These and other dimensions of interprofessional education are explored further in Chapter five.

Integrating curricula

Much effort has been invested in reframing uniprofessional curricula into multiprofessional or interprofessional curricula. Szasz, the Canadian pioneer in interprofessional education, advocated 'integrated curricula' to counter the compartmentalisation of knowledge and the adverse effects of separatist and competitive cultures resulting from academically, and often geographically, discrete health care education programmes (Szasz, 1969). Another argument, this time from the USA, is that learning together can counter the proliferation of health professions (Baldwin, 1996) (see Chapter one).

Bernstein (1971) described moves towards an integrated curriculum to create opportunities to make active connections between different subject matter in the interests of relevance to practice. For Barnett (1999), integrated curricula were vital for the cognitive development of students who would be required to respond flexibly to the needs of individuals, families and communities.

He argued that interdisciplinary education:

- Related learning to real life situations
- Created a context for new kinds of thinking
- Exposed students to a wider range of teaching strategies
- Created supra-rationality
- Developed capacity to challenge suppositions

Integrated curricula, for Beattie (1995), promised to transcend the tribalism of the health professions, while Hammick (1998) demonstrated how Bernstein's (1996) distinction between 'singular discourses', such as biology and psychology, or 'regionalisation of knowledge', as in medicine and nursing, could be used to reframe professional into interprofessional curricula.

Some of the early movements to integrate curricula were designed to combine related professions, for example social work and nursing, whereas later movements drew together the more disparate groups, such as the allied health professions and the complementary therapies (Barr, 2002). These movements can be seen as precursors for more inclusive attempts to frame common curricula across all health and social care professions.

Tope (1996) analysed the content of pre-qualifying programmes for 13 professions in South Wales: dental hygiene, dental technology, dentistry, dietetics, medicine, nursing, nutrition, occupational therapy, operating department practice, physiotherapy, podiatry, social work, speech therapy and radiography. The outcome was a list of 116 items, ranging from ageing to writing reports, whose presence or absence was then charted for each programme. Some, such as group dynamics, listening skills and verbal communication, were found in all programmes, others in the majority. Invited to identify subjects suitable for 'interdisciplinary learning', 80% or more of the teachers who took part in Tope's study included each of the following: psychology, sociology, ethics, law and practice, research methods, management, economics of health and social care, health promotion, study skills, quality issues, structural problems and computing skills.

'Common learning' rather than 'integrated curricula' has become the catchphrase in the UK, where it has been invoked to help implement the NHS Workforce Strategy as part of the modernisation agenda (Department of Health, 2000).

'Genuinely multiprofessional education' (Department of Health, 2000, pp. 1–3) would promote:

- Teamwork
- Partnership and collaboration between professions, between agencies and with patients
- Skill mix and flexible working between professions
- Opportunities to switch training pathways to expedite career progression
- New types of worker

Pre-qualifying interprofessional education programmes (known as 'common learning sites') were being piloted and embedded nationwide at the time of writing in 2005. Four 'leading edge sites' were at King's College, London, with Greenwich and London South Bank Universities, Sheffield and Sheffield Hallam Universities, Southampton and Portsmouth Universities, and Newcastle-on-Tyne, Northumbria and Sunderland Universities, each group being in partnership with surrounding health and social care agencies. Evaluations from these and other programmes should provide evidence of the effectiveness of pre-qualifying interprofessional education.

Interprofessional education has adopted and adapted a repertoire of interactive learning methods from uniprofessional education, as we discuss in Chapter seven, each of which applies principles of adult education to interactive learning.

Putting principles into practice

CAIPE (2001) commends the following principles of interprofessional education. Effective interprofessional education:

- Works to improve the quality of care
- Focuses on the needs of service users and carers
- Involves service users and carers
- Promotes interprofessional collaboration
- Encourages professions to learn with, from and about one another
- Enhances practice within professions
- Respects the integrity and contribution of each profession
- Increases professional satisfaction

Many of these refer back to earlier discussion in this chapter. Three of these stress the need for interprofessional education to reinforce the professions separately as well as corporately, so that each contributes more effectively to the whole:

- Enhances practice within professions

Interprofessional education helps each profession to improve its own practice and to understand how that is complemented by the practice of other professions.

- Respects the integrity and contribution of each profession

Interprofessional education does not threaten the identity and territory of the participant professions. It values the distinctive contribution which each brings to learning and practice, and treats all participants as equals.

- Increases professional satisfaction

Interprofessional education fosters mutual support between professions, encouraging flexible and fulfilling working practices, but also setting manageable limits on the demands made on each (as discussed in Chapter two).

The acid test is not only whether interprofessional education leads to interprofessional practice, but whether it also reinforces professional education and practice.

Checking quality

CAIPE has published guidelines designed to improve standards in interprofessional education in accordance with these principles (Barr, 2003b). They posed the following questions to help planners and evaluators test whether their programmes are measuring up to their expectations:

- Do the aims as stated promote collaboration?

to check whether a programme is interprofessional

- How do the objectives contribute towards collaboration?

to check that promises are carried through

- Do the aims and objectives contribute to improving the quality of care?

to check whether the programme treats collaboration as a means to that end

- Are aims and objectives compatible?

to check, for example, compatibility of multiprofessional and interprofessional aims

- How is interprofessional learning built into the programme?

to check how interprofessional dimensions or emphases are integrated

- Is the programme informed by a theoretical rationale?

to prompt planners, teachers and evaluators to consider and select theoretical perspectives judiciously

- Is the programme evidence-based?

to prompt use of the emerging evidence in decision making

- Is the programme informed by interprofessional values?

to prompt introduction and ownership of such values

- Does comparative learning complement common learning?

to check that comparative and common learning sequences form a coherent whole

- Are learning methods interactive?

to check use of the group to engender comparative learning

- Is small group learning included?

to ensure that interactive learning is practicable

- Will numbers from the participant professions be reasonably balanced?

to optimise interactive learning so far as practicable

- Are all the professions represented in planning and teaching?

to ensure that the needs of all the participant professions are met

- Are clients and carers involved?

to bring them in as collaborators in learning and working

- Will the interprofessional learning be assessed?

to reinforce value given to interprofessional education

- Will it count towards qualification?

to reinforce further the value given to interprofessional education

- How will the programme be evaluated?

to provide feedback to stakeholders and contribute to the evidence base

- Will findings be disseminated?

to contribute to mutual support and exchange in interprofessional education

Building on the basics

This chapter has provided the bare bones of interprofessional education on which we put flesh in later chapters, informed by findings from our review. First, however, we explain why and how we set about that review.

4 Reviewing the Evidence Base

This chapter describes the process that we followed to systematically review and assess the empirical evidence on interprofessional education. It reports key findings from this work that contribute a unique understanding of the nature of interprofessional education and how researchers have attempted to understand its impact on students, practitioners and clients.

Introduction

The need to evaluate interprofessional education and understand its effects has long been recognised. The WHO stressed that claims, to which it subscribed, that such education could promote teamwork should be subjected to critical evaluation (WHO, 1978a, b, 1988). The Council of Europe endorsed that view when it mapped developments in interprofessional education in its member states (European Health Committee, 1993). Nevertheless, occasions when interprofessional education was formally evaluated and findings made publicly available remained few, widely dispersed and largely uncoordinated. This provided the spur for our endeavours towards synthesising what was already known to inform future developments in interprofessional education and its evaluation.

Signs of mounting interest in evidence-based health care practice during the years that we have been working on our reviews reinforced that conviction. Moves towards synthesising the evidence base for practice were prompting questions as to whether similar methods might be employed to synthesise the evidence base for education, especially professional education, in preparation for such practice. Hargreaves (1996) challenged the British educational establishment to make better use of evidence to guide its practice, citing evidence-based medicine as an example to link research and practice, although his views did not go unchallenged. Teaching, critics argued, was a personal matter. The interaction between teacher, learner and subject matter was unique to every situation rendering general findings of little value (Hammersley, 1997).

Much the same reaction greeted our decision to embark upon our first systematic review. Interprofessional learning, some colleagues insisted, was at too early a stage to be exposed to critical scrutiny. Little would be found. What was found might be negative or inconclusive, undermining efforts to make interprofessional education effective by trial and error and feeding ammunition to its opponents. Some things were better taken on trust.

Exponents of interprofessional education were, however, coming under pressure to demonstrate its effectiveness. Plans were taking shape to replace small-scale, short-lived and marginal initiatives by large-scale, long-term strategies within and across professional programmes. Investment had to be justified, not only in large-scale developments, but also costly interactive learning in small groups demanding generous staff/student ratios. The case for interprofessional education had to be made afresh in more critical and cost-conscious times, as ever-larger numbers of teachers and trainers became involved. Demands for evidence grew, accompanied by expectations of 'a burden of proof' for the efficacy of interprofessional education not asked of uniprofessional education, applying tests applicable to the evaluation of clinical practice, but questionable for the evaluation of education. We therefore decided to embark on a systematic review of interprofessional education to begin synthesising evidence for its effects.

Conducting systematic reviews

Systematic reviews provide a critical synthesis of empirical evidence relating to the effects of specific 'interventions', a means to search and evaluate evidence in a comprehensive, systematic and transparent fashion. A number of review bodies now promote and disseminate systematic review work. These include:

- The Cochrane Collaboration (www.cochrane.org)
- The Campbell Collaboration (www.campbell.gse.upenn.edu)
- The Centre for Reviews and Dissemination (www.york.ac.uk/inst/crd/welcome.htm)
- The National Institute for Clinical Excellence (www.nice.org.uk/nice-web)
- The Social Care Institute for Excellence (www.scie.org.uk)
- The Evidence for Policy and Practice Information and Coordinating Centre (The EPPI-Centre (http://eppi.ioe.ac.uk/EPPIWeb/home.aspx))

The shared aim of these bodies is to build a substantive and accessible evidence base for practitioners, policy makers and service users.

Reviewing interprofessional education

We have been reviewing the evidence base of interprofessional education for over eight years. To date, we have produced two systematic reviews.[1] The first was

---

[1] We also undertook a third review that focused on UK-based evaluations of interprofessional education, which yielded 19 papers. See Barr *et al.* (2000) for further details of this work.

registered with the Cochrane Collaboration. It focused on establishing the effects of interprofessional education in relation to two outcome criteria (changes in organisational and/or patient outcomes). It was restricted to three research designs: randomised controlled trials (RCTs), controlled before-and-after studies (CBAs) and interrupted time series studies. A comprehensive search strategy was developed with support from an information scientist. Searches of two electronic bibliographic databases: Medline (1966–1998), CINAHL (1982–1998) and the grey (unpublished) literature revealed that no studies met these narrow methodological and outcome criteria. See Zwarenstein *et al.* (1999, 2001) for further details on our first review. Nevertheless, undertaking this review was very important in providing solid training and experience for subsequent work.

During our Cochrane review we found a number of studies that, despite falling outside the initial inclusion criteria, offered potentially useful insights into the wider range of effects produced from interprofessional education. Informed by our Cochrane review and interested in pursuing this work in more depth, we embarked upon a second review, the Interprofessional Education Joint Evaluation Team (JET) review. The aim of this review was to be less constrained by methodological and outcome criteria. Following new searches of four electronic databases: Medline (1966–2003), CINAHL (1982–2001), BEI (1964–2001) and ASSIA (1990–2003), we found that 353 studies met our new inclusion criteria. This chapter describes the methods we employed to search and evaluate studies of interprofessional education. We then present key findings from the review.

Revising the parameters

We expanded the parameters of this second review by:

- Reframing the research question
- Accepting a wider, more inclusive, definition of interprofessional education
- Accepting a wider range of research methodologies
- Accepting a continuum of outcomes

But this review was less inclusive than the first in two respects. First, we only included peer-reviewed papers obtained from electronic searches of databases. Second, we did not undertake hand searches or searches of the grey (unpublished) literature. We did, however, broaden our research question to read as follows:

'What types of interprofessional education under what circumstances result in what types of outcome?'

In addition, we extended the scope of the review to include informal as well as formal interprofessional education initiatives. For example, quality improvement projects such as continuous quality improvement (CQI), total quality management

(TQM) initiatives and clinical guideline development projects were included, provided that interprofessional learning was clearly recorded in the study.

We amended our initial Cochrane review definition of interprofessional education from: *'The explicit creation of an opportunity for members (or trainees) of more than one social/health occupation to learn together'* to: *'Members (or students) of two or more professions associated with health or social care engaged in learning with, from and about each other.'* This definition differs from that commended by CAIPE as used elsewhere in this book to avoid predetermining outcomes. At the same time, we embraced a wider range of research methodologies to include quantitative (e.g. RCTs, CBAs), qualitative, (e.g. case studies, ethnographies), mixed methods and action research designs.

Finally, we extended our outcome criteria to capture all the reported outcomes from an interprofessional education initiative. To do this, we developed the Kirkpatrick (1967) four-point typology of educational outcomes (learner reaction, acquisition of learning, behavioural change, changes in organisation practice) to six categories (see Table 4.1).

Table 4.1   The JET classification of interprofessional education outcomes.

Level 1 – Reaction	Learners' views on the learning experience and its interprofessional nature.
Level 2a – Modification of attitudes/perceptions	Changes in reciprocal attitudes or perceptions between participant groups. Changes in perception or attitude towards the value and/or use of team approaches to caring for a specific client group.
Level 2b – Acquisition of knowledge/skills	Including knowledge and skills linked to interprofessional collaboration.
Level 3 – Behavioural change	Identifies individuals' transfer of interprofessional learning to their practice setting and their changed professional practice.
Level 4a – Change in organisational practice	Wider changes in the organisation and delivery of care.
Level 4b – Benefits to patients/clients	Improvements in health or well-being of patients/clients.

Searching and selecting studies

The Cochrane review criteria were revised and tested to produce a wider search strategy that we could confidently use in our more inclusive review (see Appendix one). Medline, CINAHL, BEI and ASSIA were searched sequentially to ensure that the review incorporated the relevant education, health and social care literature.

Sequential searching and processing took into account substantial overlap between databases. For example, the CINAHL search identified 124 studies already located and processed through the initial Medline search. As Table 4.2 records, the CINAHL search added 55 new studies. All abstracts and papers obtained from the searches were evaluated by at least two members of the review team to reduce bias.

A two-stage process was employed in the selection of studies eligible for the review. Initially, two questions were posed with each abstract obtained from the searches:

(1) Does this study describe interprofessional education as defined by us?
(2) Has the education described in this study been evaluated?

Where both were answered in the affirmative full papers were obtained. Each full paper was scrutinised by two members of the team in a double-blind manner. If they agreed that the paper reported an evaluation of interprofessional education, it was passed to one member of the team (SR) for abstraction, coding and entering into a statistical software package. Discrepancies in judgement between different review team members, at both the abstract and full paper review stage, were resolved through discussion and, if necessary, by referral to the whole team. As a quality check, other members of the team additionally coded approximately 10% of eligible studies. By this means we obtained 10495 abstracts and retrieved 884 papers, from which 353 papers qualified for inclusion in the review. Of these studies, we assessed 107 studies to be of a higher quality (see Table 4.2).

Table 4.2   Details of searches, abstracts and papers obtained.

Database	Years searched	Abstracts retrieved	Papers retrieved	Included studies	High quality studies
Medline	1966–2000	3374	309	162	43
CINAHL	1982–2001	3054	103	55	10
BEI	1964–2001	49	5	3	3
ASSIA	1990–2003[a]	1567	121	58[d]	25
Medline (update)	2001–2003[b]	2451[c]	346	75	26

Notes
[a] Early analysis of the studies from the Medline, CINAHL and BEI searches revealed that pre-1990 work was more scant and often of a poorer quality than the post-1990 work. It was agreed to focus on post-1990 studies.
[b] Medline was searched up to April 2003.
[c] To ensure that we were capturing all possible examples of interprofessional education that were linked to a quality initiative, we expanded the search strategy for the Medline update. In comparison with the earlier searches, this modification produced an unusually large number of abstracts (See Appendix 1).
[d] Includes three duplicates (papers that report the same evaluation).

LIBRARY. UNIVERSITY OF CHESTER.

Handling the data

Data handling initially entailed transcribing key information from all included studies onto an abstraction sheet. This produced a summary of the content of each paper. Data were collected on the nature of the interprofessional education described (e.g. context, aims, content, duration, delivery, learning and teaching methods). Data were also collected on all reported outcomes from the study. In addition, aspects of the evaluation were coded. These included: rationale, methods, analytical approach and indicators of methodological quality.

Two data abstraction sheets were used for this process: one for studies employing quantitative methods and the other for studies employing qualitative methods (see Appendix two). Both were used to elicit information on mixed methods evaluations. A code book was developed which recorded agreed criteria for entries on the data abstraction sheets, thereby improving consistency.

The development of these abstraction sheets was informed by the one employed for our Cochrane review, various methodological texts/papers and our combined research experience. The process entailed each member using a small sample of studies for abstraction. This generated initial discussion. Ongoing debate led to the modification of the sheets. This process was iterative and time consuming, but important to ensure that our review work was rigorous.

The quantitative data abstraction sheet underwent six drafts to reach a design that could elicit key information effectively. This degree of development was possible due to the number of quantitative studies we found. The qualitative sheet only underwent two drafts due to the limited number of studies employing these methods.

All data from the abstraction sheets was coded and entered into a statistical software package (SPSS) to allow easy examination of all variables. To improve validity after each batch of data entry, the data was 'cleaned' (i.e. searched for data entry errors and omissions). Any relationships that emerged from the coded database were explored further by returning to the data abstraction sheets and the original papers. The remaining studies were assessed for quality (see below) so that any that would qualify for the 'higher quality' subset would be identified, abstracted and coded. None qualified.

Analysis was then undertaken, checking for problems and assessing whether data saturation had been reached. While processing our last search update (Medline 2001–2003) we found that the distribution of findings (see tables below) remained stable and we were not gaining any new insights. After careful cross-checking and discussion we agreed that data saturation had occurred. By this point 223 of the 346 studies identified by the Medline 2001–2003 review had been fully processed, including studies from each year, all geographical areas, all educational stages and a wide spectrum of fields of practice.

Assessing the quality of studies

To identify those studies that were more trustworthy and more illuminating, we added two additional variables into our data abstraction sheets: one evaluating methodological quality, the other evaluating the quality of information provided in the report.

Methodological quality

The methodological quality of a study was judged on a five-point scale, with a score of five representing the highest rating. This score took into account a number of dimensions. These included:

- Whether the evaluation design was appropriate in relation to its research aims/questions (i.e. fitness for purpose)
- Whether selection of participants was based on clear criteria
- Whether validity and reliability or authenticity and trustworthiness had been well considered

For example, where the research aims/questions were oriented towards quantifying outcomes, a well designed and conducted before-and-after study could potentially score five for methodological quality. Similarly, where the research aims/questions were oriented towards understanding processes, a well constructed and conducted ethnography could also score five.

Mid-range scores included evaluations that were competently conducted with clear objectives and inclusion/exclusion criteria, but lacked sufficient detail concerning data analysis or attention to issues of bias. Evaluations that scored only one included weak designs in relation to research questions, for example post-intervention studies, or descriptive studies that lacked detail about research aims and questions, data collection and analysis, and failed to consider issues of bias.

Quality of information

The quality of information provided by a study was also judged on a five-point scale, again with a score of five representing the highest rating. This score took into account a number of factors, such as whether a clear rationale for the evaluation was given, whether good contextual information was provided, whether there was sufficient information on sampling, ethics and possible bias, and whether the analysis had been described in sufficient detail. Further information on this aspect of the review is presented later in the chapter. Further details on our approach in developing and undertaking this systematic review can be found in Reeves *et al.* (2002).

Acknowledging the review's limitations

Although the review has provided a unique insight into the nature, that is, aims, content, focus, evaluation approach and outcomes of interprofessional education, it inevitably has limitations. Despite developing and testing a complex search strategy, terminology related to interprofessional education remains inconsistent (see page 31). Our strategy may have failed to pick up all the myriad descriptions of interprofessional education.

The geographic distribution of the journals abstracted by the databases has meant that there is an English language bias within the review. Furthermore, although the review team was able to evaluate abstracts published in English and French, we did not have resources for translation from other languages. Lack of such resources was not, however, a severe limitation since we found very few abstracts in the databases searched that were not available in English or French.

Resource constraints prevented us from fully utilising other potential sources of interprofessional education evaluations (e.g. web-based reports and papers in relevant journals not yet abstracted by the bibliographic databases). Nevertheless, other reviews and literature searches we and others have undertaken (Barr & Shaw, 1995; Barr & Waterton, 1996; Barr *et al.*, 2000; Cooper *et al.*, 2001; Reeves, 2001) have led us to believe the data set obtained from this review provides a comprehensive picture of evaluations of interprofessional education. There is an understandable bias in the published literature in favour of producing reports of positive results. This means that our data set provides only a partial understanding of the problems associated with developing and delivering interprofessional education.

As we were not gaining any new insights into our understanding of interprofessional education we only reviewed 223 of the 346 papers identified by the review. Nevertheless, a preliminary review of the papers not subjected to full abstraction indicated that none of them qualified as a higher quality study. We therefore agreed that data saturation had occurred during our last search (Medline 2001–2003).

Whilst striving to eliminate systematic error in our work, by using the various quality control mechanisms described above, there may be some random error attached to the work. In addition, at the time of writing the UK was in the middle of implementing a policy drive to promote pre-qualification interprofessional education. Major initiatives were being evaluated and were due to be published. They may well help to answer some of the questions raised by our review. It is in the nature of literature reviews that they are historical snapshots and, in a rapidly changing field such as interprofessional education, rapidly become out of date.

Focusing on the higher quality studies

A total of 353 studies (see Table 4.2) qualified for inclusion in the JET review at the point of saturation. Further examination of these studies revealed that papers

which scored below three for both 'methodological quality' and 'quality of information' contributed too little of value to be included in our analysis. We therefore
concentrate on the 107 higher quality studies that scored three or above for both of
our quality criteria. (See Appendix three for a list of the higher quality studies that
form the data set.) In subsequent chapters we integrate the review findings with
respect to the nature of interprofessional education with thematic discussion.
First, we will summarise some of the key features of the evaluation studies to
give a flavour of the data set that we are drawing upon.

When and where

Table 4.3 provides information on the geographical location of the included
studies.[2] As the table reveals, most evaluations of interprofessional education
(58 studies, 54%) were undertaken in the US. Given this emphasis, review findings must be treated with care, as they may not be directly applicable to other
health and social care education systems. Nevertheless, Europe contributed 37%
(40 studies) of the included evaluations. There was a distinct Nordic emphasis in
the evaluations from mainland Europe, which came from Sweden (Fallsberg &
Wijma, 1999; Fallsberg & Hammar, 2000), Finland (Ketola *et al.*, 2000) and Norway
(Finset *et al.*, 1995), but there was also one from the Netherlands (van Staa *et al.*,
2000).

Table 4.4 (p.49) shows an upward trend in the number of interprofessional
education evaluations published from the early 1990s onwards.

Table 4.3   Distribution of countries.

Location	Frequency
United States	58 (54%)
United Kingdom	35 (33%)
Australia	4 (4%)
Canada	4 (4%)
Sweden	2 (2%)
Ecuador	1 (1%)
Finland	1 (1%)
Norway	1 (1%)
The Netherlands	1 (1%)

Duration and qualification

Table 4.5 (p.49) shows that most studies (58, 54%) reported interprofessional
education that extended over more than seven days of interprofessional contact

---

[2] All percentages have been rounded up to the nearest whole number for ease of presentation.
Consequently, some tables contain aggregated percentage scores that exceed 100.

Table 4.4   Publication year.

Year	Frequency
1974–1990	7 (7%)
1991–1995	24 (22%)
1996–2000	45 (42%)
2001–2003	31 (29%)

Table 4.5   Duration of interprofessional education initiatives.

Duration	Frequency
Over 7 days	58 (54%)
2–7 days	26 (24%)
Under 1 day	14 (13%)
Unclear	9 (7%)

for the participants. This was generally spread over several months, often when participants undertook a series of interprofessional sessions during the implementation of a continuous quality improvement (CQI) or a total quality management (TQM) initiative (e.g. Clemmer *et al.*, 1999; Gazarian *et al.*, 2001).

Few interprofessional education initiatives led to an academic award or qualification (17 studies, 16%). Nor were they accredited for continuing professional development (CPD) (see Table 4.6).

Only ten initiatives provided some form of higher education accreditation, such as linking an interprofessional course to a pre-qualification award (e.g. Mires *et al.*, 2001) or offering a higher education award, such as a Master's degree (e.g. Stanford & Yelloly 1994).

Care sector and condition

Studies were evenly split between interprofessional initiatives that related to hospital-based care and community-based care (Table 4.7). The distribution between chronic and acute conditions was less even. While 64 studies (60%) evaluated interprofessional education focused on chronic conditions, only 31 initiatives (29%) related to acute conditions. A further eight studies (8%) encompassed both acute and chronic conditions.

Nearly half the evaluations that related to chronic conditions were undertaken within community settings, where the management of chronic conditions like asthma or arthritis is commonplace (Table 4.8). While most hospital-based interprofessional education (31 studies, 29%) related to acute conditions, such as cardiac resuscitation (Birnbaum *et al.*, 1994) or acute asthma (Gazarian *et al.*, 2001),

Table 4.6 Qualification for interprofessional education.

Type of qualification	Frequency
None	78 (73%)
Unclear	12 (11%)
Higher education award/ accreditation	10 (9%)
Continuing education credit	7 (7%)

Table 4.7 Care sector.

Care sector	Frequency
Hospital-based	48 (45%)
Community-based	48 (45%)
Mixed	8 (8%)
Not clear	3 (3%)

Table 4.8 Clinical sector and condition.

Clinical sector	Condition			
	Chronic	Acute	Mixed	Unclear
Community-based	47 (44%)	—	—	1 (1%)
Hospital-based	16 (15%)	31 (29%)	1 (1%)	—
Mixed	1 (1%)	—	7 (7%)	—
Unclear	—	—	—	3 (3%)

16 studies (15%) reported interprofessional education focused on a chronic condition, such as alcohol detoxification (Gunn *et al.*, 1995).

Most of the 35 UK studies evaluated interprofessional education related to chronic conditions (23 studies, 66%), compared with five initiatives (14%) relating to acute conditions. This contrasted with the 58 USA papers, where there was more emphasis on acute conditions (22 studies, 38%), although chronic conditions still dominated (33 studies, 57%).

Stage and participation

Table 4.9 shows that the bulk of interprofessional activities (85 studies, 79%) took place after qualification, as a health or social care professional. We expect the balance to become more even during the next few years, particularly in countries such as Canada and the UK, where government policy is promoting interprofessional education before qualification.

Table 4.9 Pre- and post-qualifying interprofessional education.

Stage of interprofessional education	Frequency
Post-qualification	85 (79%)
Pre-qualification	20 (19%)
Mixed	2 (2%)

Typically, post-qualifying interprofessional education took the form of workshops (Berman *et al.*, 2000; Rost *et al.*, 2000; Morey *et al.*, 2002) or postgraduate studies leading to university degrees, diplomas or credits (Barnes *et al.*, 2000b; Kennard, 2002). In two studies interprofessional education was offered to both pre- and post-qualification learners: medical students and nurses (Freeth & Nicol, 1998); and medical students, unspecified 'allied health' students, general practitioners, community nurses and 'allied health' practitioners (Taylor *et al.*, 2001). Participation by profession is summarised in Table 4.10.

Most interprofessional education initiatives involved nurses and doctors, as Table 4.10 shows. As the two largest practitioner groups in health and social care, it was more likely that they would be participants in interprofessional education. The 'others' included a wide range of professions working in particular fields of practice such as schoolteachers (Cobia *et al.*, 1995), police officers (Stein & Brown 1995; Cornish *et al.*, 2003) and managers or administrators (e.g. Taylor *et al.*, 2001; Bonomi *et al.*, 2002). A number of professions such as audiologists, podiatrists, optometrists and radiographers were missing. It is possible that they were included, but hidden, in the 32 studies (30%) reporting the participation of unspecified allied health professions.

Table 4.10 Professional participation.[3]

Profession	Number of studies
Nurses	95 (89%)
Doctors	88 (82%)
Others (e.g. administrators, schoolteachers)	58 (54%)
Social workers	39 (36%)
Allied health professionals (unspecified)	32 (30%)
Occupational therapists	22 (21%)
Physiotherapists	18 (17%)
Psychologists	16 (15%)
Pharmacists	13 (12%)
Dentists	5 (5%)
Midwives	6 (6%)

[3] Actual and percentage figures in this table exceed 107 and 100% respectively as a single evaluation of interprofessional education will contain two or more professions. Therefore, multiple recording of numbers is necessary.

Research design

Table 4.11 shows that of the eight research designs employed to evaluate inter-professional education, 69 studies (66%) used quasi-experimental or experimental designs: before-and-after studies; before-during-and-after studies; controlled before-and-after (CBAs) and randomised controlled trials (RCTs).

Table 4.11 Evaluation design.

Research Design	Frequency
Before-and-after	46 (44%)
Longitudinal	19 (18%)
Controlled before-and-after	12 (11%)
Post-intervention	11 (11%)
Before-during-and-after	6 (6%)
Case study	6 (6%)
Randomised control trial	5 (5%)
Action research	2 (2%)

The predominance of experimental and quasi-experimental designs was understandable given that they can provide robust detection of change (see Box 4.1 for an example of one of the five experimental designs that we found). However, many of the studies employed a before-and-after design without a control group, which lacks power when compared with CBA and RCT studies (46 studies, 44%). In addition, 11 studies (11%) used the weak post-intervention design. The popularity of these designs may be influenced by resource constraints and evaluators' expertise. Difficulties obtaining a control group may also contribute.

Nine before-and-after and three post-intervention studies strengthened their designs by the incorporation of follow-up data, collected at one point usually between three and twelve months after the interprofessional education (e.g. Itano et al., 1991; Strasser, 1995; Mohr et al., 2002; Way et al., 2002). Two of the post-intervention studies enhanced the quality of their work by the inclusion of control groups (Falconer et al., 1993; Walsh et al., 1995).

The low incidence of action research is noteworthy. Only two action research studies were found (Lacey, 1998; Atwal, 2002), both from the UK. This may be due to the demands of undertaking action research, as researchers work collaboratively with participants in cycles of evaluation and change to achieve positive change and generate theory. It may also reflect the influence of a range of factors that inhibit the publication of action research studies. Box 4.2 presents a summary of one of the two action research studies included in the review.

It was encouraging to identify 19 longitudinal studies (e.g. Clemmer et al., 1999; Milne et al., 2000; Jackson & Bircher, 2002), as this type of research design provides

---

Box 4.1   A randomised controlled trial (Thompson *et al.*, 2000).

A joint collaboration by university and service staff based in Southampton and Portsmouth in England resulted in the development of a randomised controlled trial to evaluate the impact on patient care of implementing a clinical practice guideline for the treatment of depression. Fifty-nine general practices were recruited into the trial. Practices were randomised by computer to the intervention group (made up from 29 teams of general practitioners and practice nurses) who received a four-hour interprofessional session on jointly implementing the guideline, or to a control group (made up from 30 teams). Control group participants did not receive their interprofessional sessions until completion of the trial.

To evaluate the impact of the new guideline, questionnaires were distributed to intervention and control group participants before and after the delivery of the sessions. In addition, depression scale scores of patients treated by the practitioners in both intervention and control groups were collected. It was found that the new guideline was well received by participants. In addition, 80% of participants felt their management of depression had improved as a result of its introduction. However, findings from the depression scale revealed that there was no significant change to patient depression scores following the intervention.

---

valuable accounts of the longer-term effects of interprofessional education (usually over weeks or months) on participants' collaborative practice and the quality of care.

Only six studies (all case studies) drew upon interpretivism (Bain & McKie, 1998; Fallsberg & Hammar, 2000; Reeves, 2000; Roberts *et al.*, 2000; Alderson *et al.*,

---

Box 4.2   An action research study (Lacey, 1998).

Based at the University of Birmingham, in England, this action research study was undertaken with health and social care practitioners who were participating in an interprofessional course for staff working with people with profound and multiple learning difficulties. The author worked collaboratively with course participants, as an action researcher, to enable the course to be developed to meet their needs effectively. Questionnaires, interviews, observations and documentary data were collected over the four-year period of the study.

Responses from the 109 participants, including nurses, physiotherapists, occupational therapists, speech and language therapists and social workers, indicated that the course had a positive impact on their collaborative work and relationships with colleagues working in other professions and agencies. In addition, responses were fed into the ongoing development of the course. Over time, the action research data was used to make a number of course modifications, including the use of distance learning materials and the introduction of a practical project into the course.

2002; Rubenstein *et al.*, 2002). All the studies were from Europe: five were from the UK and one was from Sweden. This may mean that the accumulating evidence from evaluations of interprofessional education begins to answer the 'what?' questions that people have, but can say very little in relation to 'how?' and 'why?' questions. This may inhibit the ability to design effective interprofessional education or to intervene appropriately when negative outcomes are detected.

Data collection and sources

Investigators tended to collect multiple forms of data (e.g. questionnaires, audit data, interviews, observations and documentary data) in their evaluations (Table 4.12). Combining methods ensures evaluation data are generated from multiple perspectives, which in turn can provide a more comprehensive insight into the nature of interprofessional education. Of the 45 multiple methods studies, most (27 studies, 60%) contained two types of data, typically questionnaires and audit data (e.g. Thompson *et al.*, 2000; Dalton *et al.*, 2001; Hermida & Robalino, 2002).

Table 4.12   Data collection methods.

Data Collected	Frequency
Multiple methods *	45 (41%)
Questionnaire	32 (30%)
Clinical audit	21 (20%)
Interview	6 (6%)
Observation	3 (3%)

* (e.g. questionnaires, interviews etc.)

Questionnaires (32 studies, 30%) and audit data (21 studies, 20%), used as the sole method of data collection within a study, were also popular. The relative ease and low expense of collecting these types of data may account for their popularity in the evaluation of interprofessional education. However, the majority of questionnaires were pilot tools that were not validated. Notable exceptions were provided by Carpenter (1995) and Carpenter & Hewstone (1996), who developed the Interprofessional Attitudes Questionnaire, and Hayward *et al.* (1996), who used the Interdisciplinary Education Perception Scale validated by Luecht *et al.* (1990). (See Freeth *et al.*, 2005, Chapter eleven for a discussion on the use of validated scales in interprofessional education.) There was a relative absence of documentary data (e.g. course/curriculum documents and student handbooks) within the studies. Documentary evidence was analysed in 17 studies (16%), usually in combination with questionnaire and interview data (e.g. Stanford & Yelloly, 1994; van Staa *et al.*, 2000; Mohr *et al.*, 2002).

Table 4.13 shows that most studies (58%) exclusively considered the learners' perspective of interprofessional education and a further 21 studies (20%) included learners' perspectives alongside at least one other. Resource limitations may have been the reason. Participants are the easiest group to access. Given the nature of their involvement, they are usually willing to provide feedback. Less attention has been given to obtaining the patient/clients' perspective (11 studies, 10%) including such data. The number of studies that include a patient/client perspective increases from 11 studies (10%) to 25 studies (24%) when account is taken of the 14 studies that drew upon multiple sources of data. Of this subset, ten studies obtained data from both patients and participants. It should, however, be noted that while learner perspectives were obtained directly from individuals, usually in the form of a questionnaire, patient perspectives were typically collected from secondary sources, such as patient notes (e.g. Birnbaum *et al.*, 1994; Morey *et al.*, 2002).

Table 4.13   Source of data.

Source of data	Frequency
Learners	62 (58%)
Clinical audit	13 (12%)
Patients/clients	11 (10%)
Learners & patients/clients	10 (10%)
Learners, patients/clients & staff	2 (2%)
Learners & staff	4 (4%)
Learners & clinical audit	3 (3%)
Learners, patients/clients & clinical audit	1 (1%)
Patients/clients & clinical audit	1 (1%)

Box 4.3 contains a rare example of a study that directly captured the patient's perspective.

Box 4.3   A study focusing on the patient's perspective
(Treadwell *et al.*, 2002).

Interprofessional collaboration between senior staff based in a children's hospital in California resulted in the development and implementation of a quality improvement initiative that aimed to enhance the delivery of pain relief to paediatric patients. The initiative involved the introduction of a paediatric pain assessment tool and a standardised pain assessment protocol. Clinical staff participated in a number of interprofessional sessions to learn how to employ these new tools in their practice. To understand the impact of the initiative, questionnaires were collected from staff and interviews were undertaken with patients or their primary carers both before and after the implementation of the quality improvement programme. Findings from the evaluation revealed that patients/carers reported improved staff responsiveness and improved levels of satisfaction with the management of their pain.

The lack of staff perspectives, for example clinical facilitators and higher education teachers, was striking. Only four studies included data from staff (Madsen *et al.*, 1988; Reeves, 2000; Roberts *et al.*, 2000; Reeves & Freeth, 2002).

Reporting limitations in the studies

Over half of the studies (54%) did not address methodological limitations (see Table 4.14). Word restrictions in journals may account for lack of attention to weaknesses associated with studies, but this detracts from their overall credibility. Less than half (46%) of studies provided some account of their methodological limitations. A useful example is provided by Lalonde *et al.* (2002), who discussed the limitations associated with the use of self-reported data in their evaluation of an interprofessional initiative for health and social care professionals working with people with HIV/AIDS. They also acknowledged the limitations resulting from the absence of a control group and the self-selection of respondents

Table 4.14 Identifying methodological limitations.

Methodological limitations	Frequency
Not discussed	58 (54%)
Multiple biases (e.g. performance, detection, selection)	19 (18%)
Performance	17 (16%)
Detection	12 (11%)
Selection	1 (1%)

Ethical considerations

Most investigations (87 studies, 81%) did not discuss the ethical issues related to their evaluations (see Table 4.15) although there was an upward trend. While none of the studies considered ethical issues from 1974 to 1990; three did so

Table 4.15 Ethical considerations.

Ethical issue	Frequency
Not addressed	87 (81%)
Formal approval	11 (10%)
Informed consent	4 (4%)
Confidentiality	2 (2%)
Anonymity	2 (2%)
Confidentiality and anonymity	1 (1%)

from 1991 to 1995; five from 1996 to 2000; and 12 from 2001 to 2003. This may be a reflection of the increasing demand for enhanced standards of research governance.

Conclusion

We have included in this chapter a selection of findings from our systematic review of evaluations of interprofessional education to provide a basic picture of the nature of interprofessional education and approaches to its evaluation. The complexity of the findings presented points towards the need to discriminate between types or domains of interprofessional education, as we do in the next chapter. This is the first of three chapters in which we interweave further data from our review to illuminate discussions, not only about models, but also about outcomes and learning methods.

5 Distinguishing Between Six Domains

This chapter is the first of three that revisit conventional wisdom about interprofessional education in the light of findings from the review. It distinguishes between six interprofessional education domains, three before and three after qualification.

Introduction

Self evidently, interprofessional education takes many forms, albeit in pursuit of the same aims and applying the same principles. It can also be classified in numerous different ways, taking into account its many dimensions. After testing the utility of alternatives, we selected a classification which enabled us to organise our data so that it highlighted the distinctive ways in which interprofessional education is commonly understood.

Dimensions of interprofessional education

In Chapters three and four we discussed some characteristics of interprofessional education, any combination of which might be included in a classification. For example:

Explicit or implicit

- Recognised or unrecognised as interprofessional education during daily work, uniprofessional or multiprofessional education

Discrete or integrated

- Freestanding or built into professional or multiprofessional education

All or part

- Wholly comprising interprofessional education or a module, elective or strand

General or particular

- Providing a generic overview of interprofessional practice or focusing on a particular client group, practice method or work setting

Individual or collective

- Focusing on the learning by the individual participant or by the group

Work-based or college-based

- In the participant's workplace or educational institution

Work-led or college-led

- Under the auspices of a service agency or an educational institution

Shorter or longer

- Lasting from minutes to years

Sooner or later

- Before qualification (earlier or later in the course), or at some stage after qualification

We combined two of these characteristics to formulate an initial classification as follows:

- College-based pre-qualifying interprofessional education
- Service-based pre-qualifying interprofessional education
- College-based post-qualifying interprofessional education
- Service-based post-qualifying interprofessional education

Careful inspection of our systematic review database and critical discussion of the conceptual differences between these categories confirmed that the distinction between pre- and post-qualification was helpful, but the utility of the distinction between college-based and work-based was questionable. Some examples were both, others were neither, that is, located in hotels and conference centres or delivered by means of electronic or open learning.

More fundamental to creating a meaningful category of interprofessional education is not where an initiative is sited but rather which setting leads to the development and quality assurance of an initiative. We identified three categories (Table 5.1, p.60) and noted the high level of service-led initiatives and relatively low level of jointly-led initiatives.

Combining pre- and post-qualification with organisational leadership creates six domains for interprofessional education as follows:

- College-led pre-qualifying interprofessional education
- Service-led pre-qualifying interprofessional education
- Jointly-led pre-qualifying interprofessional education
- College-led post-qualifying interprofessional education

Table 5.1 Interprofessional education and lead institution.

Lead institution	Frequency
College-led	37 (35%)
Service-led	56 (52%)
Jointly-led	14 (13%)

- Service-led post-qualifying interprofessional education[1]
- Jointly-led post-qualifying interprofessional education

Table 5.2 indicates how studies from the review were distributed in each of these six domains:

Table 5.2 Stage of interprofessional education and lead institution[2].

Stage of interprofessional education	Institutional lead		
	College	Service	Joint
Pre-qualification	12	—	8
Post-qualification	24	56	5

Division into these six domains enabled us to distinguish between characteristics of interprofessional education by type. Pre-qualifying studies lay foundations for post-qualifying studies along a continuum. Each, in an ideal world, would be planned to complement the other as part of progressive sequences of learning. Similarly, college-led and service-led studies would be mutually reinforcing.

Each of the six domains is discussed below, showing the relationship between uniprofessional, interprofessional and in one instance multiprofessional education.

Domain 1: college-led pre-qualifying interprofessional education

We begin by building models for the inclusion of pre-qualifying interprofessional education which is college led. Each model has a corresponding figure. Each includes five (white) rectangles representing uniprofessional programmes, show-

---

[1] More often referred to as staff development, in-house training or continuous professional development (CPD).
[2] This table excludes two 'mixed stage' (for pre- and post-qualifying students), one of which was college led and one was jointly led.

ing how interprofessional education (shaded) has been introduced. There may be more or less than five programmes in reality.

The extra-curricula model

Requirements for licence or validation, pressures on crowded curricula, and sometimes resistance from teachers, can make for difficulties in introducing interprofessional education within and between profession-specific curricula. This argues for assigning pre-qualifying interprofessional education to the margins outside class contact hours for studies required in preparation for awards, which we call the extra-curricula model (see Figure 5.1). (Alternatively, as we discuss below, interprofessional education may be undertaken outside college teaching by linking it with placements.)

Box 5.1 provides an example of the extra-curricula model. This model offers a simple, unthreatening and painless way to implant small-scale interprofessional education where institutions and their staff are not yet ready for its integration within professional programmes, or institutional support for major developments has not yet been secured. Its adoption obviates the need to negotiate changes in profession-specific curricula and to seek approval for major modifications or revalidation. Successful adoption of the extra-curricular model may pave the way for integrated models later.

Meanwhile, achievements may be modest. Students may accord less value to marginal interprofessional studies than to their mainstream professional stud-ies, especially if assessment and credit is lacking. They may also be left as best they can to resolve disjunctions between professional and interprofessional learning. Much may depend upon whether teachers, as well as students, from the professional programmes participate, the enthusiasm with which they do

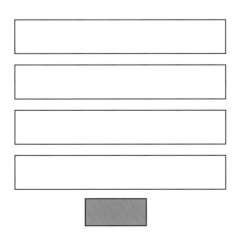

Figure 5.1 Extra-curricula model.

> **Box 5.1**   Saturday school (Gilbert *et al.*, 2000).
>
> Students of nine different health and human services professions took part in two day-long team experiences at the University of British Columbia in Canada. Objectives and content (teambuilding) complemented the professional programmes. Assessment was informal and related to teams, not individuals. It did not count towards course credits. Meetings were held on Saturdays to avoid timetabling problems. Each student was paid $100 to encourage attendance, although feedback suggested that many would have done so anyway. Recruiting teachers (with no extra payment) proved to be more difficult.

so and their readiness to help students to relate professional and interprofessional learning.

The crossbar model

A more integrated model (Figure 5.2) introduces one or more shared learning sequences represented by one or more horizontal bars across college-based pre-qualifying studies. These crossbars may extend to all professions included in the overall plan or be limited to some. They may comprise multiprofessional (light grey) and/or interprofessional studies (dark grey).

Themes, for example ethics or communications, ceded from professional courses or introduced anew, are included in crosscutting bands of study which bind the uniprofessional programmes together. Derived thus, these crossbars only become interprofessional if and when interactive and collaborative learning is built in. Changes may be necessary in profession-specific curricula, calling for

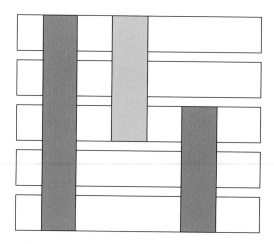

Figure 5.2   Crossbar model.

approval of modifications, but confined to mutually agreed themes or topics. Box 5.2 offers an example of the crossbar curriculum.

Box 5.2   A graduate entry programme for medical and nursing students (Queen Mary University of London, 2004).

The Graduate Entry Programme (GEP) is an interprofessional course developed by St Bartholomew's School of Nursing and Midwifery and the School of Medicine and Dentistry, Queen Mary University of London. The course offers graduate pre-qualifying students a fast-track route into either medicine or nursing. Students undertake a number of interprofessional modules that occur at certain points in their curricula. In the first year they participate in PBL sessions aimed to cover the core knowledge, skills and capabilities that are required by both professions, including the fundamentals of pathology, ethics and law, pharmacology and communication skills. In the second year (final year for the nursing students), the students share opportunities to reflect together as an interprofessional group on their experiences of a range of clinical placements. The medical students' third year is entirely uniprofessional for its college-based elements but the final year provides the opportunity to work on an interprofessional basis as students spend time in a shadow junior doctor attachment.

In some cases crosscutting curricula have been introduced as a block of joint study for an initial period, before students embark upon their profession-specific studies, as pioneered in a classic and highly acclaimed programme in Sweden (see Box 5.3, p.64) which influenced subsequent developments elsewhere.

A further development embeds the crossbar model within a multiprofessional context. In its most radical form, it starts by defining common curricula deemed to be applicable to all the professions to be included, within which profession-specific curricula are embedded. We have chosen one example from a number of the UK pre-qualifying programmes which have gone this far (see Box 5.4, p.64). Most colleges also carry responsibility for practice learning on placement during pre-qualifying studies, and interprofessional education maybe embedded here.

Another application of the crossbar model is where interprofessional education is introduced in the form of a practice placement for groups of students to visit a patient in their own home (see Box 5.5, p.65). Each student tends to see the client through different eyes, focusing on what they have been taught to see, but filtering out other things. Given skilled facilitation, differences in perception provide many and varied opportunities for interprofessional learning when each group comes back to the class.

Other programmes within this model have introduced initiatives which enable students to compare systematically what they are learning and to get to know each other in the process. This is concurrent with doing their practice learning in the same or neighbouring locations (see Box 5.6, p.65).

Box 5.3   Beginning together (Areskog, 1988, 1992, 1994, 1995a,b).

Interprofessional education was introduced in 1984 at the University of Lin-köping in Sweden for students from six professions to promote:

- A holistic approach to health and disease
- Patient-centred education
- Close contact with primary care and preventive work
- Team training
- Coverage of previously neglected research areas

Interprofessional education, it was envisaged, would create flexibility, adaptation to change in occupational roles and collaborative research. Students spent their first ten weeks in a combined programme addressing these and other issues, assisted by teachers from all six professions. Learning was problem-based throughout. Themes included life stages, cultural differences, human development, lifestyle and handicap; and was informed by health economics, health information, medical technology, sociology, social anthropology, ethics and management. After the ten-week period students entered their profession-specific programmes, but with intermittent interprofessional sessions, seminars and theme days. Common sessions were also included for two or three professions together, during clinical training, to highlight patient care from different perspectives.

Box 5.4   Embedding uniprofessional and interprofessional in multiprofessional curricula (Barrett *et al.*, 2003).

The University of the West of England, in Bristol, introduced interprofessional learning into pre-qualifying programmes for ten health and social care professions for over 700 students. The identity of the individual professions was to be preserved and, where possible, enhanced within an overall curriculum which sought to build collaborative skills.

The curriculum framework comprised:

- a variety of shared learning modules
- discrete pathway modules for each profession
- interprofessional learning

The shared learning modules were multiprofessional for those professions needing the same knowledge base. Interprofessional learning permeated the

(Continues)

whole programme throughout students' pre-qualifying education. It was interactive, using enquiry-based learning and client-centred scenarios, complemented by case-based learning on placement. Interprofessional learning was progressive. Interprofessional outcomes had to be explicit in uniprofessional pathway modules and uniprofessional practice placements.

Box 5.5   Joint observation (Anderson & Lennox, 2005).

Leicester Medical School, in England, developed a sophisticated process of observation, originally for medical students, but later extended to include nursing and social work students. The object was to give students opportunities to observe and assess patients in the social, cultural and economic context of a deprived inner-city neighbourhood. Three students, one from each of three professions, visited a patient at home and reported back. They returned to the neighbourhood to interview the patient's key worker. The complete class then planned an end of semester seminar to present their overall impressions to all the key workers although not, so far, to the patients.

Box 5.6   A process map for interprofessional learning
(D'Avray *et al.*, 2004).

First-year pre-qualifying students from medicine, nursing, radiography, physiotherapy and dietetics at King's College, London, and from Greenwich and London South Bank Universities came together on placement to explore and analyse care from the patient's point of view and to make suggestions for the improvement of services. No prior medical knowledge of the patient's condition was needed; it was the patient's experience of care that students learnt about. Facilitators helped students to investigate a patient's journey through 'process mapping'.

Four one-and-a-half-hour slots were identified in timetables to capture as many students as possible. During its first meeting, each group chose a patient experience to investigate. They defined an episode of care and agreed where investigation would begin and end. They then constructed a map to chart what was happening to the patient and who was involved, identifying gaps and conflicts in their knowledge and deciding amongst themselves how they would find out more by the next meeting.

Subgroups then visited a clinical unit that provided care for the chosen sort of patient; identified a patient, with help from ward staff; then tracked the journey, helped by interviews with the patient, caregiver and staff, and reviewing documentation. Students discussed ways to improve their patients' experiences at the second and third meetings of the group. At the fourth and final meeting, they produced a written report to staff, including recommendations to improve patients' experience.

Given the logistical difficulties in synchronising placement dates and locations for students from different professions (Cooke *et al.*, 2001), the use of this model may be challenging.

Domain 2: service-led pre-qualifying interprofessional education

Although pre-qualifying professional education is overwhelmingly college-led, it would be service-led if and when it follows an apprenticeship model. In that case, service-led pre-qualifying interprofessional education might be offered between two or more groups of apprentices. A more probable model is during concurrent placements in the same location, where the service agency introduces interprofessional education, exemplified by a classic early 'experiment' at Thamesmead in South East London (see Box 5.7).

Domain 3: jointly-led pre-qualifying interprofessional education

This domain is becoming more common, due to increased emphasis on partnership between service providers and education providers. This is a trend that we expect to continue. Useful examples of this type of interprofessional education can be found in Finland, Norway, Sweden and the UK, which have all piloted 'training wards' where students from three or more professions learn their profession-specific practice, but also common skills and teamwork (see Box 5.8). However, establishing and maintaining training wards, or similar practice-based initiatives, is a labour-intensive activity and depends upon sustained prioritisation from the host service agency. This can be difficult for service settings that have recruitment and retention difficulties, high workloads, and pressures from reorganisation or other competing initiatives. It is unlikely that this model will ever become widespread.

Box 5.7   Lunch breaks together during placements (Jaques & Higgins, 1986).

Medical, health visiting and social work students coincidentally on placement in Thamesmead met during lunchtime and for a weekend retreat. Intrusion on practice learning time was kept to a minimum, save for some half-day workshops. Sessions included icebreakers, games, exercises, role-plays and case discussions. Participation was not assessed and did not therefore count towards students' respective qualifications. Attendance in no way interfered with practice learning requirements for students from each profession.

> **Box 5.8** Acute clinical placement in Sweden
> (Wahlström *et al.*, 1996, 1998).
>
> The Linköping training ward in Sweden was an innovative clinical placement that provided final year students from nursing, medicine, occupational therapy, physiotherapy, social welfare and laboratory technology with an opportunity to work in interprofessional teams. Students collaborated to provide care to orthopaedic patients (with simple orthopaedic conditions such as hip fractures) on an eight-bedded ward. Supervision was provided by nurse facilitators who worked with the student teams. In addition, students received part-time profession-specific supervision from a consultant (who was also in overall charge of the ward), a medical registrar, an occupational therapist and a physiotherapist. Three teams of students covered the ward for a two-week period. During this time, student teams worked two shifts: mornings and afternoons. The bulk of their time was spent on the wards working together to provide care for patients. In addition, students attended team reflection sessions at the end of each morning shift. Each team's ward experience was concluded by an interprofessional care conference where all the students discussed issues relating to delivering team-based patient care.

Domain 4: college-led post-qualifying interprofessional education

Initiatives under this heading are typically introduced for one or more of the following purposes:

- To fill gaps in pre-qualifying studies by strengthening academic and research foundations
- To reinforce specialist fields across professions
- To introduce new models of care
- To prepare for progression from practice into management, teaching or research
- To facilitate interprofessional learning

They may also be introduced to deploy scarce expertise optimally and to ensure viable numbers where single professions cannot justify courses of their own.

Courses are shared by the participant professions and content is typically multiprofessional rather than interprofessional, although many multiprofessional Master's programmes in the UK have introduced interprofessional learning subsequently, in response to the changing demands of practice and pressure from participants (Storrie, 1992) (see Box 5.9).

> **Box 5.9**   An award bearing community mental health course
> (Barnes *et al.*, 2000a,b).
>
> Birmingham University offered a two-year, part-time (one day per week) interprofessional course for community mental health practitioners. The course was developed and delivered in collaboration with a number of stakeholders, including local mental health trusts, social services departments and service users (who also participated in the evaluation of the programme). Open to nurses, occupational therapists, social workers, psychologists and psychiatrists, the course offered participants teaching sessions focused on psychosocial interventions that incorporate an interprofessional focus. In addition to undertaking classroom activities, participants carried out practice-based projects in their workplace. The completion of a series of assignments and a portfolio lead to either a postgraduate certificate or diploma in community mental health. Participants could also complete a dissertation that led to the award of a Master's degree in the subject.

The cross-curricula model

At first sight the post-qualifying cross-curricula model is the same as the pre-qualifying crossbar model, but there is a critically important difference. Combined studies now comprise discrete blocks and they tend to be combined with multiprofessional education (light grey blocks) rather than with uniprofessional (white blocks), with crosscutting interprofessional education (dark grey) (see Figure 5.3).

Figure 5.3 illustrates how practitioners from each profession can mix and match discrete studies with interprofessional studies shared with colleagues from other professions. Which studies are shared with whom differs in time and place, taking into account opportunity, choice and circumstance, in a largely free market where provision is always changing, constrained only when regulatory bodies specify particular courses or impose requirements during the validation process.

Interprofessional education at the post-qualifying stage may be relatively free from requirements made by regulatory bodies and can therefore be introduced with fewer complications. It may also have more immediate impact on practice and may consequently appeal to employers and funding bodies. Nevertheless, each profession must still protect time and opportunity to refine, reinforce, update and develop profession-specific knowledge and skills.

Freestanding, post-qualifying programmes have been linked within credit accumulation schemes counting towards qualifications. This enables workers to select shorter programmes to meet priority learning needs without prolonged absence from work. Schemes such as this are particularly apposite when participants are required to include interprofessional elements in their study pathway (see Box 5.10).

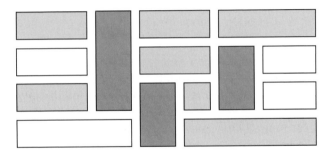

Figure 5.3   Cross-curricula model.

Box 5.10   Systemic interprofessional education (University of Westminster, 2004).

The Interprofessional Postgraduate Learning Plan (Interplan) enabled mostly part-time participants from diverse professional and occupational backgrounds such as health, social care and community development to choose between a wide range of modules to select pathways of study best suited to their needs and interests within constraints set for the award of a certificate, diploma or Master's degree. They also had to take at least one or both of the following interprofessional modules. First, Collaborative Challenge enabled students to compare collaborative practice in their employing organisations, the strategies employed, the problems encountered and the solutions found, set within the context of government policies driving such collaboration and theoretical framework. Second, Pride and Prejudice simulated interpersonal, group, inter-group and organisation relations in working life, employing psychodynamic methods. The primary focus was on facilitating participants' learning about their own, frequently unconscious attitudes and behaviour patterns and reactions towards the 'other'. For the purpose of this module, the other was located at interprofessional or inter-agency level, the intention being to enable participants to transfer learning from the module to their working lives.

  All Interplan modules had two distinctive features. First, learning was based on reflection, that is, clear links were forged between practice and theory through group discussion, which was typically interprofessional. Second, all academic work during core modules had an explicit practice focus. For example, during the policy module, as participants analysed a policy relevant to their practice they were expected to identify situations where collaboration between professions, organisations or sectors was critical to implementation.

Colleges are sometimes invited to run in-house courses, including some interprofessional courses, on behalf of service agencies or to provide teachers and facilitators (Box 5.11).

Box 5.11   A college course for staff working in spinal cord
injury units (Tepper, 1997).

Responding to the needs of local practitioners, tutors at the University of
Pennsylvania developed and delivered a three-day interprofessional course
to teams of nurses, occupational therapists, physiotherapists, doctors and
psychologists working in spinal cord injury (SCI) units. To ensure that the
course met the demands of the participants a needs assessment was undertaken
to inform its development. The aim of the course was to offer participants an
opportunity to gain knowledge and skills necessary to understand the health
care needs of people with SCIs. Participants undertook a range of experiential
interactive activities (brainstorming sessions, buzz groups, role-play) designed
to promote teambuilding, while enhancing their understanding of caring for
people with SCIs. An evaluation of the course indicated that participants
enjoyed this interprofessional learning experience. In addition, five-month
follow-up data revealed that participants considered that they collaborated in
a more coordinated fashion following their involvement in the course.

Many college-led post-qualifying courses have a practice component, but placements are the exception. College teachers are more likely to be involved in helping
course participants to plan and conduct work-related assignments. Again, these
may be interprofessional (see Box 5.12).

Box 5.12   A collaborative assignment (University of Westminster, 2004).

Students on the Master's courses within Interplan (see Box 5.10) completed a
dissertation module comprising a work-based research project supported by
their management. They identified a topic relevant to their daily working life
that involved collaboration between different occupations, professions or
agencies. An innovative feature of this module was an opportunity to involve
the clients of the service as equal participants in the research or as one of the
groups whose collaboration was observed and analysed.

Domain 5: service-led post-qualifying interprofessional education

The agenda for service-led post-qualifying interprofessional studies is primarily
driven by employment needs, although progressive employers recognise that
responding to the needs and expectations of the individual becomes enlightened self-interest where it improves motivation, work satisfaction and staff
retention.

Interprofessional education in this domain may be determined from audits and (in the UK) clinical governance, which provides a framework through which organisations are 'accountable for continually improving the quality of their services and safeguarding high standards of care by creating an environment in which excellence in clinical care will flourish' (Scally & Donaldson, 1998, p. 62). Clinical governance is inextricably linked with learning through appraisal. Models for work-led post qualifying studies are described below.

Action-learning sets

These provide a framework for work-led learning, for one or more professions within or across organisations. Participants learn together over time, usually helped by a facilitator, and calling on external learning resources as they progress (see Box 5.13).

Box 5.13   Action learning with doctors and counsellors
(Jenkins & White, 1994).

Mindful of the difficulties that general practitioners and counsellors experience when working together in primary care teams, two groups of four general practitioners and four counsellors working in Middlesex, in England, formed an action-learning set. It was agreed that a skilled external facilitator would work with both groups for the duration of their involvement in the project. The aim of both action-learning sets was to identify problems related to their collaborative work and begin to find jointly acceptable solutions. The plan was to hold six to seven meetings at four to six-weekly intervals, with each meeting lasting from two to four hours. In their initial meeting, both action-learning sets generated a number of problem areas that needed attention, including patient referrals, confidentiality issues, waiting list difficulties and funding. Subsequent meetings were spent discussing and agreeing how participants could resolve the problems through their collaborative work. Many proposals were successfully implemented.

Continuous quality improvement (CQI)

CQI has been widely introduced in the United States, supported by the Institute for Healthcare Improvement (IHI), the Joint Commission for Accreditation of Healthcare Organisations and others. Recognising the need to find new models for educating health professionals, the IHI initiated the Interdisciplinary Professional Education Collaborative in 1994 to improve health care by 'working from upstream' (Headrick et al., 1996, p. 149). Its influence has since spread to the UK, through the NHS South West Region and Bournemouth University, and to other countries, as a means to empower teams, many of them interprofessional, to effect change for the better.

Each team selects the particular improvement which it is intent on effecting and embarks on a four-stage 'plan', 'do', 'study' and 'act' (PDSA) cycle for learning and improvement (Cleghorn & Headrick, 1996), often assisted by an external facilitator. Numerous evaluations, including several published in a themed issue of the *Journal of Interprofessional Care* (Volume 14, Number 2, May 2000), demonstrate not only that the chosen objective was achieved, but also that participants learned from each other and team cohesion was strengthened (see Box 5.14).

Box 5.14　Quality improvement in a children's hospital (Gazarian *et al.*, 2001).

Staff based at Sydney Children's Hospital in Australia established a quality improvement initiative, based on the principles of PDSA, designed to enhance the delivery of care for children with acute asthma. Initially, staff worked together for a period of four months, developing evidence-based clinical guidelines for the emergency department of the hospital. Once the guidelines had been agreed, medical, nursing and pharmacy staff attended a series of interprofessional sessions where they learned how to implement them in the department. Further sessions were held in the months following their implementation, to ensure their successful adoption. Evaluation of the initiative revealed that while there was a high adherence to the guideline on managing acute asthma (captured by physician-prescribing practices), there was no overall difference in patient length of stay.

Practice Professional Development Planning

A working party led by the Chief Medical Officer for England (Department of Health, 1998) promoted Practice Professional Development Planning (PPDP) in primary care to develop the concept of the 'whole practice' as a human resource and to increase involvement in quality development. Much of the report presents CPD as a vehicle for individual and team learning, which reconciles personal and organisational learning, but it also gave added impetus to CQI initiatives (Wilcock *et al.*, 2003).

Domain 6: jointly-led post-qualifying interprofessional education

Our review found only five jointly led post-qualifying studies (Clemmer *et al.*, 1999; Thompson *et al.*, 2000; Lalonde *et al.*, 2002; Morey *et al.*, 2002; Treadwell *et al.*, 2002) but, as in domain 3, the increasing importance attached to partnership means that we expect these studies to be the beginning of a growing trend. The studies to date show interprofessional education in this domain to be a diverse activity involving a variety of different professions, learning methods, aims and settings. Examples of initiatives falling within this domain can be found in Box 5.15 and Box 4.1 in Chapter four.

Box 5.15   Interprofessional education for sexual health practitioners (Lalonde *et al.*, 2002).

University and service staff collaborated to develop and deliver an interprofessional course to health and social care practitioners working in nine sexual health community clinics across the USA. The course aimed to increase practitioners' understanding of HIV/AIDS and enhance their approaches to working together in delivering care to clients. The course consisted of a series of interactive workshops, computer-based distance learning and didactic presentations. In total, 598 health and social care practitioners from medicine, nursing, dentistry, social work, counselling and outreach work participated in these workshops. Interviews with a sample of 218 participants were undertaken. It was reported that the course had enhanced participants' ability to collaborate with other professional groups and also improved inter-agency referral rates.

Conclusion

The six-fold classification set out in this chapter was developed inductively from critical engagement with our systematic review database. It enables a large and complex dataset to be explored in meaningful and manageable subsets. The classification has proved a useful device for exploring the potential of different domains to support interprofessional learning. Although jointly-led interprofessional education was the exception, current UK developments point to its growing importance. The domains may prove to be durable, but the models associated with each may well change as programme planners invest imagination, ingenuity and innovation.

However interprofessional education may be classified, findings from the review point clearly to the need to distinguish between types of interprofessional education not only in structure but also in focus and outcome, to which we turn in the next chapter.

6 Relating Outcomes to Foci

In the first part of this chapter we analyse outcomes from the 107 studies, by a continuum of six outcomes derived from the Kirkpatrick typology. We then relate the three foci (preparing individuals for collaboration, cultivating collaboration collectively as a group/team, and improving services and the quality of care) to widely held aims for interprofessional education, with examples. Finally, we relate the outcomes of interprofessional education to the three foci.

Exploring outcomes

As we explained in Chapter four, to understand the outcomes reported in studies that qualified for our review we expanded Kirkpatrick's (1967) four-point typology into a six-point typology. To recapitulate, our six-point typology recorded the following outcomes:

- Learners' reactions
- Modification of learners' attitudes/perceptions
- Learners' acquisition of knowledge/skills
- Learners' behavioural change
- Change in organisational practice
- Benefits to patients/clients

See page 43 for a more detailed description of this typology.

Table 6.1 provides details of the (positive, mixed, neutral and negative) outcomes reported from the 107 studies included in the review.[1]

The table shows a predominance of positive findings across all six of the outcome categories. It is noteworthy that almost half of the evaluations (50 studies, 47%) reported outcomes related to learner reaction towards their interprofessional education experience. Changes in organisational practice (45 studies, 42%) and the acquisition of knowledge and skills (40 studies, 38%) were the next most commonly identified outcomes. Fewer studies reported changes in practitioner behaviour or benefits to patients/clients and attitudinal changes.

---

[1] Due to multiple reporting of outcomes in this and other tables in the chapter, combined frequencies and percentages can produce a greater overall figure than the 107 studies that were included in our review.

Table 6.1 Reported outcomes.

Level	Positive	Mixed	Neutral	Negative
1 Reaction	45 (42%)	5 (5%)	—	—
2a Attitudes/ perceptions	21 (20%)	6 (6%)	5 (5%)	—
2b Knowledge/ skills	38 (36%)	2 (2%)	—	—
3 Behaviour	21 (20%)	2 (2%)	2 (2%)	1 (1%)
4a Organisational practice	37 (35%)	6 (6%)	2 (2%)	—
4b Patient benefit	20 (19%)	7 (6%)	5 (5%)	—

Coincidence of outcomes

Most studies reported outcomes at more than one level (see Table 6.2).

Table 6.2 Coincidence of reported outcomes.

Level	1	2a	2b	3	4a	4b
1	50	20	28	16	15	8
2a	—	32	17	11	6	6
2b	—	—	40	7	6	5
3	—	—	—	26	13	4
4a	—	—	—	—	45	13
4b	—	—	—	—	—	32

Box 6.1 provides an example of a study that reports two types of outcome.

Box 6.1 A study reporting level 2a and 2b outcomes (Parsell *et al.*, 1998).

Twenty-eight final year students from occupational therapy, orthoptics, radio-therapy, nursing, physiotherapy, medicine and dentistry, based at the University of Liverpool, were offered a two-day pilot interprofessional course where they worked in small interprofessional groups, discussing a number of scenarios relating to teamwork and collaboration issues in clinical practice. The course was evaluated with pre/post questionnaires that assessed changes in student attitudes and knowledge. To track the longer-term impact of the course, six-week follow-up data were also collected. It was found that the course increased students' knowledge and understanding of teamwork and helped to develop more positive attitudes of the other professional groups.

Studies reporting college-led initiatives tended to indicate changes at levels 1, 2a and 2b, whereas studies with service-led initiatives tended to report changes at levels 4a and 4b. This contrasted with studies that were jointly college and service-led, which tend to report level 3 outcomes. Most outcomes that reported at level 3 also reported at levels 4a and 4b. This trend may be due to changes in individual practitioners' collaborative behaviour which help support wider changes in the organisation and delivery of clinical practice.

Level 1 outcomes

Of studies that reported changes at level 1 (reactions to the interprofessional education experience), reactions were typically gathered from questionnaires and recorded in terms of:

- Enjoying the interprofessional experience (e.g. Thompson *et al.*, 2000; Doyle *et al.*, 2003)
- Learner satisfaction (e.g. Milne *et al.*, 2000; Taylor *et al.*, 2001.)
- Rating the educational experience (e.g. Jones & Salmon, 2001).

Box 6.2 offers an example of a study reporting level 1 outcomes.

Box 6.2   A study reporting level 1 outcomes (Ker *et al.*, 2003).

A simulated ward environment for second-year medical and nursing students in Dundee was created to provide students with an interprofessional experience caring for simulated patients who displayed the symptoms of a variety of common medical conditions. After a briefing about the patient, students were divided into interprofessional teams and were asked to take responsibility for the ward for a shift. At the end of their shift, the students prepared a joint report, which was presented to their tutors in the form of a ward handover. Student teams then received feedback on their performance by the tutors.

  Findings from the student questionnaires indicated that students enjoyed working together in the simulated ward. It was felt that the ward provided a sufficiently realistic environment to help them learn about the demands related to interprofessional collaboration when attempting to organise and deliver medical care to a group of patients.

How important are outcomes at level 1 compared with, for example, changes to the delivery of care (level 4a) and patient benefit (level 4b)? Is it important to collect information on learner reaction? Adult learning theories (to which we turn in the next chapter) would argue that learner reactions are crucial to learning. We elaborate upon this in our companion volume, Freeth *et al.* (2005).

  The level 1 outcomes reported were almost always positive. Five studies did, however, contain mixed (positive and negative) outcomes (e.g. Cornish *et al.*, 2003) or positive, neutral and negative outcomes (e.g. van Staa *et al.*, 2000).

Level 2a outcomes

Changes in attitudes or perceptions towards another profession or towards inter-professional collaboration (level 2a) were reported in 32 studies (30%). Like the studies reporting level 1 outcomes, all studies reporting at level 2a assessed changes in attitude or perception by the use of questionnaires. Typically, level 2a outcomes were measured in terms of attitudes:

- To other professional groups (e.g. Carpenter, 1995; Reeves, 2000; Mires *et al.*, 2001)
- About teamwork (e.g. Barber *et al.*, 1997; Lacey, 1998)
- Towards working with other professions (e.g. Mohr *et al.*, 2002)

See Box 6.1 (above) for an example of a study reporting level 2a outcomes.

There were no studies that reported wholly negative outcomes at this level. However, six studies reported mixed (positive and negative) outcomes (e.g. Gibbon *et al.*, 2002) and (positive/negative/neutral) outcomes (e.g. Carpenter & Hewstone, 1996). In addition, five studies contained neutral outcomes. Morey *et al.* (2002) provided an example of a study that reported no change in attitudes following the delivery of interprofessional sessions for doctors, nurses and technicians working in emergency medical departments in the USA.

Level 2b outcomes

Forty studies (38%) reported changes in collaborative knowledge or skills (level 2b). Once more questionnaire data was the normal source for the reported outcomes. Reported changes in knowledge or skills included:

- Enhanced understanding of roles and responsibilities of other health and social care professionals (e.g. Fallsberg & Wijma, 1999; Farrell *et al.*, 2001; Alderson *et al.*, 2002)
- Improved knowledge of the nature of multidisciplinary teamwork (e.g. Roberts *et al.*, 2000; Reeves & Freeth, 2002)
- Development of teamwork skills (e.g. Schreiber *et al.*, 2002)

Box 6.1 (above) provides an example of a study reporting level 2b outcomes.

Although there were no studies reporting negative or neutral outcomes at this level, two studies reported mixed outcomes (Nash & Hoy 1993; van Staa *et al.* 2000).

Level 3 outcomes

Studies that reported level 3 behaviour change (26, 25%) tended to focus on assessments of interprofessional cooperation and communication, or development of closer links between professions (e.g. Milne *et al.*, 2000; Taylor *et al.*,

2001; Morey *et al.*, 2002; Way *et al.*, 2002; Cornish *et al.*, 2003). Box 6.3 offers an example of a study reporting level 3 outcomes.

Box 6.3   A study reporting level 3 outcomes (Kristjanson *et al.* 1997).

In response to a joint initiative between the Canadian Palliative Care Association and Health Canada, a two-week interprofessional course designed for palliative care teams working in rural settings in northern Canada was developed and delivered. The aim was to test a pilot interprofessional education experience in palliative care to improve the quality of care delivered to terminally ill cancer and AIDS patients. Participants from teams consisting of doctors, nurses and social workers undertook a series of lectures, case conferences, seminar discussions and home visits during the course. Analyses of data collected three months after the delivery of the course indicated a positive change in the participants' collaborative behaviour. Professionals reported that they could work together as an effective interprofessional team. In addition, it was reported they had developed better links with the other teams involved in the course. For many participants this meant that they were more likely to consult with colleagues in the other teams if they required advice.

In addition to the reports of positive changes in behaviour, two studies reported positive and neutral outcomes, two neutral outcomes and one (Atwal, 2002) negative outcomes resulting from an interprofessional initiative designed to enhance teamwork for hospital-based practitioners. In comparison with studies reporting other types of outcomes, measures of behaviour within these studies tended to be poorly conceptualised and operationalised. Often studies provided simple self-reported accounts of behavioural change.

Level 4a outcomes

Forty-five studies (43%) reported changes in organisational practice (level 4a). Studies reporting outcomes at this level tended to include qualified practitioners who worked on initiatives aimed at improving the quality of patient/client care. Box 6.4 provides an example.

Measures used to report changes in organisational practice included:

- Referral practices (Walsh *et al.*, 1995; Taylor *et al.*, 2001)
- Inter-organisational working patterns (Baker *et al.*, 1995; Roberts *et al.*, 2000)
- Documentation of patient records (Brown, 2000; Dalton *et al.*, 2001)
- Reduced costs (Pilon *et al.*, 1997; Overdyk *et al.*, 1998)

In addition to the reporting of positive outcomes, six studies reported mixed (positive and neutral) outcomes (e.g. Bailey, 2002) and two studies reported neutral outcomes at this level.

> **Box 6.4** A study reporting level 4a outcomes (Crawford *et al.*, 1998).
>
> To provide more effective care for patients who deliberately self-harm, a series of one-hour interprofessional workshops for doctors and nurses was established in the accident and emergency (A & E) department in a large teaching hospital in London, UK. In total 45 nurses and 15 doctors attended one of the workshops held over a three-week period.
>
> An audit of patient notes undertaken before and after the sessions indicated that A & E staff completed notes in a more accurate and comprehensive fashion following the sessions. In addition, it was found that there was an increase in interdepartmental liaison between A & E staff and the hospital's para-suicide team.

Level 4b outcomes

Thirty-two studies (30%) reported changes to patient/client care (level 4b). This group of studies focused on reporting change, which centred around:

- Clinical outcomes, such as infection rates (Horbar *et al.*, 2001), clinical error rates (Heckman *et al.*, 1998; Morey *et al.*, 2002)
- Patient satisfaction (e.g Brown, 2000; Treadwell *et al.*, 2002)
- Length of patient stay (e.g. Adamowski *et al.*, 1993; Price *et al.*, 1999; Gazarian *et al.*, 2001)

Those studies that collected clinical outcome data provided some useful insights into the effects of interprofessional education on outcomes for patients. Collection of client satisfaction and length of stay data was more problematic. This was because patient satisfaction data tended to be based upon unvalidated questionnaires (some of which were simplistic 'happy sheets'). Although data about length of stay is relatively easy to collect, it does not provide an accurate indicator of an improvement in clinical care. Indeed, it may suggest that a clinic has increased its throughput, but not necessarily provided better care.

Box 6.5 provides an example of a study reporting level 4b outcomes.

Three foci of interprofessional education

As explained in Chapter three, three central foci for interprofessional education emerged during the review. The first focuses on preparing individuals with the knowledge, skills and attitudes for collaborative practice. The second focuses on learning how to collaborate collectively as an effective member of a team or group. The third focuses on collective action to effect change and improve the quality of services and care for clients. Table 6.3 shows the distribution of these different foci across the 107 studies in the review.

> **Box 6.5** A study reporting level 4b outcomes (Jackson & Bircher, 2002).
>
> The use of the European Foundation for Quality Management (EFQM) excellence model of quality assurance provided the foundation for an interprofessional initiative that aimed to enhance the delivery of care to the patients of a general practice near Salford. A large patient list, combined with the poor organisation of the practice, led the primary care team to seek external assistance to ensure the practice could meet the needs of its patients more effectively.
>
> An external facilitator was located. Using the EFQM model he worked with team members individually and collectively to identify their current challenges and to develop an implementation plan to resolve them. Findings from an evaluation of this initiative found that a number of benefits to patient care were realised as a result of this initiative. For example:
>
> - More targeted health promotion advice to patients
> - A reduction of blood pressure for patients with chronic heart disease
> - Higher proportion of older patients receiving the influenza vaccine
> - Reduced waiting times for prescribed drugs
> - A reduction of patient waiting times to see a doctor or a nurse at the practice

Table 6.3 Focus of interprofessional education.

Focus	Frequency
Individual preparation	50 (47%)
Cultivating team/group collaboration	13 (12%)
Improving services/quality of care	44 (41%)

There was a low incidence of studies focused on cultivating team/group collaboration and we shall return to this shortly. Now we turn to each of the interprofessional education foci in turn, knitting these together with outcomes.

Focus 1: preparing individuals for collaborative practice

This first focus is emphasised most often in pre-qualifying interprofessional education, where it is often associated with one or more of the following aims.

Acquiring common and comparative knowledge

Common curricula, so the argument runs, can establish common knowledge bases for collaborative practice, common understanding of the economic, environmental and social context of practice, the organisation and delivery of services, and policies and their application. Introducing comparative learning enables participants to probe reciprocal understanding of roles, responsibilities and relationships, powers and duties, joys and sorrows, in respective working worlds, to pave the way for collaborative practice. Such learning goes beyond expounding policies and their implementation, to explore their implications for each profession and for relations between them. Not content with the objective, it can also explore the subjective – the anxieties, tensions and rivalries played out in relationships between professions.

Box 6.6 provides an example of a short interprofessional course designed to enhance the comparative knowledge and skills of medical and nursing students in breaking bad news to patients.

Comparative learning needs to encourage reflection, as students become more aware of the distinctive attributes that their profession brings to collaborative practice. It employs interactive learning to facilitate comparison, calling upon the experience of participants rather than leaving this to the teacher. In so doing, it reviews and revises reciprocal attitudes as differences in values, attitudes and perceptions are brought into the open and made accessible to change.

Box 6.6   Breaking bad news (Wakefield *et al.*, 2003).

A one-day 'breaking bad news' course was developed by staff based at the University of Manchester, in England, for medical and nursing students. The aim of the course was to enable students to experience breaking bad news as part of an interactive interprofessional programme. In doing so, it was anticipated that students would enhance their understanding of each other's roles and responsibilities when breaking bad news and develop their interprofessional and professional-patient communication skills.

Each session began with a plenary discussion around communication and interprofessional learning. Facilitators then carried out role-play exercises on how to break bad news. Following this activity, the students were asked to work together in interprofessional dyads while role-playing in a number of scenarios that involved the use of simulated patients.

Thirty-four students participated in the course. Questionnaire data revealed that the students felt the course had challenged their misconceptions of one another's profession, enhanced their knowledge of each other's roles and responsibilities in breaking bad news and enriched their communication skills.

Developing positive attitudes

Comparative learning can expose attitudes towards each other, some positive and mutually supportive, others ignorant, prejudiced or stereotypical. Approached thus, interprofessional education can overcome barriers which impede collaborative practice, as in the following example, between the participant professions (see Box 6.7).

Learning about each other, we suggest, is a precondition, without which interprofessional education may fail to achieve progressively more challenging aims because of lack of collaboration between the parties. Viewed thus, interactive learning is needed at every stage in interprofessional education, as old problems recur and new ones arise. It is needed especially when interprofessional education is used as an instrument to effect organisational change, which may strain working relations and trigger defensive reactions at the very time when collaboration is most needed. It can be preparatory, preventive and reparative.

Optional interprofessional education may attract participants already well disposed towards probing relationships with other professions. Required interprofessional education may, however, include 'reluctant joiners' who are ill at ease with activities that expose and challenge their assumptions and prejudices about other professions.

Where the profession is not represented in the group, they can be the butt of criticism. Problems may be seen through the eyes of the 'offended' party, with no

---

Box 6.7   Exposing perceptions and prejudices (Pietroni, 1991).

Medical, nursing and social work students were invited to expose perceptions of each other, first in profession-specific small groups, then with the other professions in a plenary session. Social work students described themselves as scapegoats, perceiving medical students as arrogant, immature, intelligent, beer-drinking rugby players, and nurses as hardworking but unimaginative. Medical students saw themselves as arrogant, naive, lazy and heavy-drinking rugby players, perceiving social work students as left wing, self-opinionated, immature, intelligent lesbians driving 2CVs, and nursing students as overworked smokers with chips on their shoulders. Nursing students saw themselves as apathetic, overworked and underpaid cyclists, perceiving social work students as caring vegetarians and medical students as (no surprises by now) arrogant, snobbish, rugby players.

Far from proving divisive, the degree of congruence between these reciprocal perceptions was thought to generate solidarity within the group, the significance of the exercise being thought to lie in using seemingly lighthearted observations to probe more profound perceptions and pave the way for mutual understanding and teamwork.

chance for the 'offending' party to reply and engage in efforts towards resolution. Scapegoating becomes too easy. Every effort needs to be made to ensure that all relevant parties are represented, while facilitators need to be sensitive to the danger.

Application of the contact theory (discussed more fully in Chapter nine) provides a more rigorous list of conditions to be met before interprofessional learning can be expected to modify attitudes:

- Positive expectations by participants
- Equal status of participants
- A cooperative atmosphere
- Experience of successful joint working
- Concern for an understanding of differences as well as similarities
- Perceiving other participants as typical of the profession they represent
- Organisational support, that is, from college and/or service agency

(Hewstone & Brown, 1986; Dickinson, 2003)

At issue is whether all these conditions must be met on every occasion, and to what degree, before positive changes in attitudes and relationships can be expected.

There can be no guarantee that interprofessional education will change attitudes for the better. Worst fears may be confirmed. Exposure to another profession may reinforce negative preconceptions. Progress will depend not only upon the readiness of one party to modify its attitudes towards another, but also the readiness of the other to modify those of its attitudes and its behaviours that cause offence. Interactive learning becomes a process of accommodation between the parties.

Improved relations within the group may not carry over into practice. Negative attitudes may be sustained, as work based upon contact theory suggests, if behavioural changes observed in the learning situation do not equate with those observed in members of the same profession encountered at work. They may also be sustained, not because of the attitudes and behaviours of individuals from that profession, but because of what comes to light regarding its values, codes of conduct, registration, regulation, education and institutions.

Changing attitudes, if and when accomplished, may not be sufficient. Feeling better disposed towards another profession may work in favour of collaboration, but the relationship between attitudes and behaviour is complex. Changes in attitudes may change behaviour. Conversely, changes in behaviour may change attitudes. It is possible to correlate clusters of attitudes with clusters of behaviours. The one may modify the other if:

- It is possible to create conditions where the object of the attitude can be experienced directly
- Sufficient information about the said object can be gained
- It is possible to reflect on one's own attitude
- The situation can provide an opportunity to learn about links between attitude and behaviour

(Eagly & Chaiken, 1993)

It is also important to recognise that attitudes are situation- or object-specific, which may constrain transferability of learning. A member of one profession may be positively disposed towards a member of another, but this alone does not predict a similar disposition towards another member of that profession. Experiences outside the learning environment will need to be introduced to facilitate the transfer of learning.

Formulating collaborative skills, competencies and capabilities

The case for skill-based, competence-based or capability-based outcomes for interprofessional education rests on the belief that changing attitudes alone is not enough to prepare practitioners for collaboration in complex situations. Furthermore, competence-based formulations of curricula have become widely accepted in health and social care professions, so it is natural for people to want to think of interprofessional education in these terms too.

Barr (2002) distinguished between:

- *Common competencies* – those held in common between all professions
- *Complementary competencies* – those that distinguish one profession from another
- *Collaborative competencies* – those necessary to work effectively with others

Albeit not drafted as competencies, he found that some UK occupational standards and benchmarking statements could be framed as such to help in formulating competency-based outcomes for professional and interprofessional education. He identified occupational standards set for health and social care professions in the UK necessary for collaborative practice, while Whittington (2003) identified the skills and underpinning knowledge for collaborative practice by social workers (applicable to all health and social care professions).

Combining and augmenting Barr's (2002) and Whittington's (2003) formulations the following competencies can be identified for collaborative practice:

- Cooperating and communicating between professions and between agencies
- Recognising and observing the constraints of one's roles, responsibilities and competence yet perceiving needs in a wider context
- Providing assessments of client need on which other professions can act
- Using formal and informal networks
- Managing confidentiality between professions and between agencies
- Negotiating working agreements with other professions and agencies
- Coordinating a team and conducting interprofessional meetings
- Ensuring that your professional point of view is heard
- Conveying agency policies
- Adapting to unilateral change by another profession or agency
- Coping with conflict
- Contributing to the development and knowledge of other professions
- Contributing to joint service planning, implementation, monitoring and review

- Evaluating another practitioner's assessment
- Describing one's roles and responsibilities clearly to other professions and discharging them to the satisfaction of those others
- Recognising and respecting the roles, responsibilities and competence of other professions in relation to one's own, knowing when, where and how to involve these others through agreed channels
- Working with other professions to review services, effect change, improve standards, solve problems and resolve conflict in the provision of care and treatment
- Working with other professions to assess, plan, provide and review care for individual patients and support carers
- Tolerating differences, misunderstandings, ambiguities, shortcomings and unilateral change in another profession
- Entering into interdependent relationships, teaching and sustaining other professions and learning from and being sustained by those other professions
- Facilitating interprofessional case conferences, meetings, team working and networking

Box 6.8 offers an example of an interprofessional education course that developed a number of collaborative competencies.

Box 6.8   Developing collaborative competencies for nursing and medical students (Morison *et al.*, 2003).

Senior nursing and medical students in Northern Ireland were offered an eight-week interprofessional course jointly developed by education and service, that combined both classroom and clinical learning activities. Initially, students participated in two weeks of classroom activities, specifically lectures, problem-based learning and seminar discussions to help them prepare for their subsequent six-week practice placement. Based on a hospital ward, the students' placement involved them undertaking a variety of shared ward rounds, tutorials and clinical teaching.

   The course aimed to help the students learn about the relationship between their own and other professional roles and responsibilities and also to reflect critically on how this knowledge would impact on their ability to collaborate as a team member. Student learning was assessed by a collective oral presentation based on a clinical case they studied during their practice placement. It was found that the students developed a number of collaborative competencies from their participation in this initiative. In particular, they reported improvements in their awareness of their own and fellow students' attitudes to other professions, improvements in their ability to recognise and understand their roles and responsibilities, and an enhancement of their ability to communicate and collaborate.

The Sheffield Combined Universities Interprofessional Learning Unit (2004) mapped benchmarking statements and other key UK sources to draft 'capability statements' as outcomes for pre-qualifying health and social care programmes. It preferred the term 'capability' to 'competence' to signal the need to respond to change.

The resulting Interprofessional Capability Framework was organised into the following four domains:

- Knowledge in practice
including awareness of 'others' professional regulations in the team
- Ethical practice
including client participation in decision making and the duty of care
- Interprofessional working
including assessment, communication and co-mentoring
- Reflection
including reciprocal, continuing interprofessional learning

Work continues, at the time of writing, to revise the Framework to take into account other UK sources and its application.

Collaborative skills, competencies or capabilities are not peculiar to interprofessional working. They also apply to uniprofessional working and, indeed, to everyday family, community and occupational relationships. Professionals can therefore build collaborative skills, competencies or capabilities for interprofessional working on everyday experience. This carries implications for recruitment criteria, now that collaboration is seen to be so much a part of working life, and for the accreditation of prior experiential learning. Whatever the collaborative skills, competencies or capabilities may be that the participants bring, they will need to be developed and augmented to respond to the added complexity of interprofessional practice.

Focus 2: cultivating collaborative team/group practice

While collaboration takes many other forms, teamwork is by far the best tried and tested mechanism for collaboration, enjoying a hallowed place in interprofessional practice. Substantial strides have been made towards identifying the conditions under which teamwork improves collaboration and care. Based on 400 teams with 7000 participants, Borrill et al. (2000) found that the quality of teamwork process was strongly related to team effectiveness. The clearer the team's objectives, the higher was the level of participation in the team, the greater the emphasis upon quality and the higher the support for innovation. More effective communications within teams correlated positively with lower stress levels among members.

Within and between professional groups

The purist may protest that collaboration within a profession is not interprofessional, but there are good reasons to take it into account in interprofessional education. First, experience gained, and competencies developed, in intra-professional relations can transfer into interprofessional relations. Second, competencies for collaboration between specialties within the same profession are closely akin to those needed between professions. Arguably, working relations between specialities need to be in good order before time and energy will be released for interprofessional relations.

One-to-one collaboration (co-working within and between professions) is largely neglected in the interprofessional literature, yet most collaboration involves only two practitioners. It may be fleeting (no more than a telephone call) or enduring over months or years. It may be simple or complex. It may be arms-length, with neither need nor opportunity for the workers to get to know each other, or dependent upon a close working partnership.

Teamwork receives most attention in the literature, but group collaboration also includes case conferences and committees. Networking calls for wide-ranging knowledge about agency mandates and community resources and emphases, especially the need for representative and negotiating competence.

Within and between organisations

Interprofessional education and practice took root in health and social care at a time when agencies were smaller and simpler than today. As statutory agencies grew larger, more complex and more bureaucratic, and mixed economies of welfare were created with internal markets within and between statutory, commercial and charitable sectors (Wistow et al., 1994), collaboration became more complex. Interprofessional education had to develop accordingly, paying as much attention to the inter-agency as to the interprofessional dimension.

Box 6.9 (p.88) provides an example of an interprofessional education initiative developed for staff working in teams across different health and social care organisations.

With clients

Collaboration with clients and their carers has long been associated with interprofessional working. Clients may participate in much the same way in professional and interprofessional learning. Learning can be built around clients' accounts of their experiences in the hands of the caring professions and around case studies, following client pathways as they encounter different professions and agencies. Clients may also contribute to programme planning, teaching,

> **Box 6.9**   Managing challenging behaviour – an inter-agency approach
> (Gentry *et al.*, 2001).
>
> Concern about a limited amount of specialised training available for staff who faced challenging behaviour whilst working with people with learning difficulties, led educational staff to create an experiential interprofessional course for mental health teams working in a range of care settings: hospital, community residential, day care, respite, across Northumberland, in England.
>
> The three-day programme aimed to develop team members' competence and confidence in managing difficult behaviour in their work settings. During the course, team members took part in seminar discussions based around critical incidents and role-play exercises. In addition, teams worked together to develop relevant preventive and reactive behavioural strategies in their workplace.
>
> Over one hundred nurses, social workers and support staff from nine community and acute teams took part in an evaluation of the programme. The teams identified a number of gains in terms of knowledge and skills of collaboratively managing challenging behaviour. In addition, it was reported that the behavioural strategies developed during the course were going to be implemented by each team upon their return to the workplace.

assessment and evaluation as well as being counted as team members and co-participants in interprofessional programmes. (See Box 5.9 in Chapter five for an example of client involvement in the development and delivery of an interprofessional education course for mental health practitioners.) .

In the UK, an *Expert Patient Programme* (NHS, 2004) allows patients to become equal partners with professionals to manage their long-term conditions. The initiative draws upon experience in the USA, where Stanford University School of Medicine has run a similar programme during the last 24 years, including an interprofessional course. Practitioners are strongly encouraged to bring a person with a chronic illness with them to be an equal participant (Stanford University School of Medicine, 2004).

With communities

The need for collaboration with communities has grown wherever the emphasis has shifted from hospital to community-based care, especially in highly disadvantaged urban and rural areas, which have become the setting for much work-based interprofessional education, and with minority groups (see Boxes 2.7 and 2.8 in Chapter two). Interprofessional education has introduced methods of community-based participatory inquiry (Seifer & Kauper-Brown, 2004) where local people are variously engaged with investigators in formulating research questions, planning projects, and collecting and analysing data.

Focus 3: developing services and improving care

Promoting collaboration is no longer accepted as sufficient. Interprofessional education is also expected to engage directly in service development, reinforcing workforce strategies, facilitating implementation of policies and improving the quality of services. There is room for argument about whether this aim is an updated and extended conception of interprofessional education or a more broadly based form of multiprofessional education within which interprofessional education may be embedded. Either way, many programmes in the UK integrate collaborative objectives (p.84) with service and workforce development. This chapter would therefore be less than complete, and less than helpful, if it did not take this inclusive view.

Workforce strategy

Whilst interprofessional education has long been employed to encourage a degree of flexibility between professions in a spirit of collaboration, it has more recently been invoked in the UK to implement workforce strategies that call for permeability between professions, with one substituting for another (Department of Health, 2000). At the same time, policy makers are encouraging accelerated career progression, by accrediting prior learning, to shorten education for a second professional career. These developments can raise controversial ethical and political issues. Interprofessional education provides a forum to address them.

There have quite different implications for education and training from those to encourage collaboration. If one profession is to carry responsibilities normally assigned to another then it needs to acquire the relevant knowledge and skills to the same standards. This must either be ensured through common undergraduate studies at the same level, or by further learning to enhance knowledge and skills as necessary, relevant to the duties for which the worker is to substitute. Here again benchmarking statements are helpful, enabling judgements to be made about the preparedness of a member of one profession to substitute for another, and the amount and nature of additional learning needed (see Box 6.10).

The example given in Box 6.10 prompts questions. How common is common learning if conducted by each profession, grounded in its own assumptions and applied to different roles and responsibilities in different practice settings? Does this undermine the very idea of common learning, or are variations on the theme to be encouraged as necessary interpretation in response to profession-specific needs? If the latter view prevails, how common must common learning be to ensure that one profession can substitute for another to the required standard or convincingly claim credit for prior learning? These are complex problems which may be peculiar to the UK, but are liable to arise also wherever interprofessional education is expected to help implement workforce strategies.

Box 6.10 Coping with the logistics (Universities of Southampton and Portsmouth, 2004).

The New Generation Project, based in Southampton and Portsmouth, distinguished between common learning (from content analyses of benchmarking statements) to generate a more flexible workforce and interprofessional education to promote collaboration.

Faced with horrendous logistical problems in arranging common learning for 4000 students from 13 professions, however grouped, to be in the same place at the same time, the organisers decided that common learning need not be together. Each profession would apply the same common learning curriculum separately.

The organisers stressed the advantages in treating common learning in this way, so that resources could be freed for relatively short but intensive periods of interprofessional learning: face-to-face interactive learning between the professions with the unambiguous object of promoting collaborative practice.

Recruitment and retention

Once interprofessional education had been drawn into workforce development, it was only a matter of time before it would be invoked to help recruitment and retention. This comes through most strongly in disadvantaged communities, to break the vicious circle of under-manning, chronic recruitment problems, high wastage, debilitating stress and low morale as discussed in Chapter two.

Interprofessional education may help, as we demonstrated in Chapter two, by resolving conflict, fostering mutual support and reducing stress. Job satisfaction may be enhanced and wastage reduced. Recruitment and retention should then improve, as the area gains a reputation as a supportive place to work in a learning environment. Interprofessional learning helps to reverse the downward spiral.

Substitution

Interprofessional education is also seen as a means to generate a more flexible workforce, with 'skill mix', where a practitioner from one profession can substitute for another, and 'skills escalators' (accordingly credited), where a member of one profession progresses into another.

Implementing policy

Interprofessional education can create opportunities to consider new policies from different professional perspectives, weigh implications for the roles of each profession and relations between them, and address tensions that may result (see Box 6.11).

> **Box 6.11** Interprofessional education and clinical governance
> (Foy *et al.*, 2002).
>
> The UK Government's policy on clinical governance, which stresses the need for health and social care professionals to adopt an evidence-based approach in their practice, provided the impetus for the development of an interprofessional project for members of 21 primary care teams based in and around Manchester.
>
> Participants initially attended three interprofessional critical appraisal workshops that aimed to enhance their skills in assessing research that could inform their clinical practice. During the workshops the teams also identified a clinical topic relating to their own practice and formulated a question that required further evidence to answer. They then searched the evidence and critically appraised the literature. The teams then drew up action plans and targets based on their research findings. The overall aim of this part of their training was to use the evidence they had collected to change an aspect of their professional or organisational practice.
>
> During the six months following the workshops, each team met with a facilitator to review progress on their action plan and to resolve any problems that they encountered. Participants reported team communication and service delivery improvements. For example, the evidence that one team found indicated a need to reduce antibiotic prescribing for children. A collaborative effort between the doctors and health visitors to do so resulted in an evidence-based policy on prescribing and the production of a practice leaflet explaining the new policy to clients.

Improving services and quality of care

Finally, interprofessional education has been built into methods to review and improve the quality of services and the quality of care. CQI involves interested parties, often including a number of professions, in systematic and cyclical investigation, appraisal, action and review (Gunn *et al.* 1995) as we have already discussed in Chapters four and five (see Boxes 4.3 and 5.14).

Another approach designed to improve service and the quality of care is collaborative enquiry, which, like CQI, entails systematic and cyclical review, which can be applied to quality improvement (Reason, 1994). Box 6.12 provides an example of an interprofessional initiative that employed collaborative enquiry. (See also Box 2.7 in Chapter two for the use of collaborative enquiry to improve the delivery of community services for people living in Nottingham.)

Findings from the review

Our review demonstrated an association between the focus of interprofessional education and its reported outcomes that accords with arguments and assump-

---

Box 6.12   Supervising the child protection process
(Cosier & Glennie, 1994).

Northamptonshire Social Services Department commissioned a collaborative inquiry from the Professional Development Group at the University of Nottingham into supervision in child protection. The inquiry started from the premise that ownership was a key ingredient in catalysing change. Individuals and groups needed to be empowered by active participation to explore options, based on their knowledge of the situation. A group of 11 first-line managers was convened, representing education, health, police, probation, social services and the National Society for Prevention of Cruelty to Children (NSPCC). It met seven times over four months. Priority was given, during the first meeting, to getting to know each other. Each participant interviewed another and introduced him or her to the group. Small groups then asked 'What can we contribute to the Inquiry and what do we want from it?'

An *inquiry map* was devised for subsequent sessions, to give directions and set limits. It incorporated three phases:

- Ascent: exploration of supervision as a topic
- Flight: understanding supervision in context
- Descent: relating what had been learned to current supervisory practice

Outcomes distinguished between the desirable and the achievable, taking into account special characteristics of management and supervision in child protection. The inquiry ended with a formal presentation to the Area Child Protection Committee.

---

tions discussed earlier. Table 6.4 shows that interprofessional education initiatives, with a focus on developing individuals, tend to report outcomes linked to individual change: level 1 learner reaction; level 2a attitudes/perception change; and/or level 2b acquisition of knowledge/skills. In contrast, initiatives focused on service development tend to report organisational change: level 4a professional practice and/or level 4b improvements to patient/client care.

Table 6.4   Focus and outcomes of interprofessional education.

Focus	Reported positive outcomes					
	Level 1	Level 2a	Level 2b	Level 3	Level 4a	Level 4b
Preparing individuals	31 (29%)	15 (14%)	34 (32%)	9 (8%)	9 (8%)	5 (5%)
Team/group collaboration	4 (4%)	3 (3%)	1 (1%)	2 (2%)	2 (2%)	1 (1%)
Improving services/care	10 (9%)	3 (3%)	3 (3%)	10 (9%)	26 (24%)	14 (13%)

The low incidence of initiatives focused on team/group collaboration is note-worthy. Perhaps programme developers are overlooking the focus. Perhaps this focus implies team-based training and at post-qualification level it can be very difficult to release teams from busy practice areas. Perhaps teams of colleagues are reluctant to engage in interprofessional education explicitly focused on exam-ining their teamwork and collaboration; perhaps the third focus is less threatening and implicitly includes examination of teamwork. But if, as we argue below, the three foci are interconnected and mutually reinforcing, the extent to which inter-professional education focused on team/group collaboration is a 'missing link' needs careful consideration.

The dynamics of interprofessional education

This chapter has linked our empirically tested six-fold classification of interpro-fessional education outcomes to our inductively derived scheme of three foci for interprofessional education. Some of the models discussed are long-standing, well argued, well tried and backed by evidence; others more recent, largely untried and lacking evidence so far. Relationships between them are iterative, multiple and complex.

It is tempting to conclude that the picture is so complex that it defies any attempt to introduce a pattern of relationships. But a coherent policy for inter-professional education and practice demands just that. We therefore offer a formulation, albeit tentative, for others to test against their experience and im-prove upon. Figure 6.1 represents each of the three foci as a cycle driven when all is proceeding to plan, by successful achievement of each of its subsidiary aims. Modifying attitudes through interactive learning, acquiring comparative know-ledge and enhancing collaborative competence are mutually reinforcing.

Learning to collaborate with and between professions, within and between organisations, with service users and their carers, and with communities is also reinforcing. So, too, is collaboration to generate a more flexible workforce, for implementing policies and to improve the quality of services. Each cycle also reinforces the other, adding momentum to the whole. Failure to achieve one or more foci in a cycle adversely affects the others, retarding momentum. Similarly, failure to activate positively any one of the cycles retards the others, and conse-quently undermines the achievement of a range of possible positive outcomes related to interprofessional education. In the extreme case, if one cog stops so does the whole mechanism.

This is a more sophisticated formulation than the chain reaction at the end of Chapter two. It moves beyond linear progression and introduces many more variables, within which propositions put at the end of that chapter can be intro-duced.

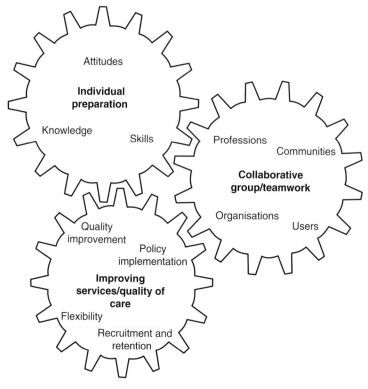

Figure 6.1   Interlinking relationship of the three foci of interprofessional education.

Conclusion

In this chapter we have complemented the classification of interprofessional education by structure to introduce focus and outcome. This has led to the formulation of a dynamic model in which the three foci were presented as holding the potential to be mutually reinforcing. In the next chapter we introduce approaches to teaching and learning.

7 Approaching Learning and Teaching

Interprofessional education, like most uniprofessional education, is grounded in adult learning principles. It has adopted and adapted a repertoire of learning methods from uniprofessional education. This chapter describes some of them. Examples are included from the review and other sources.

Introduction

Interprofessional learning builds upon adult learning methods. The more that professional education embraces adult learning, the easier it becomes for teachers and participants to engage in interprofessional learning. Participants who have become accustomed to modern learning approaches may respond easily to interprofessional learning. Others may experience more difficulty if their general and/or professional education employed mostly traditional didactic teaching, prompting them to enter into interprofessional learning as passive recipients.

Applying principles of adult learning

In this chapter we view interprofessional learning methods in the context of principles of adult learning and some of the many theories that pertain (e.g. Knowles, 1975; Kolb, 1984; Brookfield, 1986; Lave & Wenger, 1991).

Knowles (1975) said that adult learners were intrinsically motivated by the 'problems' they identified and sought to solve for themselves. Learning was therefore likely to be more permanent when knowledge had direct application to work and incorporated task-centred or problem-solving approaches. The strength with which this belief is held in professional education, and increasingly in interprofessional education, helps to explain the popularity of problem-based learning to which we refer below. Such learning is active, self-directed and (most importantly for interprofessional learning) collaborative. Learners identify gaps in their knowledge and/or skills, agree what information is needed to fill them, locate sources, assign tasks and pool findings to resolve the problem.

The notion of adult learning as cyclical is informed by the work of Kolb (1984) who identified four stages in a cycle that can be entered at different points:

- Initial experience
- Observation and reflection
- Formation of abstract concepts
- Testing concepts in new situations

Looking at the cycle with experience as a starting point, for example, the learner uses observation and reflection to convert experience into ideas, which are then tested in new situations.

Lave & Wenger (1991) argued that learners entered into 'communities of practice', where they learnt by participating in the life of a certain community and acquired knowledge from established community members. Learning was embedded or 'situated' in that specific context. It took place within a framework of participation rather than the individual mind, although Elkjaer (1999) criticised Lave & Wenger's model for emphasising the context of learning over individual learning.

Calling upon Lave & Wenger, Cable (2000) saw collaboration as 'situated activity' in which learning and doing were perceived as intimately intertwined. Learning to collaborate was a dynamic construct of working, subject to constant interpretation and reinterpretation. It was not founded on a traditional, cognitive construct of learning but had social, moral and emotional dimensions. Learning and performance could not be separated. Learning was performance and the meaning of the activities in which they occurred were a constantly negotiated and renegotiated interpretation of those held by the participants of their community of practice. Learning as participation was not simply a way of acquiring skills, but also of developing an identity and sense of belonging in a community. Differences in perspective among participants were instrumental in the generation of learning.

Organisational Learning Theory (Argyris & Schön, 1984) is closely associated with these perspectives. It is a process whereby individuals work and learn collectively to improve the quality of their working environment and the products or services they deliver. This theory underpins total quality management (TQM) and continuous quality improvement (CQI), which feature so strongly amongst work-based examples of interprofessional education found during our searches of the literature. Both these approaches (discussed more fully in Chapter nine) employ Organisational Learning Theory to enable an organisation to improve its performance as it strengthens staff morale and interprofessional collaboration, and uses resources more effectively to enhance consumer satisfaction.

We find the following analysis by Brookfield (1986) a useful springboard for reflection on the nature of interprofessional education. We add our own observations in italics with reference to interprofessional education.

- The adult learner is a self-directed, autonomous learner. The outcome of the learning is more likely to be positive if the learner chooses the direction, content and methods. *This poses immediate challenges for interprofessional education. Participants may need to explore whether their perceived learning needs and desired outcomes are in harmony and whether their preferred approaches to learning coincide. Mismatches may lead to negotiation and provide excellent opportunities for collaborative learning.*

- Teachers and facilitators need to respect adult learners' needs, personalities and learning preferences. *In interprofessional education, participants and facilitators from different professions need to accept and celebrate the diversity in the group and learn from it.*

- The experience of the learner is paramount. Life experience is both the substrata for learning and defines the particular learning needs of the individual. *Lived professional experiences, and their influence on professional attitudes and behaviour, provide bases for interprofessional exchange, as participants compare perspectives and experience, and sometimes challenge each other.*

- Active learning is at the heart of adult learning. *This applies especially to professional and interprofessional learning. Passive acquisition of knowledge translates poorly into practice. Active learning implies change, which may only occur if previously held attitudes and beliefs are open to challenge in a safe, supportive and cooperative learning environment.*

- Learning has to be relevant. *Interprofessional education may be instigated in response to the perceived needs of the team, the organisation, the professions or the overall service delivery system. Effective learning, however, depends upon demonstrating relevance to each participant individually.*

- Pressure to learn needs to be internalised before the participant will be motivated to learn. *Again, this is a powerful reminder that interprofessional education, albeit designed for groups, is, in the final analysis, for individuals.*

- The learner needs to be ready and receptive. This may result from a degree of discomfiture, where dissonance between the desired knowledge or skill and their current state is sufficient to prompt motivation to learn and change. *Effective interprofessional education generates such discomfort but in a supportive environment.*

Some approaches to interprofessional education

The following list of approaches to interprofessional education has its origin in earlier work by one of us (Barr, 2002). We now revisit each of the categories in the light of the arguments, assumptions and evidence explored in this book. The list is not exhaustive; it needs to be adapted and extended as new methods come to attention and as teachers innovate. No one method is preferable; experienced teachers ring the changes depending upon students' learning needs at the time and to hold their attention. The categories are mutually reinforcing, not mutually exclusive.

Exchange-based learning

Numerous means are employed to enable participants to expose feelings, compare perspectives and exchange experience. Debates about ethical issues can expose underlying value differences between professions, to critical review. Games, which play out working relationships between professions and between organisations, can lighten the learning, but contain serious content. Case studies can enable participants from different professions to introduce different insights and suggest different interventions as the group works towards a collaborative response.

See Box 6.1 (Chapter six) for an example of an exchange-based interprofessional education initiative for occupational therapy, orthoptics, radiotherapy, nursing, physiotherapy, medical and dentistry students based in Liverpool. See also Box 6.11 (Chapter six) for another example of an exchange-based initiative, involving primary care teams working in the Manchester region.

Narrative-based learning is an example of exchange-based learning, which encourages participants to recount stories to each other. Appreciative enquiry is one way in which narrative-based learning is employed in interprofessional education, which shifts the emphasis from problematic aspects of working relationships by inviting participants to share good experiences, for example in working with other professions (McGruder Watkins & Mohr, 2001). See Box 7.1 for an example of narrative-based learning within an interprofessional programme for students from four different professional groups.

Box 7.1   Narrative-based learning (Turner *et al.*, 2000).

Medical, nursing, social work and rehabilitation therapy students based at the University of Southampton participated in a four-hour interprofessional workshop in which they listened to a family carer's experiences of caring for a relative with a terminal illness. The workshop was divided into two parts. In the first part, in small interprofessional groups, students talked to one another about the similarities and differences in their respective roles and courses. In the second part, students remained in their small groups and were introduced to family carers. Students then talked to the carers to elicit their experiences, before presenting their findings for a plenary discussion. Interviews and observations were collected with students and carers. It was found that participants, both students and carers, valued the opportunity to talk to one another. In addition, the students felt their interprofessional experiences had enhanced their understanding of teamwork.

Action-based learning

Under this heading we will consider interprofessional problem-based learning, which works well at pre-qualification and post-qualification levels, and service-led post-qualification interprofessional education that occurs through quality improvement initiatives and practice guideline development.

Problem-based learning (PBL), or enquiry-based learning (EBL), is eminently suitable for interprofessional education, calling, as it does, on participants' experience and real life situations, and requiring group cooperation. It is not designed to resolve current problems, rather to stimulate critical evaluation of a problematic situation and to mobilise necessary learning in an autonomous and systematic manner.

PBL originated in the 1970s and was commended by the WHO as the preferred learning method for interprofessional education (1988). Box 7.2 contains an example of how PBL was employed for Canadian health and social care professionals.

Box 7.2   Problem-based learning (Mann *et al.*, 1996).

PBL was selected for an interprofessional course involving community-based doctors, nurses, dieticians, social workers and pharmacists working in Nova Scotia. The aim of the course was to improve professionals' understanding of health promotion issues and the role of interprofessional collaboration in this area. Working in small interprofessional groups, participants discussed four problem-based cases linked to various aspects of health promotion and agreed 'solutions' to the problems contained in each case. An evaluation of the course revealed that participants enjoyed their interprofessional PBL and felt they had acquired a better understanding of each other's roles in relation to heart health promotion. The authors concluded that the use of PBL was an effective means of gaining knowledge about how professionals can work together in health promotion. Indeed, the emphasis of PBL on using collaboration to generate knowledge and 'solve' problems meant that it was considered highly appropriate for this interprofessional course.

The evidence suggests that PBL encourages independence, teamworking, better integration of knowledge and deeper learning (Foldevi *et al.*, 1994; Bligh, 1995). It clearly stimulates participants' interest (Spratley, 1989; Davidson & Lucas, 1995). Hughes & Lucas (1997) found that PBL was effective in achieving interprofessional education goals, such as learning about roles and improving interprofessional communication skills. Similarly, Howkins & Allison (1997), in their analysis of interprofessional education events, found that PBL, combined with a reflective process, was the cornerstone of success. Lucas (1997), however, warned that PBL was expensive. Staff–student ratios were greater (one to eight) compared with other learning methods, where at least 15 participants could be catered for in the same group, although contact hours were less than for traditional modes of learning.

Action-based learning also includes learning during collaborative enquiry (Reason, 1994), continuous quality improvement projects (Wilcock & Headrick, 2000) and action research. In the course of our review work we became increasingly aware of the frequency with which professions worked together to develop practice guidelines, during which process interprofessional learning was recognised as occurring or necessary. In the latter case, the provision of interprofessional continuing professional education then becomes the next logical step in the quality improvement cycle. Thus, interprofessional practice guideline development may be regarded as a vehicle for interprofessional learning: a form of interprofessional education.

Practice-based learning

There is room for argument in interprofessional education, as in uniprofessional education, as to whether practice learning should be treated as method or setting. We include it here as method, in accordance with general usage in the interprofessional literature, but recognise that it is also one of the settings in which other learning methods are employed. Interprofessional practice-based learning takes many forms – out-placement in another professional setting, linked learning for students concurrently on placement in adjoining workplaces, joint placements in the same setting and purpose designed learning environments, such as training wards (Reeves & Freeth, 2002; Ponzer *et al.*, 2004). See Box 5.8 (Chapter five) for an example of a practice-based placement developed for nursing, medicine, occupational therapy, physiotherapy, social welfare and laboratory technology students.

Simulation-based learning

Again, this takes many forms. Role-play can be adapted to expose working relationships between professions, as participants take the parts of client, carer or practitioner from their own or another profession's perspective. The latter may leave the more lasting impression – how else can one get inside someone else's head? See Box 6.6 (Chapter Six) for an example of an interprofessional course that offered nursing and medical students at the University of Manchester the opportunity to role-play in a number of 'breaking bad news' scenarios with simulated patients. Skills laboratories introduced into professional education, for example in medicine and nursing, can be developed to include two or more professions and interprofessional perspectives on diagnosis and treatment. Working life can be simulated to create a learning environment in which one-to-one, group and inter-group, organisational and inter-organisational relationships can be acted out. See Box 6.2 (Chapter six) for an example of a simulated interprofessional learning experience for nursing and medical students based in Dundee.

Observation-based learning

This ranges from the relatively simple opportunities to shadow a worker (or fellow student) from another profession or observe a multidisciplinary team meeting, to the more sophisticated application of observational studies methods from psychodynamic theory, employed in training for psychotherapists. See Box 7.3 for an example of observation-based learning within a practice placement for nursing and medical students.

> **Box 7.3**   Observation-based learning (Guest *et al.*, 2002).
>
> Staff at the University of Sheffield developed an interprofessional practice placement for senior nursing students and junior medical students to provide them with an opportunity to learn together within an acute paediatric setting. It aimed to enhance their understanding of each other's role and responsibilities and to nurture mutual respect for each other's professional contribution to paediatric care. A key activity during the placement was the 'shadowing' of nursing students by the medical students. This allowed them to observe the nurse's role and appreciate the demands of delivering care to paediatric patients. The students' ward-based learning experiences were later discussed within seminar discussions. Findings from an evaluation of the placement indicated that all participants valued their interprofessional learning experiences on the ward. They also felt that there were improvements in their knowledge of one another's roles and responsibilities and their clinical skills.

E-based learning

The increasingly widespread introduction of e-based and 'blended' learning for health and social care professions has much extended opportunities for interprofessional education. As professional education capitalises upon advances in educational technology this is also being introduced into interprofessional education to complement and reinforce face-to-face teaching or to substitute for it. While we have included e-learning as a method, as we noted with practice learning, it could also be viewed as setting. The electronic environment can be viewed as a 'place' where approaches to teaching and learning discussed elsewhere in this chapter are undertaken. Box 7.4 exemplifies this.

> **Box 7.4**   Video conferencing (Cornish *et al.*, 2003).
>
> Mental health professionals working separately in remote rural locations across Canada undertook a short interprofessional course that employed video-conferencing technology. The course allowed 34 physicians, nurses and social workers to participate in presentations and discussions on issues linked to the care of patients with mental health problems.
>
> Although participants found the use of video-conferencing technology helpful for enhancing interprofessional cohesion the reliability of the equipment could be poor. Nevertheless, following a number of technical refinements, it is hoped that this programme can be expanded to incorporate other health and social care practitioners located in rural settings in the country.

Richardson and Cooper (2003) described an interprofessional blended learning course for research students at the University of East Anglia that incorporated virtual on-line seminars via the Internet with 'real' seminars. Box 7.5 also offers an example of blended learning.

Box 7.5　Computer-mediated interdisciplinary teams
(Vroman & Kovacich, 2002).

The Interdisciplinary Training for Health Care in Rural Areas Project, located at the University of Maine, was developed by a team drawn from the humanities, social sciences and health care disciplines, as an asynchronous, computer-mediated curricula, comprising rural, interprofessional, problem and case-study-based distance learning.

　　Teams met face to face early in their development, to discuss the project and to facilitate team development. Postings following meetings showed how personal relationships had been enhanced and carried over into computer-mediated communication.

Received learning

Arguably, received learning or didactic teaching has no place in interprofessional education. By definition, such education employs interactive learning methods such as those that we have been describing – a threshold criterion we followed in our systematic review. Received learning, nevertheless, still has a place, used sparingly, for example to respond to informational needs by way of background, or to questions arising from interactive learning.

Findings from the review

In our systematic review we classified approaches to learning and teaching as follows:

- E-learning and blended learning
- Exchange (e.g. seminar and workshop discussions)
- Guideline development
- Observation (e.g. work shadowing or site visits)
- Practice learning (e.g. student placements)
- Problem-focused (PBL or problem-solving activities)
- Received (e.g. lectures or presentations)[1]
- Simulation (e.g. role-play)

---

[1] Studies were only included in the review if received learning was combined with at least one interactive approach.

Guideline development and problem-focused learning were discussed together under the heading 'action learning'.

Table 7.1 summarises the approaches to learning of teaching within the interprofessional education, reported in the 107 studies retained from our systematic review. Almost half the examples of interprofessional education (51, 48%) employed a single approach, for example:

- Guideline development (e.g. Heckman *et al.*, 1998; Rubenstein *et al.*, 2002)
- Seminar discussions (e.g. Perkins & Tryssenaar, 1994; Rost *et al.*, 2000)
- Practice-based learning (e.g. Taylor *et al.*, 2001; Schreiber *et al.*, 2002)

Table 7.1 Approaches to interprofessional learning and teaching.

Learning methods	Frequency[a]
Exchange	56 (52%)
Received	42 (39%)
Guideline development	38 (35%)
Practice	21 (20%)
Problem-focused	15 (14%)
Simulation	9 (8%)
Observation	7 (7%)
E-learning	1 (1%)
Not given	5 (5%)

[a]Totals exceed 107 (100%) due to the use of multiple approaches

Twenty three studies (21%) reported combining two approaches to learning and teaching, nineteen studies (18%) reported three approaches and nine studies (8%) reported four approaches.

Received (didactic) learning alone does not qualify as interprofessional education. Where employed, it was combined with interactive learning methods (27 studies, 25%); the most popular combination (15 studies, 14%) being lectures (received learning) and seminar discussions (exchange-based learning) (e.g. Lennox *et al.*, 1998; Berman *et al.*, 2000; Alderson *et al.*, 2002). Seminar discussions were often combined with a range of other methods, such as problem solving and role-play (e.g. Long, 1996; DePoy *et al.*, 1997; Farrell *et al.*, 2001; Bailey, 2002).

The initiatives that focused on guideline development drew upon the principles of TQM or CQI to varying degrees (see Chapter nine). Most (26 studies, 24%) were located in the USA. In addition, it was found that interprofessional initiatives that employed this approach tended to report changes to organisational practice (level 4a, 22 studies, 20%) or improvements to the delivery of patient/client care (level 4b, 13 studies, 12%). See Box 4.1 (Chapter four) for an example of an interprofessional initiative that developed a clinical guideline and Boxes 4.3 (Chapter four) and 5.14 (Chapter five) for examples of interprofessional initiatives that employed quality improvement methods.

Conclusion

Approaches to learning and teaching in interprofessional education were examined through the lens of adult learning theories. Chapter nine will look at other theoretical perspectives that have been brought to bear on interprofessional education. Earlier work by Barr (2002) was revisited in the light of the arguments, assumptions and evidence examined in this book. To a great extent, the approaches to teaching and learning selected for interprofessional education are influenced by the domain in which it is located (Chapter five), its focus (Chapter four) and the values it seeks to address, as considered in the next chapter.

8 Reconciling Values

Values are implicit in many of the themes running through preceding chapters, some of which we make explicit in this chapter. Reference to values was almost invariably lacking from studies in our review. We have therefore called on sources from the wider literature. These include: values in the development of interprofessional curricula; sociological critiques of the professions in contemporary society; and moves to establish common values for health and social care, which we complement with our own attempt to draft a value base for interprofessional education.

Reframing attitudes as values

There is more in the interprofessional literature about attitudes than about the values that prompt them, attitudes which nonetheless value or devalue the object of their attention. Intelligent collaboration invites critical appraisal of other professions as partners, appraisal which may be well judged or prejudiced. Recourse to negative stereotypes can be seen as the means by which one profession characterises (or caricatures) another, with intent to detract and devalue.

Oppenheim (1992) suggested that values are deeper and more enduring than attitudes or opinions, and of a higher order in the human psyche. They are more persistent, laid down earlier in a person's development and influence clusters of attitudes. Viewed thus, conflicting attitudes to the same object may be determined by differing underlying values.

Internalising values

Health and social care professions may, as we suggest later in this chapter, be closer to a consensus about a common value base than the following discussion might suggest, but account does need to be taken of differences in values held by different professions, which influence their attitudes and behaviour played out in their collaboration with each other. In Chapter three we suggested that these differences could, in part, be attributed to the process of socialisation during pre-qualifying education, as students identified with the customs, mores and traditions of their chosen profession. Values are internalised and espoused. Conformity is rewarded. Preferment goes to those whose attitudes, behaviour and values best exemplify those of their profession, albeit sometimes at the expense of other professions subjected to invidious comparison.

Interprofessional education works to redress the downside of socialisation. But it also respects the undoubted benefits of socialisation to practitioners, clients and public, imbuing a sense of worth (or value) for practitioners, enhancing self-esteem, cultivating professional identity and *esprit* (Becker *et al.*, 1961; Melia, 1987; Sinclair, 1997) and protecting clients, through standards reinforced by peer pressure. In turn, this invites the confidence of the public.

Powerful though the socialisation process may be in shaping values, the seeds of difference between professions may have already been sown before students enter their professional programmes, by admission and recruitment policies. There are established traditions in recruitment that widening access initiatives and valuing diversity will take time to alter.

Relative status, earnings and career progression, for example, differ between professions, which have traditionally and predominantly recruited men or women (Hugman, 1991). Differences may be diminishing where professions long dominated by men, such as medicine, now recruit more women. This is accompanied by concern about the falling status of medicine, changes in retention rate patterns and calls for increased student numbers to accommodate these (Evans *et al.*, 2002; McMurray *et al.*, 2002).

All professional programmes are based in values derived in part from the academic disciplines that contribute to their knowledge base. Professions mainly grounded in the natural sciences, such as physics and chemistry, are more likely to subscribe to the values of the positivist scientific method, perceiving treatment as an intervention towards a predetermined goal. Professions that draw mostly upon the social sciences, such as anthropology and sociology, are more disposed to recognise the value of knowledge from the interpretive and change paradigms, where environmental and contextual understanding are privileged. These are, of course, generalisations. Diversity of epistemology is not only inter- but also intra-professional.

But to attribute value differences between professionals exclusively to their educational experience, without reference also to the relative strength and prestige of their professional associations and their relative status in the workplace, would be simplistic. Some associations are better endowed and enjoy more political influence than others, such as those granted the prestigious title of 'Royal College' in the UK. Status and esteem in the workplace is influenced by remuneration and opportunities for career progression, but most obviously by conferment of autonomous practice and self-regulation, traditionally deemed to be the distinguishing marks of professions (Freidson, 1970; Johnson, 1972; Larson, 1977).

Value may also be accorded, although not necessarily equated with status, to those professions perceived by self and others as vocational. But professions act from dual motives, to provide service and to use their knowledge for economic gain (see, for example, Krause, 1996). Balancing these two, said Evetts (1999), was critical to interprofessional collaboration. Values associated with the vocational ideal may bond professions together, but may also be used to test whether another bears the hallmark of a profession.

Value differences within professions, for example between specialties, may be as great as between professions. Furthermore, values change in time and place as professions update them to reflect current social mores and subscribe to values in different countries in keeping with their cultures, customs, religions and political ideologies.

Exposing differing value perspectives between stakeholders

Value differences within interprofessional education may be greater between other stakeholders – policy makers, managers, professions, teachers, students, clients and regulatory bodies, than between the participants. Differences between stakeholders may become apparent in the values that they ascribe to themselves and to other stakeholder groups during the joint planning and management of interprofessional education programmes. Atkins (1998) reminded all those engaged in interprofessional education of the powerful emotions evoked during its planning, as much as its provision, especially the potential loss of professional identity, engendering reactions of loss and grief which must not be ignored.

Policy makers

Albeit rarely engaging directly in programme planning, policy makers in countries such as Canada, Finland, Norway, the UK and the USA drive the interprofessional education agenda. Carrier & Kendall (1995) construed this as a device to introduce bureaucratic control over collaboration. Meads & Ashcroft (2005), on the other hand, saw it as means to effect reforms in health and social care delivery, whose implementation calls for flexible deployment of the workforce. Whatever the motivation, the influence of policy makers on interprofessional education is evident in official documents and earmarked funding.

Regulatory bodies

Like policy makers, regulatory bodies rarely participate directly in programme planning. Their approval nevertheless needs to be secured before a programme can be delivered. Membership of regulatory bodies and their visiting panels differs between professions and between countries. Some may exclusively comprise representatives of the relevant profession, others a cross-section of stakeholders, which may generate tension within a panel but also add credence to their judgements.

In the UK, all major regulatory bodies for the health and social care professions support interprofessional education in principle. Encouraging though that is, it does not ensure that assessment panels include members conversant with, and sympathetic towards, interprofessional education.

Underlying value constructs are thrown into a sharp relief, said Shakespeare (1997), when dual validation of courses is required. There is therefore a strong case for establishing agreed procedures and criteria where a programme requires approval by more than one regulatory body, based on the advice of a joint panel on which each is represented (as we elaborate in Chapter eight of Freeth *et al.*, 2005).

Service and education managers

Service managers are often viewed as agents for the policy makers, sharing much the same values. In accordance with their role, they necessarily put organisational values before the interests of particular professions and their members. They see interprofessional education not so much as a means to effect collaboration between professions based on traditional roles and boundaries, as to deploy the overall workforce flexibly. The agenda for interprofessional education becomes correspondingly more ambitious, with the attendant risk that resistance may be encountered if and when professions feel threatened.

Educational managers may look for ways to rationalise programme provision to gain economies of scale and to use scarce specialist expertise to optimum effect (Barr, 1994), influenced by the expectations of funding bodies. Like service managers, some may value professionalism writ large more than the individual professions; in which case they may be predisposed to look for commonalities across professions.

Managers who argue for a wider view of professionalism risk being seen by practitioners, rightly or wrongly, as anti-professional. If challenged, they may assert their support for professionalism *per se* while challenging seemingly restrictive practices between professions whose functions and boundaries have been historically determined and fail to equate with the needs of modern service delivery. They may also make the case for rationalisation to counter the proliferation of professions (as discussed in Chapter one), in the interests of the workers as much as the delivery of services. Fewer and larger professions, they may suggest, will improve career mobility and progression, while a broader education will be more personally enriching for students. Far from antipathetic, such managers may present themselves as friends and allies, concerned to amalgamate the smaller and weaker professions into fewer and larger groupings in their own interests.

The professions

Pirrie *et al.* (1999) like others (e.g. Freidson, 1970; Larson, 1977) saw professional associations as conservative, intent on maintaining and defending professional identity and culture threatened by blurring traditional boundaries and changing professional roles. That may drive professional institutions on/to the defensive, but it is at variance, in our experience, with the positive stance towards interprofessional education and practice which many practising professionals and their associations seek to maintain. They may, nevertheless, need to be persuaded that interprofessional learning can and will reinforce profession-specific learning and that the case put for interprofessional education will benefit workers and clients as well as service agencies (see Chapter two).

Each profession may protect its own members, but unite in arguing for education which is responsive to practice as well as policy. Asserting the values of practice may, however, devalue college-based education, adding credence to arguments that the only effective interprofessional education is in the workplace (see Chapter nine).

The students

It may fall to representatives of the professions to assert the value of a student focus, to help service managers to anticipate the point when staff are being released to, or recruited from, the programme being planned. It is they who may also need to remind educational institutions of their contractual obligation to each participant as student, if and when this seems to be in tension with contractual obligations entered into with service agencies and funding bodies, which emphasise workforce strategies and categories of worker rather than individuals. That is easier when students are also included in the planning process, although it is unusual, in our experience, for them to be given a voice until the programme is operational and a consultative group has perhaps been installed. For example, the student voice helped to shape initial and continuing development of an interprofessional education programme in mental health at the University of York, UK (see Freeth *et al.*, 2005, Chapter one and Box 1.2). See Box 8.1 (p.110) for details on this.

The organisations

Allowance must also be made for differences in values, customs and culture between types of organisation from which the stakeholders are drawn: statutory, commercial and charitable; education, health and social care. Statutory bodies may be exercised about meeting legal obligations, commercial bodies with profit and voluntary bodies with advocacy and provision of specific services. Different organisational cultures can impede collaboration, for example between health and social care (Peck *et al.*, 2001).

The clients and carers

Much lip service is paid to involving clients and carers in programme planning and delivery, asserting the central value accorded to client-centred care as much as their potential contribution to learning. Their involvement is, however, still the exception and often rudimentary, although Barnes *et al.* (2000a,b) provided a good example where clients were an integral part of the programme development. Such involvement can be a powerful reminder of the need to focus on

> **Box 8.1**   Involving students in course planning and review
> (University of York, 2004).
>
> The Collaborative Practice in Mental Health module at the University of York
> in the north of England had a developmental evaluation strategy. Results from
> the formative evaluation were discussed by an Advisory Group of service
> users and providers, a carer, student and faculty representatives, a member of
> the university teaching and learning committee and an external advisor. In the
> third year, this group still included the student representatives from the first
> and second run of the module, by then practitioners able to reflect on the
> impact of their interprofessional learning on their practice.
>
> The perspectives of these different stakeholders were pivotal in ensuring
> that the module aims remained relevant and were the driving force behind the
> teaching and learning arrangements. Their views have also led to changes,
> such as having fewer students in the working groups, whole day sessions to
> encourage attendance and enhanced information to students about the
> module's purpose. Work is now in progress to implement intra-modular
> collection of students' views and thus, where possible, to shape the module
> to the needs of the learners during its delivery, rather than only making
> changes for the following cohort of students.

client-centred care and quality of practice at all times (Beresford & Trevillion,
1995), while perhaps making it harder for other stakeholders to indulge in disputes (see Freeth *et al.*, 2005, Chapter four).

Observing the planning process

Reeves (2005) observed the collaborative process between educational and clinical
managers as they developed and delivered an interprofessional education initiative, over two years. He found that enthusiasm for interprofessional education
facilitated positive group relations and supported the development and delivery
of the initiative, but also resulted in a lack of critical analysis amongst members,
which resembled the characteristics of groupthink. This, Reeves observed,
resulted in ambiguity about respective roles, lack of debate between members
about the development of the initiative and failure to undertake group maintenance activities, which undermined the quality of members' work together, and
generated tensions. Reeves also noted that external challenges, notably re-organ-
isation in the hospital where the programme was due to be delivered, undermined the group's collaborative work.

These observations point to the need to include observation of the critical role of
programme development in studies that seek to understand how competition,
collaboration, conflict, collusion and power are played out between stakeholders.

Employers propose and colleges dispose. So says conventional wisdom, power-fully reinforced when employers hold the budget to commission education. But teachers can also exercise power born of an authoritative grasp of their subject. This becomes apparent where they have a more developed understanding of interprofessional education than do employers' representatives, although that may be challenged.

Responsibility for curriculum planning, within the agreed framework, is usu-ally passed to the teachers from the participating professions. Common ground between them will almost certainly be commitment to practice. Beyond that, each may be predisposed to safeguard the interests of his or her profession. Those with practice experience (past or concurrent) bring to their teaching positive and negative experiences of collaborative practice with other professions. Unhelpful baggage should be set aside, but acknowledging differences born of past experi-ence can also be used to heighten sensitivity to interprofessional tensions and inform teaching from which students can learn. All teachers need opportunity to explore value differences between their professions so that insights gained may be used to improve teaching, learning materials and programme development. We discuss such staff development in Chapter seven and programme development in Chapters three to six of Freeth *et al*. (2005).

Probing values during interprofessional education

It is a matter of judgement when, where and how to explore similarities and differences in values between professions during interprofessional education. In-depth exploration may be more appropriate in longer college-led programmes with time and opportunity for reflection.

All education is value laden, including uniprofessional, multiprofessional and interprofessional education. It is hard to think of content typically included in interprofessional education in health and social care which is not. There is, therefore, no lack of opportunities to prompt participants to probe ethical dimen-sions, moral dilemmas and conflicts. This helps to make their values (personal and professional) accessible to comparison and debate. Examples include values prompting reforms in health and social policy internationally and nationally, including global policies for health, enshrined in WHO papers such as *Health for all in the Twenty-first Century* (WHO, 1998), grounded in equality and human rights, elaborated later with specific global goals (WHO, 2000).

Participants may be prompted to debate the ethical and moral issues in subjects ranging from *in vitro* fertilisation to euthanasia, from DNA testing to protection of privacy, and from respect for the client to the UN *Declaration of Human Rights* (United Nations, 1948). Underlying value differences are often brought into the open during such debates, but the most effective may be issues that arise naturally during teaching, and from practice learning or concurrent work experience.

Interviews with senior health care, police and social services personnel in an accident and emergency unit in the Netherlands and the UK (Hunt & van der Arend, 2002) returned recurrently to the following themes:

- Information sharing and confidentiality
- Consent
- Professional values and autonomy
- Human rights
- Accountability
- Policies and protocols
- Staff safety
- Public safety

Scenarios reported during interviews included: the youth with a stab wound unwilling to volunteer an explanation; reported rape where the victim does not wish the police to be informed; and the mentally disordered offender who poses a threat to staff. Few settings offer more compelling examples to engage students in many and varied ethical and moral issues.

Help may well be enlisted from the range of participant professions in planning the study of ethics and values in clinical practice, as examples from the USA and the UK demonstrate. The first two of these (see Boxes 8.2 and 8.3) suggest how teachers from each of the professions can contribute to curriculum development.

Box 8.2   Involving seven professions in formulating ethical curricula.
(Stone *et al.*, 2004)

Teachers in Portland, Maine were asked two questions, for the seven professions to be included in a 15-week interprofessional ethics course:

- What content areas should be considered for inclusion?
- What design framework, format or structure would best fit the content chosen?

An interprofessional faculty design team conducted a comparative analysis of codes of ethics for the seven professions. It then grouped topics as responsibility to: the person, profession, client, health care team, employer, research and practice, and the public.

Throughout the course, videos, case examples and articles about ethical issues concerning the specific professions were utilised for discussion and decision making. Assignments moved participants along a continuum from profession-specific projects to interprofessional projects.

Two more examples (Boxes 8.4 and 8.5) move beyond curriculum planning to show how teaching about values has been introduced into interprofessional education.

Box 8.3   Identifying core topics in health care ethics
(Aveyard *et al.*, 2005).

Teachers at Oxford Brookes University, in England, used a nominal group technique to identify ethical topics to be included in seven uni-professional programmes, including those that might appropriately be included in inter-professional education. All participants were taught ethics in health care during pre-registration studies by a visiting ethicist.

Seven core topics were identified for all professions:

- Ethical theory
- The professional duty of care, codes of practice and accountability
- Informed consent and client refusal
- Confidentiality
- The vulnerable patient
- Research ethics
- Rationing

Box 8.4   Ethical consequences of advances in genetics
(Alderson *et al.*, 2002).

Eleven interprofessional ethics seminars were offered to staff working at two hospitals (one inner city, the other suburban) in and around London, England. The aim of the seminars was to improve participants' understanding of dilemmas arising from social and ethical consequences of advances in genetics and their impact on health care policy and practice. The programme was developed from a series of interviews with staff to understand their key concerns about the advancement of genetics in health care.

The seminars were facilitated by an ethicist who encouraged participants to debate critically, question and probe each other's comments and re-examine their assumptions in relation to the ethical issues of genetics. Fifty-six staff from a range of different professional groups, including doctors, nurses, midwives, health visitors and psychologists, participated in the sessions.

Interviews undertaken after the delivery of the seminars indicated that the participants enjoyed the sessions. They particularly enjoyed the time they had to learn from one another and reflect together on one another's personal and professional values in relation to genetics. In addition, participants felt that they had become more aware of each other's professional roles and responsibilities as a result of their involvement in the programme.

Comparing codes of ethics

Wilmot (1995) distinguished between ethical values found in formal codes in the literature (to which we now turn), in the theory base of the professions and in practitioners themselves, all of which could inform interprofessional discourse.

> **Box 8.5**   Religious and spiritual issues in health care (Dombeck, 1989).
>
> Nursing, medical and divinity students took part in an interprofessional course in Rochester, New York, to explore religious responses to human suffering and to examine the role of different health care professionals with regard to spiritual concerns of clients.
>
> Students identified symbols associated with their own and the other professions, recounted myths and re-enacted rituals which had social and emotional meaning for themselves and for their clients. Symbols associated with physicians included the stethoscope, with nurses the thermometer and the syringe, with clergy the stole and with counsellors the couch. Rituals associated with physicians included the physical examination and the pronouncement of death, with nurses the morning bath, with the clergy the laying on of hands and counsellors listening for 50 minutes.
>
> Students teased each other: physicians had to 'play God', nurses to be 'bleeding hearts', clergy to be 'Alices-in-Wonderland' or 'Pollyannas' and counsellors 'poker-faced clock-watchers'.

Interprofessional education may compare professional codes of ethics to identify similarities and differences in the values underlying these. Hewison & Sim (1998) provided a helpful starting point with their exploration of the potential in codes of ethics to help or hinder interprofessional working, balancing injunctions to collaborate with other professions against emphasis put on differences and demarcations.

Citing Wall (1995), they listed five principles generally found in codes of ethics:

- Respecting a person's individuality
- Endeavouring to do good
- Not doing harm
- Telling the truth
- Being fair

Three position statements have been reported so far, which invite health and, in one case, social care professions to subscribe to common values and ethics.

First, a group of Anglo-American scholars (Berwick *et al.*, 1997, 2001) formulated a common ethical code to which they invited all health and social care professions to subscribe, based on the following principles:

- *Rights* – people have a right to health and social care
- *Balance* – care of individual patients is central, but the health of populations is also of concern to the professions
- *Comprehensiveness* – in addition to treating illness, professions have an obligation to ease suffering, minimise disability, prevent disease and promote health
- *Cooperation* – health care succeeds only if professions cooperate with those served, with each other, and with those in other sectors

- *Improvement* – improving health care is a serious and continuing responsibility
- *Safety* – do no harm
- *Openness* – being open, honest and trustworthy is vital in health care

Second, a statement drafted for the UK Health Regulatory Bodies asserted that all health care professionals were personally accountable for their decisions and actions (UKCC, 2001).

They must:

- Be open with patients and clients and show respect for their dignity, individuality and privacy, and for their right to make decisions about their treatment and health care
- Justify public trust and confidence by being honest and trustworthy
- Act quickly to protect patients, clients and colleagues from risk of harm
- Provide good standards of practice and care
- Cooperate with colleagues from their own and other professions

Third, the United Kingdom Quality Assurance Agency for Higher Education (QAA, 2004) included the values for health and social care under the following headings in its draft statement of Common Purpose for Subject Benchmarks:

- Respect for clients' and patients' individuality, dignity and privacy
- Clients' and patients' right to be involved in decisions about their health and social care
- Justify public trust and confidence
- Set high standards of practice
- Protect clients and patients from risk of harm
- Cooperate and collaborate with colleagues
- Contribute, where appropriate, to the education of others

These statements suggest that reaching agreement about a common ethical code for all health and social care professions as a basis for consultation need be neither difficult nor protracted. Meanwhile, they offer excellent interprofessional learning material, against which codes of practice for particular professions can be compared and contrasted.

Ethical critiques of health care, according to Irvine *et al.* (2002), frequently adopt one of a number of normative approaches: principle-based, consequentialist, deontological or virtue-based. While these may be appropriate when examining specific clinical issues, none, according to Irvine and his colleagues, provide a sufficient basis for understanding the complexities of interprofessionalism, which demanded an appreciation of the multiplicity of subject positions within and between health care professions.

Competing agendas for interprofessional education

What, then, should interprofessionalism be?

- A closing of ranks to safeguard collective self-interest in an age when professionalism and its claims to elitism and privilege are under threat
- A coming together of professions to respond more effectively to the needs of their shared clientele, each voluntarily ceding some of their autonomy to realise more fully the altruistic values underpinning their common professionalism
- A response to modernisation policies to reform the professions, countering the downside of professionalism which stands in the way of reform and the strengthening of public accountability

The first of these propositions, in our experience, bears no relationship to the values which the interprofessional movement espouses. The second more accurately characterises the emerging interprofessional movement worldwide. The third demands more of interprofessional education than it can deliver alone, although it may contribute as part of a strategy of workforce reforms.

Interprofessional education must demonstrate not only that it can be an effective vehicle to resolve issues that divide professions, but also to resolve these competing perceptions about its very nature and purpose. At issue is whether interprofessional education, by resolving problems pertaining to its own identity, can modernise professionalism.

Different perceptions of professionalism and interprofessionalism, sometimes compounded by tensions between professions, are played out during programme planning and continue throughout its delivery. The common learning ethos exerts pressure to reconcile values as the parties find common cause, but comparative learning argues sometimes for honest acknowledgement of differences to be reconciled, at other times to be tolerated and for it to be built into the learning when helpful. The danger lies in overlooking the powerful influence of values, or in denying or fudging differences.

Establishing interprofessional education values

Interprofessional education may be contested territory but, as the discussion above has shown, its learners, their professions and agencies all espouse values that impact on its effectiveness. It is timely for interprofessional education to establish a value base for its development, delivery and evaluation. In Chapter two we showed the links in the chain that leads from effective interprofessional education to partnerships in health. We developed that further in Chapter three with a model of interprofessional education that extended the linear concept into an interlocking and interdependent relationship between the individual, the collaborating team and the delivery of care and a service. Values of interprofessionality are essential to the harmony between these links and relationships. We suggest a framework for these, built on values to inform the interprofessional learning environment and process, and built on three pillars: shaping the learning environment, perspectives taken in the learning process and concepts underpinning that process.

Shaping the learning environment

Androgological

Interprofessional education is based upon principles of adult learning including androgogy. It values what participants bring from their respective fields and from their life experience. It advocates interactive learning to equip participants with the knowledge, skills and attitudes to work independently and collaboratively and with the capability to know which of these modes of practice is in the best interest of clients in any given situation.

Professional

Interprofessional education values the contribution of each profession. It respects the need for division of labour, not least to accommodate growth in professionally relevant knowledge. It seeks to protect and reinforce the integrity and identity of each profession, while recognising that boundaries must be permeable and negotiable in response to the changing demands and expectations of policy and client.

Pan-professional

Interprofessional education reaches beyond mutual respect, in search of a definition of professionalism wider than any one profession or family of professions. It reinterprets the concept of professionalism in its contemporary context, taking aboard public accountability, external control, the interface with management and client participation. It wrestles with the need to balance the general and the particular, the development of a broad-based and flexible professional workforce and the preservation of the integrity of the constituent professions, whilst accepting the need for each to change in relation to the others.

Perspectives on the learning process

Client-centred

Interprofessional education values the contribution of clients. Acting on the belief that good practice (professional and interprofessional) is client-centred, it looks for ways to include clients and carers in developing, delivering and evaluating programmes, in assessment and as co-participants. It seeks to harmonise those values generated by professional socialisation and values underpinning the delivery of client care.

Holistic

Interprofessional education challenges compartmentalisation of the human condition according to predetermined specialities. It recognises the need to integrate mind, body and spirit, and person, family, neighbourhood, community, society and environment. It aligns itself with systemic practice with families and communities and with ecological movements.

Change-oriented

Interprofessional education seeks to make services better, prepared to embrace new approaches to service delivery and open to innovation. It recognises the value of service changes that enhance job satisfaction and improve recruitment and retention amongst all staff.

Concepts underpinning the learning process

Collaborative

Interprofessional education values collaboration over competition, but is realistic enough to know that they coexist. It works to constrain and counter the harmful effects of excessive competition within a wider collaborative framework.

Inclusive

Interprofessional education errs on the side of inclusion. It is predisposed towards widening inclusion in collaborative education and practice, unless and until there are compelling grounds to the contrary. It recognises that the practice of all professions benefits from critical scrutiny by self and others, and testing against evidence.

Equality and diversity

Interprofessional education espouses equality and values diversity. It extends the application of principles of equal opportunities and anti-oppressive practice to relations between professions, encouraging mutual respect and parity of esteem as learners, and seeking to reduce status differentials in the workplace. It celebrates difference, capitalising on the distinctive contribution that each profession and organisation brings. Accustomed to moving between professional cultures, exponents of interprofessional education are disposed to work between ethnic, religious and national cultures.

Conclusion

In this chapter we have exposed hidden and ill-documented value differences between professions and between stakeholders in interprofessional education, in the belief that they must be acknowledged before they can be addressed and reconciled. We have, however, gone further, drawing attention to moves towards common values and codes of practice and suggesting key components to be included in developing a value base for interprofessional education.

9 Thinking Theory

Like Chapter eight, this chapter enters into territory which goes beyond findings from our review. It draws selectively on the wider literature to identify theoretical perspectives to illumine interprofessional education and practice. Other theories introduced into interprofessional education, but less well developed in that context, are mentioned briefly. We make no claim to be exhaustive. The theoretical base for interprofessional education continues to evolve rapidly. Our exploration of explicit and implicit theoretical influences on the development of interprofessional education may be a useful first step in synthesising a theoretical base for a maturing conception of interprofessional education.

Introducing theory

Numerous theoretical perspectives have been introduced into interprofessional education from different academic disciplines. Interprofessional education errs on the side of inclusion, weighing each theoretical perspective on its merits, regardless of the academic discipline or practice profession from whence it comes. Few, however, have gained general currency so far, save perhaps for the influence of adult learning theories on the design and delivery of most interprofessional learning opportunities (Chapter seven).

Nor is the case for theory universally accepted. Some exponents, in our experience, are eager to strengthen the explicit theoretical base of interprofessional initiatives. Others resist the very idea of theory-based interprofessional education, stressing, instead, its roots in practice and fearing academic drift. We view unease at examining theoretical perspectives as misplaced, subscribing to the view (Schön, 1987) that practitioners constantly reflect on action and use this reflection to explain and predict phenomena and to shape future actions – that is they theorise.

Making theory explicit encourages systematic, disciplined and critical thinking. It informs decisions and generates propositions which can be tested. Theory, like much in interprofessional education, is contested territory.

Noting theoretical perspectives from the review

It was unusual for any of the 107 studies in our review to refer directly to a particular theoretical framework for interprofessional education (Table 9.1).

Table 9.1 Underpinning theory.

Underpinning theory	Frequency
Made explicit	
Learning organisation	13 (12%)
Adult learning	8 (8%)
Contact theory	3 (3%)
Implicit in report	
Adult learning	55 (51%)
Learning organisation	28 (26%)

While only 24 studies (22%) explicitly cited the use of an underpinning theory in the development or delivery of the interprofessional education, the descriptions of initiatives indicated widespread implicit use of the general tenets of adult learning theories (discussed in Chapter seven and below). Quality improvement initiatives that did not explicitly discuss an underpinning theoretical perspective were classified as making implicit use of the learning organisation perspective.

Studies that explicitly drew upon learning organisation theory tended to use principles of Total Quality Management (TQM) (e.g. Townes *et al.*, 1995) or Continuous Quality Improvement CQI (e.g. Bonomi *et al.*, 2002).

Of the small group of studies that explicitly drew upon theoretical perspectives from adult learning, five incorporated problem-based learning (e.g. Mann *et al.*, 1996); while the remainder incorporated Knowles' theory of adult learning, Kolb's theory of experiential learning and/or Schön's theory of reflective practice (Lia-Hoagberg *et al.*, 1997; Freeth & Nicol, 1998; Parsell *et al.*, 1998).

Theoretical perspectives on interprofessional education

Many theoretical perspectives have the potential to guide the development of interprofessional education and to aid understanding of interprofessional learning. We have selected those mentioned in the interprofessional literature. Encompassing a range of disciplinary traditions, they work best when they resonate with the practice context for interprofessional education and can be explained persuasively to stakeholders.

We assign these perspectives to the three foci for interprofessional education (see Chapter three), according to the main emphasis, but also taking into account overlap. For example, most theoretical perspectives that emphasise individuals also provide insights into interprofessional group collaboration.

(1) Preparing individuals for collaborative practice

- Adult learning
- Contact
- Social identity
- Self-categorisation
- Realistic conflict
- Self-presentation
- Loss and change
- Social defence
- Relational awareness
- Social exchange
- Negotiation
- Cooperation

(2) Cultivating collaboration in groups and teams

- Work-group mentality
- Group development
- Team learning

(3) Improving services and the quality of care

- Systems
- Organisational learning
- Activity

We also return to discourse analysis, on which we touched lightly in Chapter one, in view of its application in understanding interaction within and between inter-professional education and practice, and its relevance to communication studies.

Focus 1: preparing individuals for collaborative practice

This set of theories shares an emphasis upon the individual, but with implications often for their behaviour in groups and teams. Some are invoked to instigate change, others to understand the effect that change has on professions and their relationships with each other.

The tenets of adult learning theories are perhaps the most pervasive in the design and delivery of interprofessional education. For example, active learning is enshrined in the definition of interprofessional education and reflected back in countless examples, such as those in this book. In Chapter seven we couched approaches to interprofessional learning and teaching in the context of principles of adult learning as set out by some of the more influential late twentieth century writers in the field. Adult learning, according to those educationalists, is problem-centred, cyclical, situated, shared and intimately entwined with doing; in short, the type of learning that improves individuals' performance in areas that matter to them. Adopting this perspective, interprofessional education can be expected to succeed where interprofessional collaboration matters to participants, the educational experience is active, valuing and building upon prior knowledge and practice experience, and is recognised as relevant to participants' developmental needs.

Perspectives from social psychology

But application of adult learning theories alone is not enough to underpin interprofessional education. There are a number of theories from social psychology which help inform interprofessional education, notably *contact theory*. Carpenter (1995) and Dickinson (2003), amongst others, introduce this theoretical perspective into the development and evaluation of interprofessional education, which is then more clearly seen as a means to modify attitudes and negative stereotypes.

Contact theory, developed from the work of Allport (1979), examined the origins of prejudice between different social groups, where members identify with their own group to the detriment of their relationships with others. For him, the most effective way to reduce tension between groups was contact between their members, but hard experience, for example in seeking to ease racial tension in the Deep South of the United States, taught that simply bringing individuals from the groups together was insufficient to effect change. Three conditions, Allport concluded, had to be met before prejudice between them could be reduced: equality of status between the groups; group members working towards common goals; and cooperation during the contact. Hewstone & Brown (1986) added three other conditions, with particular reference to interprofessional education: positive expectations by participants; successful experience of joint working; and a focus on understanding differences as well as similarities between themselves (see p. 83).

Hewstone & Brown (1986) also identified the essential aspects of stereotyping, which application of contact theory is intended to modify. Individuals are categorised during the stereotyping process. Attributes are then ascribed to members of that category. Everyone who belongs to the group is then assumed to be similar to each other and different from those in other groups. Out-groups tend to be seen as homogeneous but in-groups as more diverse. Stereotypes also set up expectations of behaviour. Disconfirming evidence tends to be ignored, but confirming evidence to be remembered. Contact situations can therefore become self-fulfilling prophecies, which may explain why contact alone is not enough to change individuals' attitudes towards members of other groups.

A more complex formulation is needed to relate attitudes to behaviour (see Chapter six), where attitudes are exposed and challenged in face-to-face encounters with clients and with colleagues from other professions. We have found it helpful to apply work by Eagly & Chaiken (1993), which leads us to suggest that conditions deemed necessary for the contact theory to take effect have to be augmented before behaviour will change. The extended list then needs to be tested, either in college by simulating practice or in the workplace, to establish whether behaviour is modified.

A number of other theoretical perspectives from social psychology, related to individual and group identities, illuminate processes associated with interprofessional education. Help in understanding the significance of identification with one's own group (or profession) rather than another group (or profession) comes from *social identity theory*. This theory includes an interpersonal, inter-group dimension, where a person's behaviour is determined by individual characteristics at one end of the spectrum and by the group to which he or she belongs at the other (Tajfel & Turner, 1986; Ellemers *et al.*, 1999).

Brown & Williams (1984) identified three models of social identity theory:

- *The decategorisation model*, which plays down distinctions between groups and their members during inter-group encounters
- *The common group in-group identity model*, which establishes a super-ordinate group that members of the previously competing groups can join
- *The salient category model*, which maximises the group nature of contact as opposed to the personal

Choosing between these models is critical in distinguishing between intended outcomes from interprofessional education insofar as it seeks to change professional identity.

Should interprofessional education:

- Play down uniprofessional identities?
- Promote a supra-identity as health professions, to which uniprofessional identities become secondary?
- Reinforce and utilise uniprofessional identities?

Emphasis on one or more of these may differ between interprofessional education programmes, but inclusion of the last is essential, as included in our formulation of interprofessional values in the last chapter.

In self-categorisation theory, Turner (1999) builds on social identity theory. It retains the focus on self and group identity, but perceives them as lying along a continuum. Turner asserted that it was a mistaken assumption to think that social identity theory directly equated in-group bias with aggression between groups. The relationship was more complex, involving, among other factors, the social (or health) context as a possible mediating variable. This perspective is an antidote to oversimplified formulations of inter-group relations introduced, in our experience, into interprofessional education. It points to the need to understand groups or teams, and relations between them in their organisational context.

Social Identity theory also bears comparison with *realistic conflict theory,* which proposes that inter-group attitudes and behaviour reflect the objectives that each hold in their shared relationships. Where groups hold divergent objectives they will have hostile and discriminatory inter-group relationships. Conversely, where groups have common objectives conciliatory behaviour between groups will emerge (Brown *et al.*, 1986; Spears *et al.*, 1997). This theory shifts the emphasis from the identity of the members to the objectives of the group. It signals the need for interprofessional education to address the varying objectives that members believe that the group should have.

Three other social psychology theories: *social exchange theory, cooperation theory* and *relational awareness theory*, also focus on the development of the individual for collaborative practice, but take a different perspective from that explored so far.

The realisation that exchange carries meaning beyond its market value for the participants prompted social scientists to formulate social exchange theory, which argues for reciprocity in social relations, a calculation of return. The success of an exchange, for example bargaining or negotiating, is seen to be dependent either upon benefit to the parties or to a third party. There is therefore often an element of self-interest, but also the incurring of obligation or indebtedness (Challis *et al.*, 1988). This theory may help practitioners to look beyond the immediate consequences of their interactions with other professions to take into account the longer-term implications for themselves and for their professions. It may be employed in interprofessional education to cultivate an understanding of how collaborative relationships are created and maintained between individuals and between groups.

Believing that only cooperation will ensure the survival of the species, Axelrod (1984) sought the conditions that would make it possible between self-interested egoists in a complex world. He called this cooperation theory, into which he introduced *games theory*, as used, for example, by Rowley & Welsh (1994) in interprofessional learning materials in community care. This is a mathematical theory setting out the optimum choice of strategy in conflicts of interest. The parties do better, according to these theories, by cooperation than they do by working alone. Defection from an agreement brings retaliation. Knowing that they will meet again, said Axelrod, leads participants to conclude that, unless there is cooperative behaviour by both parties, there will be loss to the overall enterprise and to the parties themselves. This last proposition clearly applies within a team, but not necessarily in more ephemeral and more diffuse working relations, where behaviour may be less constrained by the prospect of renewed contact.

Relational awareness theory, developed from research and consultancy with health care teams by Drinka *et al.* (1996), helps to explain when and how the behaviour of members changes under different conditions. They analysed the individual motivational styles of team members by profession. The predominant motivational style of members was 'altruistic-nurturing' under normal conditions, but 'analytic and autonomising' under conflict conditions (p. 51). Interprofessional education that promotes learning about these styles and associated conditions can help participants to understand their own behaviour and that of others in their teams, and prompt action to control the working environment to reduce the risk of counterproductive behaviour.

Perspectives from dynamic psychology

A similar perspective to relational awareness theory comes from psychodynamic theory, namely *social defence theory*, exemplified by Menzies (1970). She found that nurses who normally collaborated well with other professions became defensive at times of anxiety when they were working under stress, withholding collaboration and working according to prescribed procedures. Denial, splitting and projection were the key mechanisms in play, whereby the other, be it junior or senior nurse, would be held responsible for the workers' inability to relieve the pain and suffering of the patients. Obholzer (1994) later identified the same mechanisms at work in interprofessional relations, where managers or doctors were the target of projections that could impede collaboration. Box 9.1 provides an example of an interprofessional initiative that drew upon this theoretical perspective.

Box 9.1   Understanding underlying feelings (Trowell, 1994).

An in-depth analysis of a child protection course at the Tavistock Clinic explored dynamics underlying group interactions. Child protection, it was found, evoked deep and powerful feelings, as the children affected were vulnerable. It was all too easy for the workers in this field to experience feelings such as dependency, confused sexual responses and anger, which surfaced during the course and interfered with learning. Interprofessional tensions emerged as one way of dealing with the discomfort evoked, nurses frequently becoming the repository for negative projections. To deal with these challenges, both the learners and the facilitators needed to be mature enough to acknowledge the areas of conflict and the underlying dynamics, and to learn from the process involved.

Social defence theory has been invoked in interprofessional education (e.g. University of Westminster, 2004), on the one hand to help participants understand their own and colleagues' behaviour under stress and, on the other hand, to reaffirm the need for a safe and comfortable learning environment to mitigate or contain anxiety and stress, where participants can open up and productive working relationships can be generated.

Another psychodynamic perspective introduced into interprofessional education is *loss and change theory*. Stress may be generated where interprofessional learning results in loss or change in professional identity (Atkins, 1998 citing Marris, 1986), which may in turn generate resistance, strained relationships or defensive behaviour. Box 9.2 (p.127) offers an example of how loss and change theory was incorporated into the evaluation of an interprofessional education programme.

Perspectives from sociology

Three sociological theories illuminate further the utility of theory in understanding interprofessional education. The first of these, *practice theory*, introduced by Almas (2004), taken from Bourdieu & Passeron (1990), helps to understand the processes by which entrants to the health professions come to hold a collective identity through 'common learning'.

Capital, especially cultural capital, is viewed as a product of education by which the person becomes cultivated and acquires the ability to talk and move within the

---

Box 9.2   Coping with anxiety, loss and change (Holman & Jackson, 2001).

Marris' theory of loss and change was used in an evaluation of interprofessional workshops for staff caring for older adults in London. The study found that, although participants enjoyed the sessions, they reported that their participation had not altered the way they worked with either their colleagues or patients/carers. Based on Marris' theory, the researchers argued that lack of impact in changing practice could be attributed to resistance due to unconscious feelings of anxiety connected with possible change.

---

community where that culture is performed and appreciated. It includes a set of prevailing values, traditions and competencies. Each profession, and each of its schools, has its own cultural capital. Identity is the meeting between culture and self. Central to Bourdieu's work is the concept of *habitus*, a system of 'dispositions' allowing individuals to act, think and become oriented in the social world. *Habitus* is the product of social experience, acquired not inherent, a disposition to act in a particular way. It internalises the principle of cultural arbitrariness learnt from socialising agents like teachers and mentors. The application of this theoretical perspective has yet to be fully developed in relation to interprofessional education and collaboration, but it promises to provide a much needed environmental context to complement the progress made in applying interactive learning methods.

Identity is closely akin to self-image. *Self-presentation theory* (Goffman, 1963) is therefore a helpful adjuvant to this discussion. According to Goffman, individuals present themselves to others by over-communicating gestures that reinforce their desired self-image and under-communicating gestures that they wish to detract from their self-image. He called this 'impression management'. He also distinguished between 'front stage performances', for example meetings between colleagues or consultations with clients, and 'back stage performances', for example interactions with family and friends. The front stage is more formal and more restrained in nature. The back stage is more relaxed, with opportunities to step outside front stage character and where individuals could prepare for their front stage performances. Adopting Goffman's perspective, interprofessional learning may be more effective when it generates informality and friendship conducive to back stage performance, complemented by front stage performance in practice or on placement (Reeves, 2005).

Negotiation theory (Strauss, 1978) is another useful sociological perspective, which holds that formal roles are generally applied flexibly as individuals engage in trade-offs between their personal goals, those of others and the formal rules of the organisation. Application of this theory becomes more complex when negotiations are interprofessional and/or inter-organisational as well as interpersonal. It has been applied in health care settings to explain how negotiations have shaped the nature of interprofessional relations between doctors and nurses (Svensson, 1996; Allen, 1997). It was also used by Reeves (2005) to help explain how processes of negotiation were employed between project steering group members and their students during the development and delivery of a practice-based interprofessional education programme. This study revealed the role of negotiation in the process of discussion and bargaining that occurred between members and their senior managers. Negotiation, in the form of reflective team discussions, was found to be vital in shaping the collaborative work of the students who participated in the programme.

Focus 2: cultivating group/team collaboration

The discussion above has shown how theories focusing on the individual nevertheless also help to understand behaviour between groups. We turn now to theories which focus on collaboration within the group, as distinct from between groups. These perspectives may help participants to understand better the group or team within which they are learning or working and help teachers in creating conditions favourable to such learning.

Work-group mentality theory

Bion (1961) identified two forms of group functioning from a psychodynamic perspective, one where a group is addressing the task at hand, which he called 'work-group mentality' and the other where a group is avoiding such a task, which he calls 'basic assumption mentality'. *Work-group mentality theory*, as it is known, has provided a powerful tool for analysis of groups and organisations that malfunction, where they are unable to deal with what Bion called 'primary task', that is the central task on which the group has consciously agreed.

Amongst others, Stokes (1994) has extended this analysis to interprofessional relations. He suggested that interprofessional team meetings can frequently be wasteful of time, where no decisions will be reached as a false sense of collaboration prevents members from tackling potentially difficult issues.

The experiential workshops entitled 'Pride and Prejudice' offered at the University of Westminster (see Box 5.10, Chapter five) have a group dynamic format. The focus is on group functioning, but specific emphasis is placed on allowing the participants to reflect on unconscious forces that shape interprofessional relations. It is not unusual for the doctors or police officers to become the focus of anger, for what appears to be lack of progress in the group: according to Bion a fight or flight basic dependence mentality comes into action if and when this occurs. The task of the group facilitator is to highlight such dynamics that tend to be mobilised, with the intent that the participants would then become sensitive to these forces in their own workplace.

Group development

Another perspective, this time from social psychology, is *group development theory*, collated from numerous sources by Tuckman (1965), which explains how groups progress over time during four stages:

- *Forming*, characterised by ambiguity and confusion as the group struggles to begin to work together
- *Storming*, when friction is generated between members as they begin to adopt roles and negotiate how they can work together
- *Norming*, as members work towards a consensus about the division of labour in the team
- *Performing*, as members understand one another and work together in a well coordinated fashion

In a later paper, Tuckman & Jensen (1977) added a fifth 'adjourning' stage, when the task has either been completed or membership is disrupted.

Applying this model, relationships between learners during an interprofessional education programme need to be addressed especially during the first three stages before effective co-working can be achieved during the fourth.

Support for this perspective in the teamwork literature comes from Øvretveit (1997), who said that teams needed to spend time undertaking preparatory work, making opportunities to discuss and agree how they are going to work together in an effective, efficient and mutually satisfying manner. An important outcome of this preparatory work is the development of a team policy, which should explicitly record the collective aims, roles and responsibilities of the members. For Øvretveit, ongoing discussion within the team is required to ensure that the policy is regularly updated and amended if, for example, a new member joins or there is a need to modify a previously agreed policy.

West (1996) argued that time spent together reflecting upon collaborative work can ensure that the team becomes 'reflexive', integrated and better coordinated.

> 'Reflexivity involves the members of the team standing back and critically examining themselves, their processes and their performance to communicate about these issues and to make appropriate changes.' (p.13)

The development of a reflexive approach within a team, said West, could help ensure that members became more able to adapt, respond to change and work together in a more effective and efficient manner. A key aspect to achieving a reflexive approach was the creation of an environment where members valued one another's contributions, felt safe to share their ideas openly and trusted each other as they acknowledged their shortfalls and mistakes. While West noted that the development of a reflexive approach to teamwork entailed both time and effort by members, the benefit gained from this input was worthwhile.

Team learning

The notion of the learning team has been developed from that of the learning organisation (Senge, 1990) (as discussed below). Such a team synthesises theories from adult learning and group dynamics, seeing individual learning as necessary, but collective learning as essential for an organisation to survive and flourish. The learning team moves beyond teambuilding as a linear progression towards a predetermined goal, making realistic allowance for chronic instability in many teams. It protects 'process time' to reflect upon what is going on within the dynamics of the group and to explore the wider significance of matters in hand.

Dechant et al. (1993) presented a model of team learning in industry. They acted on the guiding assumption that teams rather than individuals were the main learning units in modern organisations. Individual learning was necessary but not sufficient for organisations to survive and flourish. Their model takes into account instability as team members come and go. Bond (Bond & Hart, 1998; Bond, 1999) applied the work of Dechant et al. to teams in the UK National Health Service.

Acknowledging, though they did, that there was no substitute for practice experience, Hart & Fletcher (1999) argued that learning how to change was immeasurably enriched when combined with theory. It was better, they contended, to use a flawed theory critically and with discrimination than none at all. However well motivated the members may be, team learning does not arise spontaneously, but in response to systematic endeavours by teams to improve their work, characterised, according to Jackson & Burton (2003), by:

- Good communications
- Peer support
- Peer learning
- Shared values
- An appropriate mix of learning opportunities
- Some learning driven by members' needs and met within the team
- Some learning taking place outside the team and disseminated within it
- Learning resources, for example access to libraries
- Protected time for learning

Box 9.3 (p. 131) gives an example which develops a learning team as a vehicle for interprofessional learning.

Learning in teams can be valuable, but weakened when it assumes idealised notions of teamwork grounded in stable, enduring and cohesive working relations, which may be the exception. Many teams in health and social care settings are inherently unstable, while many workers are required to work in situations which fit neither the traditional notion of teamwork nor of networking (Engestrom et al., 1999, see below).

Focus 3: improving services and the quality of care

Turning, finally, to the third focus, we begin with a discussion about systems theory as an approach to understanding the interrelated nature of individuals to their social environments. We then go on to consider the learning organisation as a vehicle for interprofessional learning as a change agent, before discussing theories behind two important processes: Total Quality Management (TQM) and Continuous Quality Improvement (CQI). Finally, we explore the potential

---

Box 9.3   Establishing a learning team (Bateman *et al.*, 2003).

A newly created primary care team near Cambridge, England, comprised, in addition to GPs and nurses, a pharmacist, a Well Family Service coordinator, a service development manager, a research and learning officer, a patient participation coordinator, an information technology coordinator and administrative staff.

Many were attracted by the chance to develop new approaches to practice, but developed doubts about their ability to handle their new roles, especially that of nurse practitioner. One-to-one discussions were arranged in an attempt to understand the problems, and relevant training opportunities were identified and mobilised.

Team members were encouraged to maintain strong and continuing links with their respective professions, reinforced by external mentoring from that profession.

Potential conflicts, resulting from allegiances and accountability outside the team, were addressed by canvassing the views of 'partner employers' to understand better their expectations. A 360-degree reflective development process encompassed some of the appraisal requirements operated by these external partners within the one developed for the practice.

Problems rarely presented themselves clearly. Undercurrents of concern and discomfort were identified, which called for teamwork towards closer understanding.

---

use of activity theory which, still early in its formulation, promises to understand change in a more comprehensive manner.

Systems theory

Von Bertalanffy (1971) and his successors developed the concept of 'system' as an antidote to the limitations of specialist disciplines in addressing complex problems. It could be applied across all disciplines, from physics and biology, to the social and behavioural sciences, seeing wholes as more than the sum of their parts, interactions between parties as purposeful, boundaries between them as permeable, and cause and effect as interdependent not linear. The underlying philosophy of *systems theory* is the unity of nature, governed by the same fundamental laws in all its realms. Intervention by one profession at one point in the system affects the whole in ways that can only be anticipated from multiple professional perspectives.

The biopsychosocial model is an application of systems thinking developed by Engel (1977) which relates the whole person to his or her environment. It bears comparison with the notion of holistic care, often incorporated into interprofessional education as the ideal to which collaborative practice aspires. Systems theory has multiple applications in interprofessional education and practice. It

offers a unifying and dynamic framework within which all the participant professions can relate: person, family, community and environment, one or more of
which may be points of intervention interacting with the whole. It can also be
used to understand relationships within and between professions, between service agencies, between education and practice, and between stakeholders planning and managing programmes. Systems theory can offer diverse perspectives
on interprofessional education and practice.

The learning organisation

Interprofessional (and uniprofessional) learning may occur during everyday
work, but it is often inaccessible and liable, in consequence, to be devalued or
discounted. Learning organisation theory not only sheds light, but also encourages organisational development and management styles that encourage such
learning.

A learning organisation fosters a culture of questioning and enquiry. It is
innovative, with facilitative leadership (Anderson, 1992), proactive, capable of
continuous change, yet retaining its specific identity (Swieringa & Wierdsma,
1992), reframing information as learning, and adopting a cyclical process of
change. A learning organisation respects workers' differing roles, experience
and expertise, and values them as learning assets, mobilising its own capacity to
respond to learning needs from its internal teaching resources, while recognising
its limitations, bringing in college and freelance teachers when needed and
valuing the distinctive qualities of extra-mural learning by making provision to
release staff to attend courses. It responds as a good employer to the needs and
expectations of the worker, within and beyond his or her present post, as well as
those of the organisation.

The organisation facilitates the learning of all its members and continuously
transforms itself (Garratt, 1990) through a process-based definition which rests
firmly in the social-emotional area, with none of the traditional hard edges of
management. It is more than just doing a lot of training: it is a free-flow of learning
and information, dependent on satisfying the following five conditions:

- A perception of learning as a cyclical process
- An acceptance of the different roles of policy, strategy and operations within
  the organisation
- Free-flowing information
- The ability to value people as the key asset for organisational learning
- The ability to reframe information at strategic levels: first and second order
  change

The concept of the learning organisation developed from *organisational theory*,
which included the idea of double loop learning. Single loop learning for Argyris
& Schön (1974, 1984) was part of the traditional behaviour pattern designed to
enhance an individual's position and progress in competition with others. Double
loop learning was appropriate in a changing environment which required a

flexible response that only the coordinated and committed action of a team or organisation could produce. It should be conducive to creating a professional (or interprofessional) community which undertakes explicit, public and cumulative learning.

Double loop learning, added Brown & Sommerland (1992), entailed learning-in-action to explore organisational norms through collaborative enquiry, moving away from 'espoused theories', which represented a publicly acknowledged and accepted set of propositions. Education and training within a learning organisation was:

- A continuous learning process
- Essential for organisation survival
- Linked to organisation strategy and organisational goals
- On-the-job plus specialist courses
- Line managers' responsibility
- Tolerant of risk taking and mistakes

The dynamics of the learning organisation are informed by behavioural and social psychology. Lewin (1952) identified three stages:

- Unfreezing – creation of motivation to change
- Moving – developing new attitudes, values, beliefs, and behaviour patterns on the basis of new information obtained and cognitive redefinition
- Refreezing – stabilising and integrating new beliefs, attitudes, values and behaviour patterns into the rest of the system

Management mechanisms can set the learning agenda. At best, performance appraisal creates a positive opportunity to identify the learning needs of both individuals and groups. So, too, can clinical governance, as introduced in the UK, when it exposes shortfalls in services which call for more skilled workers to effect improvement.

The whole workforce stands to benefit in a learning organisation, including those workers deemed to be professionals. Such an organisation generates the conditions under which interprofessional education learning can flourish in the workplace.

Total quality management

Effecting organisational change has been made more systematic by the application of two related theories, of which TQM was introduced first. TQM (Oakland, 1993; Morgan, 1997) originated in manufacturing industries, but has been adapted for service industries.

Its essential requirements have been summarised by Kogan *et al.* (1991) as:

- Corporate planning – medium to long-term
- Staff commitment throughout the organisation
- Breaking down barriers between departments and professions

- Continuous redefinition of targets and standards
- Identification of the customer
- Facilitation and coordination
- Commitment to continuous monitoring and evaluation of progress
- Balancing input costs against effectiveness
- High quality information systems
- Valuing all staff and their contribution to change
- Education and training

Box 9.4 provides an example of a TQM initiative that included interprofessional education linked to improving the quality of care delivered to patients based in three hospital departments.

Box 9.4   TQM in three hospital departments (Townes *et al.*, 1995).

Three departments: surgery, anaesthesiology and operating room services, based in a hospital in Kentucky, combined to implement a TQM initiative to enhance the delivery of patient care. Initially, staff received interprofessional training to develop their understanding of the TQM approach and its application. Following this training staff formed two project teams. Project team 1 examined hold-ups linked to patient care activities that occurred in the area where patients waited for their operations. Project team 2 studied the delays that occurred while patients were evaluated for surgery in the outpatient clinic. Both teams created mission statements focused on how they would reorganise their working practices to reduce unnecessary delays and therefore improve patients' experience while in hospital. Data collected following the implementation of the TQM initiative found that patient delays in both areas were reduced. Despite these successes, it is noted that a number of difficulties were encountered during the implementation of this change programme. It was found that staff, in particular the surgeons, were initially resistant to the changes proposed in the TQM mission statements. Nevertheless, it was pointed out that the involvement of professional leaders and the use of regular updates on implementation process helped overcome these early challenges.

Continuous quality improvement

In our review we found more examples of CQI than of TQM. The operational differences between them may be subtle. CQI, said Wilcock *et al.* (2003), is a set of principles and methods that enables people to improve the processes and systems within which they work. At its core is the use of knowledge to identify changes, plan and assess outcomes. Its distinctive feature is the development of a framework which can be used by practitioners in their everyday work to produce improvements which they themselves considered relevant to their clients. The CQI process is a PDSA cyclical – plan, do, study and act. The 'trick' is to attempt

small changes which can be made quickly, followed by progressively more difficult ones.

See Box 5.14 (Chapter five) for an initiative in an Australian Children's hospital
designed to improve the care of children with acute asthma, Box 4.3 (Chapter
four) for a CQI initiative aimed at enhancing the delivery of pain relief to
paediatric patients in a USA hospital and Box 6.5 (Chapter six) for an initiative
that improved the quality of care to patients at a general practice in Salford (UK).
Interprofessional learning within an organisation becomes more purposeful, more
systematic and more sustained where methods such as TQM, CQI and collaborative inquiry are employed.

Activity theory

Albeit encouraging rigour and logical progression, TQM and CQI are typically
employed in health and social care to effect small-scale change rather than intervention designed to effect wide-ranging systemic change. Activity theory promises to
go further. It is a means to understand and intervene in relations at micro and macro
levels, applicable to effecting change in interpersonal, interprofessional and inter-
agency relations, developed by Engestrom (1999a,b; Engestrom *et al.*, 1999). Engestrom developed Vigotsky's (1978) concept of mediation in a triangle of individual
relationships: subject, object and mediating artefact, to examine systems of activity
at the macro level of collective and community in preference to the micro. He
introduced community, rules and division of labour into the activity system, interaction between them becoming the focus for analysis.

Joint activity, not individual activity, is the unit of analysis in activity theory,
with instability (internal tensions) and contradiction the motive force for change
and development (Il'enkov, 1977). Mediated activity not only changed the object
but also the environment. The reflective appropriation of advanced models and
tools were presented as ways out of internal contradictions that result in new
activity systems. Activity theory is still evolving, but may prove to be a significant
advance beyond TQM and CQI to instigate major strategies for change, provided
that its language can be translated and tools developed which managers and
practitioners can employ.

Discourse analysis

Less explored than it merits in interprofessional education, *discourse analysis* holds
much potential. We began in Chapter one by discussing differences in language
widely held to account for failures in communication between professions, but
questioned whether semantics alone were an adequate explanation and found
discourse theory helpful. The better discourse is understood, the more its pervasive and often hidden influence on interprofessional and inter-agency relations
may be understood.

Discourse analysis is, however, a complex concept (Van Dijk, 1997) capable of a
number of applications in interprofessional learning and working. On the one

hand, it draws on the Anglo-Saxon tradition of linguistics as means of representation, where the analyst is concerned with structures to account for meanings that might be culturally or situationally determined. On the other hand, it belongs in the continental European social science tradition as a phenomenon that takes on an active role in interpersonal and wider societal interactions. We find it helpful from both perspectives.

From the first, tension and sometimes conflict between professions may be analysed in terms of failure to understand each other's discourses. Relations may improve where one profession comes to understand better the discourse employed by another. This is most apparent where practitioners from one profession work with another on their territory. For example, the social worker outposted to the psychiatric clinic not only acquires relevant specialist knowledge, but also a facility in understanding and contributing to discourse, typically initiated and controlled by the psychiatrist. A mark of interprofessional maturity may be the degree to which the social worker is also able to introduce his or her discourse as an aid to mutual understanding.

Interprofessional education creates opportunities for participants to become more alive to differences in discourse and the problems that they can generate. Each profession may become more aware of its own discourses and how they are received by others, to learn to check the comprehension of those others when necessary and to develop the interpersonal and interprofessional skills to employ alternative discourses. Interprofessional education generates its own discourses, during planning and teaching, and through it burgeoning literature, of which this book and its accompanying volumes (Freeth *et al.*, 2005; Meads & Ashcroft, 2005) are some of many examples.

Adopting the second perspective, the analyst looks for the role and function of discourse, how it positions parties in the communication process and what impact it has on the outcome of the interaction. The context is social and organisational, the focus is what the parties bring to the interchange within it.

Foucault (1972) has developed a concept of discourse that represents a subtle and continuous interplay between the language, the means of communication and the context in which it is employed. Fairclough (1992) has operationalised this concept as an analytic tool which Koppel (2003) used to uncover prevalent discourses in continuing professional development and interprofessional education. Koppel demonstrated how three main discourses shaped the thinking and behaviour of the main parties in the education field, namely the discourses of management, professions and education.

For example, Koppel (2003) observed the interaction between representatives of education providers and practising professionals for nursing, health visiting and general practice, with health authority managers and advisers, to review current provision of post-qualifying education and to share ideas for new educational developments. The agenda was driven by the Health Service managers, who held the purse strings. Nursing representatives expressed anxiety that funds would be siphoned off from their uniprofessional courses, but GP representatives did not, since their funding was not threatened. Koppel saw this situation as exposing the conflict between management discourse, manifest in the intent to drive the change agenda through control of funds, and professional discourse, that values independence.

Discourse analysis provides a tool with which to analyse processes of exchange between organisations, taking into account their cultures and power. Active at all levels, discourse:

- Shapes individual thinking
- Finds expression in team or group interaction, during a struggle to find common ground; and when common action is mediated through discourse
- Defines organisational culture that creates its own discourse with explicit and implicit rules and values

Relating theories to foci

Although the theories that we have presented in this chapter can be assigned to our three foci, many, as we noted at the outset, span two or all three. Figure 9.1 summarises.

Theory	IPE focus		
	Preparing individuals	Cultivating group/team collaboration	Improving service/quality of care
Adult learning	×	×	
Contact	×	×	
Social identity	×	×	
Self-categorisation	×	×	
Realistic conflict	×	×	
Social exchange	×	×	
Cooperation	×	×	
Relational awareness	×	×	
Social defence	×	×	
Loss and change	×	×	
Practice	×	×	×
Self-presentation	×	×	
Negotiation	×	×	
Work-group mentality	×	×	
Group development	×	×	
Team learning	×	×	
Systems	×	×	×
Learning organisation	×	×	×
Total Quality Management	×	×	×
Continuous Quality Improvement	×	×	×
Activity	×	×	×
Discourse analysis	×	×	×

Figure 9.1 Relating theories to foci.

Towards a general theory of interprofessional education?

Some readers may be impatient to formulate a general theory of interprofessional education; others may question whether one can ever be formulated in the absence of an overarching theory of education.

For Eraut (1994), professional knowledge is a conglomerate of theories, practical knowledge and skills combined with personal beliefs. For Usher & Bryant (1989), it rested on shaky theoretical foundations, drawing on academic disciplines such as sociology, psychology and philosophy each of which is in a state of turmoil, and offered a competing paradigm or perspective. They questioned whether it was possible to find or formulate a respectable scientific theory beyond the immediate circle of its exponents.

Approached thus, any attempt to establish a general theory of interprofessional education reliant on an admixture of behavioural and social sciences is doomed to failure. We argue strongly that for such a complex field, where different groups of learners meet for a variety of purposes at different stages of their professional development, no single theory will suffice.

Conclusion

Despite ambivalence, the theoretical base for interprofessional education is being assembled: new perspectives are being brought to bear, casting existing ones in a fresh light. Teachers are invoking theories from their respective disciplines in an attempt to elucidate interprofessional education in terms to which they can relate and to inform learning about interprofessional practice by their students. Helpful though this can be, it becomes problematic when the claims of one discipline or one theory are pressed at the expense of others. In our view, no one perspective should take precedence. The task, as we see it, is not to apply theory to practice, but to employ theory derived from education and practice to understand better the relationship between them. Theory then becomes an aid to reflection.

10 Drawing the Threads Together

Finally, we draw together the threads from earlier chapters and mark up action points for future attention. We discuss the implications of our findings for interprofessional education policy and practice, and for future systematic reviews. We touch on ways in which methodology may be improved to evaluate interprofessional education, but leave substantive questions about programme development, delivery and evaluation for discussion in our companion book (Freeth *et al.*, 2005). We collate models and classifications offered. We end by highlighting some of the tensions held in interprofessional education, creative tensions whose energy can be harnessed.

Collating findings from the review

We have analysed and synthesised 107 higher quality evaluations of interprofessional education in health and social care from published sources, to enable us to comment on the current state of knowledge about its effectiveness. Those findings enabled us to revisit some of the many and varied arguments and assumptions made about interprofessional education.

The data assembled, with numerous examples, demonstrated how interprofessional education is responding to each of the many issues in health and social care summarised in Chapter one. Our review found some evidence for three (emboldened below) of the nine links set out in the chain reaction in Chapter two (see outcomes reported in Chapter six) based on the modified Kirkpatrick classification:

- **Creates positive interaction** (level 3, see Chapter six)
- Engenders mutual trust and support
- **Encourages collaboration between professions** (level 3, see Chapter six)
- Limits demands made on any one profession
- Reduces stress
- Enhances job satisfaction
- Improves recruitment and retention
- **Improves client care** (level 4b, see Chapter six)

Valuable though we found the modified Kirkpatrick classification, there is a persuasive argument for including the remaining six links in a reformulation of outcomes. This would prepare the ground to test hypotheses relating these outcomes.

We commend our three foci: preparing individuals, cultivating group/team collaboration and improving services and quality of care, as a simple, practicable and easily remembered classification of interprofessional education. It has also proved possible to refine earlier attempts to identify dimensions of interprofessional education. Key dimensions, for purposes of our analysis, were the stage which participants had reached in their professional experience, that is, pre- or post-qualification, and leadership of interprofessional education development by college or service agency; resulting in six domains for interprofessional education. Joint leadership, albeit gaining ground during the period under review, was not yet sufficiently established to attract the evaluation which it now clearly merits.

Our findings confirmed the distinction between intermediate outcomes attainable from college-led interprofessional education: laying foundations of knowledge and skills and modifying attitudes and perceptions; and ultimate objectives attainable from service-led interprofessional education: changing practice and improving the experience of clients.

Our search criteria excluded studies where interactive learning was absent. The review therefore reveals nothing about the possible effects of received (or didactic) learning alone in improving collaborative practice and the quality of services. It does, however, demonstrate that interactive learning can achieve those ends. Data are incomplete, and numbers too small, to show which interactive learning methods are more or less effective.

Information provided about approaches to learning and teaching was minimal, studies generally reporting outcomes more fully than process. Oft commended methods, such as PBL, were rarely mentioned. We were, however, encouraged to note a tendency to employ multiple learning approaches.

Values, with noteworthy exceptions, were neglected in the studies reported. We therefore turned to other sources to compare and contrast values held by different stakeholders and by different professions participating in interprofessional education, played out during planning and interprofessional learning. Preliminary formulations (see Chapter eight) nevertheless encouraged us to believe that the road towards a common value base for the health and social care professions need neither be long nor tortuous. Although theory was under-reported in many of the studies, numerous theoretical perspectives are being introduced by a limited number of scholars as interprofessional education gains ground in higher education. The relevance of some theoretical perspectives, like adult learning, reflective practice and contact theory, was better articulated than others. Again, with noteworthy exceptions, the application of theories has yet to be evaluated.

Synthesising the current state of knowledge

We respect those of our fellow researchers for whom nothing less than rigorously controlled experimental research methods will suffice, but note that they approach educational research from the perspective of clinical research. We opted for a more inclusive approach, embracing a range of methodologies commonly employed in educational research, subjecting each study to a systematic quality check, but in the final analysis leaving the reader to decide how much credence he or she is prepared to accord our findings.

Nothing in our work during the last eight years leads us to expect a dramatic break through in establishing the evidence base for interprofessional education. The way forward lies in weighing evidence painstakingly assembled, regarding process and outcome, from studies into diverse types of interprofessional education, employing diverse research methods and generating a continuum of outcomes.

It would be mistaken to treat initiatives included in our review as typical of the generality of interprofessional education. They are atypical by virtue of having been evaluated, in meeting requirements for publication, being selected for inclusion in the review and further selected for inclusion in the subsample of higher quality studies. They are biased in favour of English-language journals, which report mainly, but not exclusively, from English-speaking countries. They are also biased in favour of so-called developed countries, with the resources to conduct evaluations and outlets to publish them. The result is a nucleus of more rigorous and higher quality studies upon which to call for experience in designing future evaluation, as we do in our companion volume (Freeth *et al.*, 2005).

Improving methodology

The number of evaluations of interprofessional education reported is rising year by year, generating more opportunities to cross-fertilise experience. There is much to be learned from the best; hence our decision to include references for all 107 higher quality studies in Appendix 3.

Interprofessional education is more likely to be subject to systematic evaluation when it is college led. Such evaluation may employ approaches and criteria well honed for professional education. Helpful though that is, as a starting point, it stops short if it fails to take into account the distinctive attributes of interprofessional education (see Freeth *et al.*, 2005). It is here that reports such as this can be helpful. Work, however, remains to be done to advise and assist colleges and regulatory bodies in defining and applying evidence-based criteria. Similarly, funding bodies need help in deciding when and where to establish or evaluate interprofessional education programmes.

If only all the evaluations were as good as the best. There is much to be said for levelling up standards. Some evaluations will, however, always be better than others, where, for example, they have access to earmarked funds and can retain researchers with special expertise. The challenge lies in raising the general standard by improving advice to teachers about ways in which they can evaluate their programmes more effectively, while selecting some programmes for more systematic, more sustained and probably more costly evaluation, hiring independent researchers or building in external and expert consultancy.

Criteria for selecting interprofessional education initiatives for more rigorous evaluation need to be debated. In some countries, such as Canada and the UK, they may be those programmes according most closely with government initiatives. In others, such as the USA, they may be parts of series of programmes funded by charitable foundations. There will, however, always be innovative programmes outside the mainstream of development, whose evaluation merits particular attention to learn lessons which may have wider application. This suggests the need for funds to be held, whether by government, research institutions or charitable foundations, for which application may be made from any interprofessional education programme able to demonstrate that it is breaking new ground. Obvious 'candidates' include the application of e-learning and evaluation of the long-term impact of interprofessional education. Funds also need to be available to support the development of robust tools and innovative ways to evaluate interprofessional education.

We confine ourselves here to general observations about methodology, referring readers wishing to look more closely at evaluation to our companion book (Freeth et al., 2005). Arid debates about the relative merits of quantitative and qualitative research methods are best avoided. Given the range of unanswered questions posed by stakeholders about interprofessional education there is need for robust evaluation employing all paradigms. The secret lies in playing to the strengths of various approaches in response to those questions; and in the careful synthesis of findings from different perspectives.

Qualitative methods, such as observation, are applicable in evaluating learning processes, but are relatively underdeveloped in interprofessional education. Quantitative methods are required to measure change before, during and after the learning experience, with a heavy reliance on questionnaires. Validated instruments for this purpose are few and not always relevant to the purpose, prompting efforts to produce 'homemade' instruments that sometimes lack validity and reliability.

We draw attention, too, to the need for more longitudinal studies which follow interprofessional education participants through and beyond the programme. These need resources to trace and involve those participants after completion of their studies so that attrition may be minimised.

Informing future policy and practice

Health and social care policy and practice are often based on less than adequate evidence. Policy to inform interprofessional education is no exception. Evidence is nevertheless being assembled to which this book has contributed. We know, as a result of the review, that pre-qualifying interprofessional education primarily focuses on preparing the individual for collaboration. Studies reported demonstrate that, under favourable conditions, such education lays foundations for collaborative practice.

Can and should pre-qualifying programmes try to do more? We suggest two ways in which this may well be possible, neither of which came through strongly in the pre-qualifying studies in our review. The first is the development of competency-based, pre-qualifying, interprofessional education, that is, pursuit of a model that synthesises attitudinal, knowledge and skills-based learning, to deliver identified competencies as outcomes (Barr, 1998; Whittington, 2003). The second is teaching collaboration, which brings in the second of our three foci, including teamwork, which Miller *et al.* (2001) found to be neglected. These may well be achievable goals.

We counsell caution in trying to go further. We question the ethics and the practicality of expecting students immediately following qualification to become change agents. They have enough to do in applying and reinforcing their learning to practice, without imposing burdens that properly rest with experienced colleagues. But pre-qualifying interprofessional education can encourage receptivity to innovation, motivating and enabling newly qualified workers to respond.

Findings from our review underline the need to do better. Learning outcomes from pre-qualifying interprofessional education can, as we have suggested, be taken beyond acquisition of knowledge and attitudinal change, but will remain essentially preparatory. Much therefore depends upon the manner in which they are applied during first appointment. The need to reinforce learning following pre-qualifying education programmes is now widely accepted by the professions and employers. The literature is, however, silent about ways in which this reinforces and applies interprofessional learning. Identifying when, where and how this should be done merits research and development, lest the benefits of pre-qualifying interprofessional learning be lost.

Continuing interprofessional development (CIPD) is a vehicle to build on the foundations laid during pre-qualifying interprofessional education. The need for uniprofessional continuing education to update and reinforce profession specific knowledge and skills remains. Multiprofessional continuing education has become more widespread, where much the same updating is needed across professions. Uniprofessional and multiprofessional continuing education need to be reviewed from an interprofessional perspective, to identify and exploit opportunities to enhance learning between the participant professions to inform collaboration in practice.

We found that CQI and TQM initiatives played a greater role in interprofessional education than we had envisaged. This drew attention to a powerful vehicle for work-based interprofessional learning as a change agent, but risks overshadowing many other opportunities for such learning, as yet ill-understood, still less exploited.

We made every effort to highlight the most recently reported evaluations, but development is always ahead of the literature, especially in a field such as interprofessional education, which is subject to exponential growth. Evidence can inform innovation, innovation which calls for the exercise of judgement, confidence and courage.

Much emphasis has been put, in recent years, on pre-qualifying interprofessional education, redressing the previous emphasis on post-qualifying. Our evidence points clearly to the need to develop a continuum of career-long interprofessional education weaving in college and service-led components throughout. Hard though that may be, it is as nothing compared with the need to interweave uniprofessional, multiprofessional and interprofessional education within a single and workable rationale. If findings from our review have helped to establish what interprofessional education can contribute then that will be a first step.

Informing future systematic reviews

Methodology for systematic reviews is now well rehearsed and much used in clinical studies. Reviews such as ours should clearly be replicated, but there are three questions: how soon, how widely and applying what criteria? While the growing number of interprofessional education evaluations published would make a further review feasible quite soon, innovations and trends are more likely to be apparent after an interval of, perhaps, three to five years.

The scope of future reviews may become ever wider as fields of interprofessional education multiply and expand. The investment needed to scan sources will grow correspondingly, although the yield of useable evaluations may remain comparatively small. An alternative would be a number of more focused reviews of predetermined types of interprofessional education, for example in different fields or with different client groups, comparable to our UK-focused review (Barr *et al.*, 2000). Such reviews might well be interspersed, pending a major review comparable to that which we have reported in this book. We are updating the Cochrane review. Meanwhile, our review has identified a few studies which meet at least one of its two criteria for inclusion (see Chapter four).

Introducing shape and coherence

We have devised models and classifications in an attempt to make an inherently complex field more coherent. These included:

- An hypothesised chain reaction of outcomes (Chapter two)
- An empirical six-fold classification of outcomes (Chapter four)
- Three foci (Chapter three onwards)
- Curricula models (Chapter five)

- A dynamic model of outcomes (Chapter six) beyond the chain reaction in (Chapter two)

We have been more cautious in organising value and theoretical bases for inter-professional education, preferring to expose our thoughts to critical review, to enable others to introduce greater coherence as perspectives fall into place. Helpful though models and classifications may prove to be, we counsell against their overzealous adoption in an evolving field, where a degree of fluidity may aid creativity and make it easier to value and exchange different perspectives.

Holding the tension

Much in interprofessional education has changed during the eight years in which we have been undertaking our reviews. It has grown immeasurably in scale and scope in ever more countries. It has come in from the cold. No longer on the margins, it has secured its place in the mainstream of higher education with new opportunities to influence curricula, but also new threats to its ill-understood and half-developed methods.

Interprofessional education is exposed to closer scrutiny in an intellectually more rigorous world than ever before, challenged to explain its theoretical bases and to substantiate its claims with evidence. We captured that tension in the title of this book, more precisely in its subtitle – *argument, assumption and evidence*. We have exposed arguments for, and assumptions about, its place to critical review in the light of the evidence, a process which challenges as much as it confirms.

Exposing interprofessional education to academic study may add to fears among policy makers, managers and practitioners that it is becoming too remote from practice and too academic for its own good. If this book has reinforced those fears we have failed; our purpose throughout has been to apply systematic scholarship to improve education and, through it, practice.

But the more interprofessional education becomes an agent of change, the more it generates its own inner tension. Far from being a problem, that tension can be converted into creative energy. We have lived with these tensions throughout the review process and especially the writing up, as we struggled to develop a discourse which policy makers, managers, practitioners, educators and researchers can share. Let others judge whether we have succeeded. Win or lose, we are left in no doubt that the effective development of interprofessional education depends critically upon candid communication between all the stakeholders, not just between the professions for whom it is designed.

Only then will interprofessional education become an effective instrument to implement education, health and social care policy, and to respond to the needs of both workers and clients.

LIBRARY, UNIVERSITY OF CHESTE

Appendix 1 Search Strategies

Below is the search strategy we devised for our first electronic bibliographic database search on Medline (1966–2000), which was adapted for the later searches: CINAHL (1982–2001), BEI (1964–2001), ASSSIA (1990–2003), to reflect differences in the indexing of terms between these databases.

1 INTER-PROFESSION* or INTERPROFESSION*
2 INTER-DISCIPLIN* or INTERDISCIPLIN*
3 INTER-OCCUPATION* or INTEROCCUPATION*
4 INTER-INSTITUTION* or INTERINSTITUTION*
5 INTER-AGEN* or INTERAGEN*
6 INTER-SECTOR* or INTERSECTOR*
7 INTER-DEPARTMENT* or INTERDEPARTMENT*
8 INTER-ORGANISATION* or INTERORGANISATION*
9 INTERPROFESSIONAL RELATIONS
10 TEAM*
11 1 or 2 or 3 or 4 or 5 or 6 or 7 or 8 or 9 or 10
12 MULTI-PROFESSION* or MULTIPROFESSION*
13 MULTI-DISCIPLIN* or MULTIDISCIPLIN*
14 MULTI-INSTITUTION* or MULTIINSTITUTION*
15 MULTI-OCCUPATION* or MULTIOCCUPATION*
16 MULTI-AGEN* or MULTIAGEN*
17 MULTI-SECTOR* or MULTISECTOR*
18 MULTI-ORGANISATION* or MULTIORGANISATION*
19 PROFESSIONAL-PATIENT RELATION*
20 12 or 13 or 14 or 15 or 16 or 17 or 18 or 19
21 11 or 20
22 EDUCATION* or TRAIN* or LEARN* or TEACH* or COURSE*
23 QUALITY ASSURANCE or TQM or CQI or GUIDELINE DEVELOPMENT
24 22 or 23
25 20 and 24
26 STUDENT PERFORMANCE APPRAISAL
27 COURSE EVALUATION
28 PROGRAM* EVALUATION
29 EVALUATION RESEARCH
30 EVALUATION METHODS
31 HEALTH CARE OUTCOME*

32 SOCIAL CARE OUTCOME*
33 EDUCATION* OUTCOME*
34 LEARNING OUTCOME*
35 26 or 27 or 28 or 29 or 30 or 31 or 32 or 33 or 34
36 25 and 35

In addition, to ensure we could access potentially illuminating interprofessional education evaluations linked to CQI and TQM initiatives, we added the following terms in the later ASSIA, BEI, CINAHL and Medline update (2001–2003) searches.

37 QUALITY IMPROVEMENT PROGRAM* or QUALITY OF CARE RESEARCH
38 QUALITY OF HEALTH CARE or QUALITY ASSESSMENT*
39 QUALITY ASSURANCE or QUALITY CIRCLE*
40 QUALITY IMPROVEMENT or QUALITY MANAGEMENT
41 MEDICAL AUDIT* or NURSING AUDIT*
42 PEER REVIEW or QUALITY ASSURANCE
43 HEALTH CARE GUIDELINE* or BENCHMARKING GUIDELINE*
44 PRACTICE GUIDELINE* or TOTAL QUALITY MANAGEMENT
45 37 or 38 or 39 or 40 or 41 or 42 or 43 or 44
46 36 and 45

Again, these additional search terms were adapted to reflect differences in the indexing of terms between the databases.

Appendix 2 Abstraction of Studies

As noted in Chapter four, to record information from the studies that were included in the review we developed two abstraction sheets: one for quantitative studies and one for qualitative studies. Both sheets were used to record information on multi-method studies.

Each data abstraction sheet had an associated set of guidance notes for its completion. These notes reminded team members of decisions made relating to the criteria we used to abstract information from each study.

Quantitative Data Abstraction Sheet

CRITERIA	COMMENTS
Ref. No.:	
Citation	
Type (including grey literature)	
Educational Initiative	
Aim/objective of IPE (implicit/explicit)	
Type of IPE	
Content	
Duration	
Method of learning/teaching	
Location	
Participants (number and type)	
Sector	
Level/stage	
Qualification	
IPE Context	
Rationale for IPE (implicit or explicit)	
Outcomes	
Explicit/implicit	
Level 1: Reaction	
Level 2a: Attitudes	
Level 2b: Skills	
Level 3: Behaviour	
Level 4a: Practice	
Level 4b: Patients	
Other/unspecified	
Methods of Evaluation	
Aim of evaluation (implicit/explicit)	
Research design	
Data collection method	
Ethics	
Source of data	
Data analysis method	
Number of groups (in study)	
Unit of study (1, 2, or more individuals)	
Method of allocation	
Allocation concealment	
Blinding	
Power calculation	
(Original) Sample size	
Loss to follow-up	
Significance measures	
Reported biases	
Strength of design	
Strength of number	
Quality of study	
Quality of information	
Overall weighting	

Qualitative Data Abstraction Sheet

CRITERIA	COMMENTS

Ref. No.:
Citation
Type (including, grey literature)
Educational Initiative
Aim/objective of IPE (implicit/explicit)
Type of IPE
Content
Duration
Method of learning/teaching
Location
Participants (number and type)
Sector
Level/stage
Qualification
IPE Context
Rationale for IPE (implicit or explicit)
Outcomes
Explicit/implicit
Level 1: Reaction
Level 2a: Attitudes
Level 2b: Skills
Level 3: Behaviour
Level 4a: Practice
Level 4b: Patients
Other/unspecified
Methods of evaluation
Aim of evaluation
Sampling
Data collection
Data analysis
Research relations
Ethics
Findings
Transferability
Relevance and usefulness
Quality of study
Quality of information
Overall weighting

Appendix 3 Higher Quality Studies

Below is a list of the 107 higher quality studies that qualified for inclusion in our review. The term 'studies' equates almost with 'publications'. Three papers included multiple evaluations that were coded separately: Stanford & Yelloly *et al.* (1994) – two studies; Mitchell *et al.* (1996) – three studies; Singh *et al.* (2002) – two studies.

Adamowski, K., Dickinson, G., Weitzman, B., Roessler, C. & Carter-Snell, C. (1993) Sudden unexpected death in the emergency department: caring for the survivors. *Canadian Medical Association Journal*, **149** (10), 1445–51.

Alderson, P., Farsides, B. & Williams, C. (2002) Examining ethics in practice: health service professionals' evaluations of in-hospital ethics seminars. *Nursing Ethics*, **9** (5), 508–521.

Allison, M. & Toy, P. (1996) A quality improvement team on autologous and directed-donor blood availability. *Joint Commission Journal on Quality Improvement*, **22** (12), 801–810.

Anderson, L., Persky, N., Whall, A., *et al.* (1994) Interdisciplinary team training in geriatrics: reaching out to small and medium-size communities. *Gerontologist*, **34** (6), 833–8.

Atwal, A. (2002) Getting the evidence into practice: the challenges and successes of action research. *British Journal of Occupational Therapy*, **65** (7), 335–41.

Bailey, D. (2002) Training together – part II: an exploration of the evaluation of a shared learning programme on dual diagnosis for specialist drugs workers and approved social workers (ASWs). *Social Work Education*, **21** (6), 685–99.

Bain, N. & McKie, L. (1998) Stages of change training for opportunistic smoking intervention by the primary health care team: part II: qualitative evaluation of long-term impact on professionals' reported behaviour. *Health Education Journal*, **57** (2), 150–59.

Baker, R., Sorrie, R., Reddish, S. & Hearnshaw, H. (1995) The facilitation of multi-professional clinical audit in primary health care teams – from audit to quality assurance. *Journal of Interprofessional Care*, **9** (3), 237–44.

Barber, G., Borders, K., Holland, B. & Roberts, K. (1997) Life span forum: an interdisciplinary training experience. *Gerontology & Geriatrics Education*, **18** (1), 47–59.

Barnes, D., Carpenter, J. & Dickinson, C. (2000) Interprofessional education for community mental health: attitudes to community care and professional stereotypes. *Social Work Education*, **19** (6), 565–83.

Berman, S., Miller, C., Rosen, C. & Bicchieri, S. (2000) Assessment training and team functioning for treating children with disabilities. *Archives of Physical and Medical Rehabilitation*, **81** (5), 628–33.

Birnbaum, M., Robinson, N., Kuska, B., Stone, H., Fryback, D. & Rose, J. (1994) Effect of advanced cardiac life-support training in rural, community hospitals. *Critical Care Medicine*, **22** (5), 741–9.

Bluespruce, J., Dodge, W., Grothaus, L., *et al.* (2001) HIV prevention in primary care: impact of a clinical intervention. *AIDS Patient Care & Studies*, **15** (5), 243–53.

Bonomi, A.E., Wagner, E.H., Glasgow, R.E. & VonKorff, M. (2002) Assessment of chronic illness care (ACIC): a practical tool to measure quality improvement. *Health Services Research*, **37** (3), 791–820.

Brown, S.T. (2000) Outcomes analysis of a pain management project for two rural hospitals. *Journal of Nursing Care Quality*, **14** (4), 28–34.

Bultema, J.K., Mailliard, L., Getzfrid, M.K., Lerner, R.D. & Colone, M. (1996) Geriatric patients with depression. Improving outcomes using a multidisciplinary clinical path model. *Journal of Nursing Administration*, **26** (1), 31–8.

Carpenter, J. (1995) Interprofessional education for medical and nursing students: evaluation of a programme. *Medical Education*, **29** (4), 265–72.

Carpenter, J. & Hewstone, M. (1996) Shared learning for doctors and social workers: evaluation of a programme. *British Journal of Social Work*, **26**, 239–57.

Clemmer, T.P., Spuhler, V.J., Oniki, T.A. & Horn, S.D. (1999) Results of a collaborative quality improvement program on outcomes and costs in a tertiary critical care unit. *Critical Care Medicine*, **27** (9), 1768–74.

Cobia, D.C., Center, H., Buckhalt, J.A. & Meadows, M.E. (1995) An interprofessional model for serving youth at risk for substance abuse: the team case study. *Journal of Drug Education*, **25** (2), 99–109.

Cornish, P.A., Church, E., Callanan, T., Bethune, C., Robbins, C. & Miller, R. (2003) Rural interdisciplinary mental health team building via satellite: a demonstration project. *Telemedicine Journal & E-Health*, **9** (1), 63–71.

Cox, S., Wilcock, P. & Young, J. (1999) Improving the repeat prescribing process in a busy general practice. A study using continuous quality improvement methodology. *Quality in Health Care*, **8** (2), 119–25.

Crawford, M.J., Turnbull, G. & Wessely, S. (1998) Deliberate self-harm assessment by accident and emergency staff – an intervention study. *Journal of Accident & Emergency Medicine*, **15** (1), 18–22.

Dalton, J.A., Carlson, J., Blau, W., Lindley, C., Greer, S.M. & Youngblood, R. (2001) Documentation of pain assessment and treatment: how are we doing? *Pain Management Nursing*, **2** (2), 54–64.

DePoy, E., Wood, C. & Miller, M. (1997) Educating rural allied health professionals: an interdisciplinary effort. *Journal of Allied Health*, **26** (3), 127–32.

Dienst, E.R. & Byl, N. (1981) Evaluation of an educational program in health care teams. *Journal of Community Health*, **6** (4), 282–98.

Doyle, M., Earnshaw, P. & Galloway, A. (2003) Developing, delivering and evaluating interprofessional clinical risk training in mental health services. *Psychiatric Bulletin*, **27** (2), 73–6.

Dufault, M.A. & Sullivan, M. (2000) A collaborative research utilisation approach to evaluate the effects of pain management standards on patient outcomes. *Journal of Professional Nursing*, **16** (4), 240–50.

Dunbar, J.M., Neufeld, R.R., White, H.C. & Libow, L.S. (1996) Retrain, don't restrain: the educational intervention of the National Nursing Home Restraint Removal Project. *Gerontologist*, **36** (4), 539–42.

Edinberg, M.A., Dodson, S.E. & Veach, T.L. (1978) A preliminary study of student learning in interdisciplinary health teams. *Journal of Medical Education*, **53** (8), 667–71.

Elliott, R.A., Woodward, M.C. & Oborne, C.A. (2002) Antithrombotic prescribing in atrial fibrillation: application of a prescribing indicator and multidisciplinary feedback to improve prescribing. *Age and Ageing*, **31** (5), 391–6.

Falconer, J.A., Roth, E.J., Sutin, J.A., Strasser, D.C. & Chang, R.W. (1993) The critical path method in stroke rehabilitation: lessons from an experiment in cost containment and outcome improvement. *Quality Review Bulletin*, **19** (1), 8–16.

Fallsberg, M.B. & Hammar, M. (2000) Strategies and focus at an integrated, interprofessional training ward. *Journal of Interprofessional Care*, **14** (4), 337–50.

Fallsberg, M.B. & Wijma, K. (1999) Student attitudes towards the goals of an inter-professional training ward. *Medical Teacher*, **21** (6), 576–81.

Farrell, M., Ryan, S. & Langrick, B. (2001) Breaking bad news within a paediatric setting: an evaluation report of a collaborative education workshop to support health professionals. *Journal of Advanced Nursing*, **36** (6), 765–75.

Ferrell, B.R., Dean, G.E., Grant, M. & Coluzzi, P. (1995) An institutional commitment to pain management. *Journal of Clinical Oncology*, **13** (9), 2158–65.

Finset, A., Krogstad, J.M., Hansen, H., *et al.* (1995) Team development and memory training in traumatic brain injury rehabilitation: two birds with one stone. *Brain Injury*, **9** (5), 495–507.

Fraser, S., Wilson, T., Burch, K., Osborne, M.A. & Knightley, M. (2002) Using collaborative improvement in a single organisation: improving anticoagulant care. *International Journal of Health Care Quality Assurance*, **15** (4), 152–8.

Freeth, D. & Nicol, M. (1998) Learning clinical skills: an interprofessional approach. *Nurse Education Today*, **18** (6), 455–61.

Gazarian, M., Henry, R.L., Wales, S.R., *et al.* (2001) Evaluating the effectiveness of evidence-based guidelines for the use of spacer devices in children with acute asthma. *Medical Journal of Australia*, **174** (8), 394–7.

Gibbon, B., Watkins, C., Barer, D., *et al.* (2002) Can staff attitudes to teamworking in stroke care be improved? *Journal of Advanced Nursing*, **40** (1), 105–111.

Glanz, K., Brekke, M., Harper, D., Bache-Wiig, M. & Hunninghake, D.B. (1992) Evaluation of implementation of a cholesterol management program in physicians' offices. *Health Education Research*, **7** (2), 151–64.

Gunn, S.R., Hanisch, P. & Wood, D. (1995) CQI action team: responding to the detoxification patient. *Joint Commission Journal on Quality Improvement*, **21** (10), 531–40.

Hayward, K.S., Powell, L.T. & McRoberts, J. (1996) Changes in student perceptions of interdisciplinary practice in the rural setting. *Journal of Allied Health*, **25** (4), 315–27.

Heckman, M., Ajdari, S.Y., Esquivel, M., *et al.* (1998) Quality improvement principles in practice: the reduction of umbilical cord blood errors in the labor and delivery suite, *Journal of Nursing Care Quality*, **12 (3), 47–54.**

Hermida, J. & Robalino, M. (2002) Increasing compliance with maternal and child care quality standards in Ecuador. *International Journal for Quality in Health Care*, **14** (Suppl 1), 25–34.

Hickey, M., Kleefield, S.S., Pearson, S.D., *et al.* (1996) Payer-hospital collaboration to improve patient satisfaction with hospital discharge. *Joint Commission Journal on Quality Improvement*, **22** (5), 336–44.

Horbar, J.D., Rogowski, J., Plsek, P.E., *et al.* (2001) Collaborative quality improvement for neonatal intensive care. NIC/Q Project Investigators of the Vermont Oxford Network. *Pediatrics*, **107** (1), 14–22.

Hunter, M. & Love, C. (1996) Total quality management and the reduction of inpatient violence and costs in a forensic psychiatric hospital. *Psychiatric Services*, **47** (7), 751–4.

Itano, J.K., Williams, J., Deaton, M.D. & Oishi, N. (1991) Impact of a student interdisciplinary oncology team project. *Journal of Cancer Education*, **6** (4), 219–26.

Jackson, S. & Bircher, R. (2002) Transforming a run-down general practice into a leading edge primary care organisation with the help of the EFQM excellence model. *International Journal of Health Care Quality Assurance*, **6** (7), 255–67.

Jones, M. & Salmon, D. (2001) The practitioner as policy analyst: a study of student reflections of an interprofessional course in higher education. *Journal of Interprofessional Care*, **15** (1), 67–77.

Jones, P. & Dunn, E. (1974) Education for the health team: a pilot project. *International Journal of Nursing Studies*, **11** (1), 61–9.

Kennard, J. (2002) Illuminating the relationship between shared learning and the workplace. *Medical Teacher*, **24** (4), 379–84.

Ketola, E., Sipila, R., Makela, M. & Klockars, M. (2000) Quality improvement programme for cardiovascular disease risk factor recording in primary care. *Quality in Health Care*, **9** (3), 175–80.

Kristjanson, L., Dudgeon, D., Nelson, F., Henteleff, P. & Balneaves, L. (1997) Evaluation of an interdisciplinary training program in palliative care: addressing the needs of rural and northern communities. *Journal of Palliative Care*, **13** (3), 5–12.

Lacey, P. (1998) Interdisciplinary training for staff working with people with profound and multiple learning disabilities. *Journal of Interprofessional Care*, **12** (1), 43–52.

Lalonde, B., Uldall, K.K., Huba, G.J., *et al.* (2002) Impact of HIV/AIDS education on health care provider practice: results from nine grantees of the Special Projects of National Significance Program. *Evaluation & the Health Professions*, **25** (3), 302–320.

LaSala, K.B., Hopper, S.K., Rissmeyer, D.J. & Shipe, D.P. (1997) Rural health care and interdisciplinary education. *Nursing and Health Care Perspectives*, **18** (6), 292–8.

Leininger, L. & Earp, J. (1993) The effect of training staff in office based smoking cessation counseling. *Patient Education & Counseling*, **20** (1), 17–25.

Lennox, A.S., Bain, N., Taylor, R.J., McKie, L., Donnan, P.T. & Groves, J. (1998) Stages of change training for opportunistic smoking intervention by the primary health care team: part I: randomised controlled trial of the effect of training on patient smoking outcomes and health professional behaviour as recalled by patients. *Health Education Journal*, **14** (2), 140–49.

Lia-Hoagberg, B., Nelson, P. & Chase, R.A. (1997) An interdisciplinary health team training program for school staff in Minnesota. *Journal of School Health*, **67** (3), 94–7.

Long, S. (1996) Primary health care team workshop: team members' perspectives. *Journal of Advanced Nursing*, **23** (5), 935–41.

Madsen, M.K., Gresch, A.M., Petterson, B.J., & Taugher, M.P. (1988) An interdisciplinary clinic for neurogenically impaired adults: a pilot project for educating students. *Journal of Allied Health*, **17** (2), 135–41.

Mann, K.V., Viscount, P.W., Cogdon, A., Davidson, K., Langille, D.B. & Maccara, M.E. (1996) Multidisciplinary learning in continuing professional education: the Heart Health Nova Scotia experience. *Journal of Continuing Education in the Health Professions*, **16**, 50–60.

Midence, K. (1991) Improving engagement level and staff-resident interaction in a new therapeutic day unit. *British Journal of Occupational Therapy*, **54** (2), 61–4.

Milne, D.L., Keegan, D., Westerman, C. & Dudley, M. (2000) Systematic process and outcome evaluation of brief staff training in psychosocial interventions for severe mental illness. *Journal of Behavior Therapy and Experimental Psychiatry*, **31** (2), 87–101.

Mires, G., Williams, F., Harden, R. & Howie, P. (2001) The benefits of a multi-professional education programme can be sustained. *Medical Teacher*, **23** (3), 300–304.

Mitchell, L., Fife, S., Chothia, A.A., *et al.* (1996) Three teams improving thrombolytic therapy. *Joint Commission Journal on Quality Improvement*, **22** (6), 379–90.

Mohr, C., Phillips, A., Curran, J. & Rymill, A. (2002) Inter-agency training in dual disability. *Australasian Psychiatry*, **10** (4), 356–64.

Morey, J.C., Simon, R., Jay, G.D., *et al.* (2002) Error reduction and performance improvement in the emergency department through formal teamwork training: evaluation results of the MedTeams project. *Health Services Research*, **37** (6), 1553–81.

Nash, A. & Hoy, A. (1993) Terminal care in the community – an evaluation of residential workshops for general practitioner/district nurse teams. *Palliative Medicine*, **7** (1), 5–17.

O'Boyle, M., Paniagua, F.A., Wassef, A. & Holzer, C. (1995) Training health professionals in the recognition and treatment of depression. *Psychiatric Services*, **46** (6), 616–8.

Overdyk, F.J., Harvey, S.C., Fishman, R.L. & Shippey, F. (1998) Successful strategies for improving operating room efficiency at academic institutions. *Anesthesia & Analgesia*, **86** (4), 896–906.

Parsell, G., Spalding, R. & Bligh, J. (1998) Shared goals, shared learning: evaluation of a multi-professional course for undergraduate students. *Medical Education*, **32** (3), 304–311.

Perkins, J. & Tryssenaar, J. (1994) Making interdisciplinary education effective for rehabilitation students. *Journal of Allied Health*, **23** (3), 133–41.

Pilon, C.S., Leathley, M., London, R., *et al.* (1997) Practice guideline for arterial blood gas measurement in the intensive care unit decreases numbers and increases appropriateness of tests. *Critical Care Medicine*, **25** (8), 1308–313.

Price, J., Ekleberry, A., Grover, A., *et al.* (1999) Evaluation of clinical practice guidelines on outcome of infection in patients in the surgical intensive care unit. *Critical Care Medicine*, **27** (10), 2118–24.

Reeves, S. (2000) Community-based interprofessional education for medical, nursing and dental students. *Health and Social Care in the Community*, **8** (4), 269–76.

Reeves, S. & Freeth, D. (2002) The London training ward: an innovative interprofessional learning initiative. *Journal of Interprofessional Care*, **16** (1), 41–52.

Roberts, C., Howe, A., Winterburn, S. & Fox, N. (2000) Not so easy as it sounds: a qualitative study of a shared learning project between medical and nursing undergraduate students. *Medical Teacher*, **22** (4), 386–7.

Rost, K., Nutting, P.A., Smith, J. & Werner, J.J. (2000) Designing and implementing a primary care intervention trial to improve the quality and outcome of care for major depression. *General Hospital Psychiatry*, **22** (2), 66–77.

Rubenstein, L.V., Parker, L.E., Meredith, L.S., *et al.* (2002) Understanding team-based quality improvement for depression in primary care. *Health Services Research*, **37** (4), 1009–1029.

Rutter, D.R. & Hagart, J. (1990) Alcohol training in south-east England: a survey and evaluation. *Alcohol & Alcoholism*, **25** (6), 699–709.

Schreiber, M.A., Holcomb, J.B., Conaway, C.W., Campbell, K.D., Wall, M. & Mattox, K.L. (2002) Military trauma training performed in a civilian trauma center. *Journal of Surgical Research*, **104** (1), 8–14.

Shafer, M.A., Tebb, K.P., Pantell, R.H., *et al.* (2002) Effect of a clinical practice improvement intervention on chlamydial screening among adolescent girls. *Journal of American Medical Association*, **288** (22), 2846–52.

Singh, N.N., Wechsler, H.A., Curtis, W.J., Sabaawi, M., Myers, R.E. & Singh, S.D. (2002) Effects of role-play and mindfulness training on enhancing the family friendliness of the admissions treatment team process. *Journal of Emotional and Behavioral Disorders*, **10** (2), 90–98.

Skovholt, C., Lia-Hoagberg, B., Mullett, S., *et al.* (1994) The Minnesota Prenatal Care Coordination Project: successes and obstacles. *Public Health Reports*, **109** (6), 774–81.

Solberg, L.I., Kottke, T.E., & Brekke, M.L. (1998) Will primary care clinics organise themselves to improve the delivery of preventive services? A randomised controlled trial. *Preventive Medicine*, **27** (4), 623–31.

Stanford, R. & Yelloly, M. (1994) *Shared Learning in Child Protection*. Central Council for Education and Training in Social Work and English National Board for Nursing, Midwifery and Health Visiting, London.

Stark, R., Yeo, G., Fordyce, M., *et al.* (1984) An interdisciplinary teaching program in geriatrics for physician's assistants. *Journal of Allied Health*, **13** (4), 280–287.

Stein, J. & Brown, H. (1995) 'All in this together': an evaluation of joint training on the abuse of adults with learning disabilities. *Health & Social Care in the Community*, **3** (4), 205–214.

Strasser, R. (1995) Innovative interactive multidisciplinary workshops. *Australian Journal of Rural Health*, **3**, 56–61.

Sullivan, R. & Clancy, T. (1990) An experimental evaluation of interdisciplinary training in intervention with sexually abused adolescents. *Health & Social Work*, **15** (3), 207–214.

Taylor, J., Blue, I. & Misan, G. (2001) Approach to sustainable primary health care service delivery for rural and remote South Australia. *Australian Journal of Rural Health*, **9** (6), 304–310.

Tepper, M. (1997) Providing comprehensive sexual health care in spinal cord injury: implementation and evaluation of a new curriculum for health professionals. *Sexuality & Disability*, **15** (3), 131–65.

Thompson, C., Kinmonth, A., Stevens, L., *et al.* (2000) Effects of a clinical-practice guideline and practice-based education on detection and outcome of depression in primary care: Hampshire Depression Project randomised controlled trial. *Lancet*, **355** (9199), 185–91.

Townes, C., Petit, B. & Young, B. (1995) Implementing total quality management in an academic surgery setting: lessons learned. *Swiss Surgery*, **1** (1), 15–23.

Treadwell, M.J., Franck, L.S. & Vichinsky, E. (2002) Using quality improvement strategies to enhance pediatric pain assessment. *International Journal for Quality in Health Care*, **14** (1), 39–47.

van der Horst, M., Turpie, I., Nelson, W., *et al.* (1995) St Joseph's Community Health Centre model of community-based interdisciplinary health care team. *Health and Social Care in the Community*, **3**, 33–42.

van Staa, A., Visser, A. & van der, Z. (2000) Caring for caregivers: experiences and evaluation of interventions for a palliative care team. *Patient Education & Counseling*, **41** (1), 93–105.

Walsh, P., Garbs, C., Goodwin, M. & Wolff, E. (1995) An impact evaluation of a VA geriatric team development program. *Gerontology and Geriatrics Education*, **15**, 19–35.

Way, B., Stone, B., Schwager, M., Wagoner, D. & Bassman, R. (2002) Effectiveness of the New York State Office of Mental Health Core Curriculum: direct care staff training. *Psychiatric Rehabilitation Journal*, **25** (4), 398–402.

References

Acheson, D. (1998) *Independent Inquiry into Inequalities in Health Report*, The Stationery Office, London.

Adamowski, K., Dickinson, G., Weitzman, B., Roessler, C. & Carter-Snell, C. (1993) Sudden unexpected death in the emergency department: caring for the survivors. *Canadian Medical Association Journal*, **149** (10), 1445–51.

Alderson, P., Farsides, B. & Williams, C. (2002) Examining ethics in practice: health service professionals' evaluations of in-hospital ethics seminars. *Nursing Ethics*, **9** (5), 508–521.

Allen, D. (1997) The nursing–medical boundary: a negotiated order? *Sociology of Health and Illness*, **19**, 498–520.

Allport, G.W. (1979) *The Nature of Prejudice*, 25th edn, Perseus Books Publishing L.L.C., Cambridge, Mass.

Almas, S.H. (2004) Personal communication.

Anderson, E. & Lennox, A. (2005) Unpublished. Private communication.

Anderson, L.A., Persky, N.W., Whall, A.L., *et al.* (1994) Interdisciplinary team training in geriatrics: reaching out to small and medium-size communities. *Gerontologist*, **34** (6), 833–8.

Anderson, N.R. (1992) Work group innovation: state-of-the-art review. In: *Organisational Change and Innovation* (eds D.M. Hosking & N.R. Anderson), pp. 149–60. Routledge, London.

Areskog, N.-H. (1988) The need for multi-professional healthy education in undergraduate studies. *Medical Education*, **22**, 251–2.

Areskog, N.-H. (1992) The new medical education at the Faculty of Health Sciences, Linköping University – a challenge for both students and teachers. *Scandinavian Journal of Medical Education*, **2**, 1–4.

Areskog, N.-H. (1994) Multi-professional education at the undergraduate level – the Linköping model. *Journal of Interprofessional Care*, **8** (3), 279–82.

Areskog, N.-H. (1995a) The Linköping case: a transition from traditional to innovative medical school. *Medical Teacher*, **17** (4), 371–6.

Areskog, N.-H. (1995b) Multi-professional education at the undergraduate level. In: *Interprofessional Relations in Health Care* (eds K. Soothill, L. Mackay & C. Webb), Chapter nine, pp. 125–39. Edward Arnold, London.

Argyris, C. & Schön, D.A. (1974) *Theory in Practice: Increasing Professional Effectiveness*. Jossey-Bass, San Francisco.

Argyris, C. & Schön, D.A. (1984), Organisational learning. In: *Organisation Theory*, (ed. D.S. Pugh), 2nd edn. pp. 352–71 Penguin, Harmondsworth.

Ashburner, L. & Fitzgerald, L. (1996) Beleaguered professionals: clinicians and institutional change in the NHS. In: *The Management of Expertise*. (ed. H. Scarborough), Chapter eight, pp. 190–216. MacMillan, London.

Atkins, J. (1998) Tribalism, loss and grief: issues for multi-professional education. *Journal of Interprofessional Care*, **12** (3), 303–307.

Atwal, A. (2002) Getting the evidence into practice: the challenges and successes of action research. *British Journal of Occupational Therapy*, **65** (7), 335–41.

Aveyard, H., Edwards, S. & West, S. (2005) The identification of core topics for health care ethics that can be taught through interprofessional education. *Journal of Interprofessional Care*, **19** (1), 63–79.

Axelrod, R. (1984) *The Evolution of Cooperation*. Basic Books, New York.

Baggs, J.G. & Ryan, S.A. (1990) ICU nurse-physician collaboration and satisfaction. *Nursing Economics*, **8** (6), 386–93.

Baggs, J.G., Schmitt, M., Mushlin, A.I., Eldredge, D.H., Oakes, D. & Hutson, A.D. (1997) Nurse-physician collaboration and satisfaction with the decision-making process in three critical care units. *American Journal of Critical Care*, **6** (5), 393–9.

Bailey, D. (2002) Training together – part II: an exploration of the evaluation of a shared learning programme on dual diagnosis for specialist drugs workers and approved social workers (ASWs). *Social Work Education*, **21** (6), 685–99.

Bain, N. & McKie, L. (1998) Stages of change training for opportunistic smoking intervention by the primary health care team: part II: qualitative evaluation of long-term impact on professionals' reported behaviour. *Health Education Journal*, **57** (2), 150–9.

Baker, R., Sorrie, R., Reddish, S. & Hearnshaw, H. (1995) The facilitation of multi-professional clinical audit in primary health care teams – from audit to quality assurance. *Journal of Interprofessional Care*, **9** (3), 237–44.

Baldwin Jr, D.W.C. (1996) Some historical notes on interdisciplinary and interprofessional education and practice in health care in the USA. *Journal of Interprofessional Care*, **10** (2), 173–87.

Barber, G., Borders, K., Holland, B. & Roberts, K. (1997) Life span forum: an interdisciplinary training experience. *Gerontology & Geriatrics Education*, **18** (1), 47–59.

Barnes, D., Carpenter, J. & Dickinson, C. (2000a) Interprofessional education for community mental health: attitudes to community care and professional stereotypes. *Social Work Education*, **19** (6), 565–83.

Barnes, D., Carpenter, J. & Bailey, D. (2000b) Partnerships with service users in interprofessional education for community mental health: a case study. *Journal of Interprofessional Care*, **14**, 189–200.

Barnett, R. (1999) *The Idea of Higher Education*. Open University Press, Buckingham.

Barr, H. (1994) *Perspectives on Shared Learning*. Centre for Advancement of Interprofessional Education, London.

Barr, H. (1998) Competent to collaborate: towards a competency-based model for interprofessional education. *Journal of Interprofessional Care*, **12** (2), 181–8.

Barr, H. (2002) *Interprofessional Education: Today, Yesterday and Tomorrow*. Learning and Support Network: Centre for Health Sciences and Practice, London.

Barr, H. (2003a) Interprofessional issues and work-based learning. In: *Worked-based Learning in Primary Care* (eds J. Burton & N. Jackson). pp. 73–86. Radcliffe Medical Press, Oxford.

Barr, H. (2003b) Ensuring quality in interprofessional education. *CAIPE Bulletin*, 22, 2–3.

Barr, H., Freeth, D., Hammick, M., Koppel, I. & Reeves, S. (2000) *Evaluations of Interprofessional Education: a United Kingdom Review for Health and Social Care*. BERA/CAIPE, London.

Barr, H., Gower, S., McGruer, C., Whiteman J. & O'Connell, J. (1998) *Interprofessional Learning in Primary Care: Developments in North West London*. Department of Postgraduate General Practice, Imperial School of Medicine, London.

Barr, H. & Shaw, I. (1995) *Shared Learning: Selected Examples from the Literature*. CAIPE, London.

Barr, H. & Waterton, S. (1996) *Interprofessional Education in Health and Social Care in the United Kingdom: a Report of a CAIPE Survey*. Centre for Advancement of Interprofessional Education, London.

Barrett, G., Greenwood, R. & Ross, K. (2003) Integrating interprofessional education into ten health and social care programmes. *Journal of Interprofessional Care*, **17** (3), 293–301.

Bateman, H., Bailey, P. & McLellan, H. (2003) Of rocks and safe channels: learning to navigate as an interprofessional team. *Journal of Interprofessional Care*, **17** (2), 141–50.

Beattie, A. (1995) War and peace among health tribes. In: *Interprofessional Relations in Health Care* (eds K. Soothill, L. Mackay, & C. Webb) pp. 11–26. Edward Arnold, London.

Becker, H., Geer, B., Hughes, E. & Strauss, A. (1961) *Boys in White: Student Culture in Medical School*. University of Chicago, Chicago.

Beresford, P. & Trevillion, S. (1995) *Developing Skills for Community Care – a Collaborative Approach*. Arena, Aldershot.

Berman, S., Miller, A.C., Rosen, C. & Bicchieri, S. (2000) Assessment training and team functioning for treating children with disabilities. *Archives of Physical Medicine & Rehabilitation*, **81** (5), pp. 628–33.

Bernstein, B. (1971) *Class, Codes and Control*. Routledge, London.

Bernstein, B. (1996) *Pedagogy, Symbolic Control and Identity: Theory, Research, Critique*. Taylor & Francis, London.

Berwick, D., Davidoff, F., Hiatt, H. & Smith, R. (2001) Refining and implementing the Tavistock principles for everybody in health care. *British Medical Journal*, **323** (7313), 616–20.

Berwick, D., Hiatt, H., Janeway, P. & Smith, R. (1997) An ethical code for everybody in health care. *British Medical Journal*, **315** (7123), 1633–4.

Bion, W.R. (1961) *Experiences in Groups and other Papers*. Tavistock Publications, London.

Birchall, E. & Hallett, C. (1995) *Working Together in Child Protection*. HMSO, London.

Birnbaum, M.L., Robinson, N.E., Kuska, B.M., Stone, H.L., Fryback, D.G. & Rose, J.H. (1994) Effect of advanced cardiac life-support training in rural, community hospitals. *Critical Care Medicine*, **22** (5), 741–9.

Black, D., Morris, J.N., Smith, C. & Whitehead, M. (1988) *Inequalities in Health: the Black Report and the Health Divide*. Penguin, London.

Bligh, J. (1995) Problem-based, small-group learning. *British Medical Journal*, **311**, 342–3.

Boelen, C. (2000) Education to create unity in health: an educational programme to support the TUFH Project. *Towards Unity for Health*, 2.

Bond, M. (1999) Placing poverty on the agenda of a primary health care team: an evaluation of an action research project. *Health & Social Care in the Community*, **7** (1), 9–16.

Bond, M. & Hart, E. (1998) Exploring the roles and contributions of outside evaluators in an Action Research project: a case study. *Social Sciences in Health*, **4**, 176–86.

Bonomi, A.E., Wagner, E.H., Glasgow, R.E. & VonKorff, M. (2002) Assessment of chronic illness care (ACIC): a practical tool to measure quality improvement. *Health Services Research*, **37** (3), 791–820.

Borrill, C., Carletta, J., Carter, A., *et al.* (2001) *The Effectiveness of Health Care Teams in the National Health Service*. Aston University, Birmingham.

Borrill, C.S, West, M.A., Shapiro, D. & Rees, A. (2000) Teamworking and effectiveness in health care. *British Journal of Health Care Management*. **6**, 364–71.

Bourdieu, P. & Passeron, J.C. (1990) *Reproduction in Education, Society, and Culture*. Sage, London.

Brookfield, S.D. (1986) *Understanding and Facilitating Adult Learning: a Comprehensive Analysis of Principles and Effective Practice*. Open University Press, Milton Keynes.

Brown, B., Crawford, P. & Darongkamas, J. (2000) Blurred roles and permeable boundaries: the experience of multidisciplinary working in community mental health. *Health and Social Care in the Community*, **8**, 425–35.

Brown, H. & Sommerland, E. (1992), Staff development in higher education – towards the learning organisation? *Higher Education Quarterly*, **46**(2), 174–90.

Brown, R., Condor, S., Mathews, A., Wade, G. & Williams, J. (1986) Explaining intergroup differentiation in an industrial organisation. *Journal of Occupational Psychology*, **59**, 273–86.

Brown, R. & Williams, J. (1984) Group identification: the same thing to all people? *Human Relations*, **37**, 547–64.

Brown, S. T. (2000) Outcomes analysis of a pain management project for two rural hospitals. *Journal of Nursing Care Quality*, **14**(4), 28–34.

Cable, S. (2000) Clinical experience. Preparation of Medical and Nursing Students for Collaborative Practice. Unpublished Ph.D. thesis, University of Dundee.

CAIPE (1997) *Interprofessional Education: a Definition*. Centre for Advancement of Interprofessional Education, London.

CAIPE (2001) *Principles of Interprofessional Education*. Centre for Advancement of Interprofessional Education, London.

Carpenter, J. (1995) Interprofessional education for medical and nursing students: evaluation of a programme. *Medical Education*, **29**(4), 265–72.

Carpenter, J. & Hewstone, M. (1996) Shared learning for doctors and social workers: evaluation of a programme. *British Journal of Social Work*, **26**(2), 239–57.

Carrier, J. & Kendall, I. (1995) Professionalism and interprofessionalism in health and community care: some theoretical issues. In: *Interprofesional Issues in Community & Primary Health Care* (eds P. Owens, J. Carrier & J. Horder). MacMillan Press Ltd, London.

Casto, R.M., Harsh, S.A., & Cunningham, & L.L. (1998) Shifting the paradigm for interprofessional education at the Ohio State University and beyond. In: *Universities and Communities: Remaking Professional Interprofessional Education for the next Century*, (eds J. McCroskey & S.D. Einbinder) Chapter four. Praeger, Westport, Conn.

Challis, L., Fuller, S., Henwood, M., *et al.* (1988) *Joint Approaches to Social Policy*. Cambridge University Press, Cambridge.

Charters, A.N. & Blakely, R. J. (1973) The management of continuing learning: a model of continuing education as a problem-solving strategy for health manpower. In: *In Project Continuing Education for Health Manpower, Fostering the Growing Need to Learn: Monographs and Annotated Bibliography on Continuing Education and Health Manpower* (ed. P.H.S. Health Resources Administration). US Department of Health, Education and Welfare, Rockville, Md.

Chief Secretary to the Treasury (2003) *Every Child Matters*. Cmnd. 5860. HMSO, London.

Cleghorn, G.D. & Headrick, L.A. (1996) The PDSA cycle at the core of learning in health professions education: plan-do-study-act. *Joint Commission Journal on Quality Improvement*, **22**(3), 206–212.

Clemmer, T., Spuhler, V., Oniki, T. & Horn, S. (1999) Results of a collaborative quality improvement program on outcomes and costs in a tertiary critical care unit. *Critical Care Medicine*, **27** (9), 1768–74.

Cleveland Report (1988) *Report of the Inquiry into Child Abuse in Cleveland*. Cmnd. 412. HMSO, London.

Cobia, D.C., Center, H., Buckhalt, J.A. & Meadows, M.E. (1995) An interprofessional model for serving youth at risk for substance abuse: the team case study. *Journal of Drug Education*, **25** (2), 99–109.

Cooke, A., Davis, J. & Vanclay, L. (2001) Shared learning in practice placements for health and social work students: a feasibility study. *Journal of Interprofessional Care*, **36** (2), 185–190.

Cooper, H., Carlisle, C., Gibbs, T. & Watkins, C. (2001) Developing an evidence base for interdisciplinary learning: a systematic review. *Journal of Advanced Nursing*, **36** (2), 228–37.

Cornish, P.A., Church, E., Callanan, T., Bethune, C., Robbins, C. & Miller, R. (2003) Rural interdisciplinary mental health teambuilding via satellite: a demonstration project. *Telemedicine Journal & E-Health*, **9**(1), 63–71.

Cosier, J. & Glennie, S. (1994) Supervising the child protection process. In: *Participation in Human Inquiry* (ed. P. Reason), pp. 99–120. Sage, London.

Counsell, S.R., Kennedy, R.D., Szwabo, P., Wadsworth, N.S. & Wohlgemuth, C. (1999) Curriculum recommendations for resident training in geriatric interdisciplinary team care. *Journal of the American Geriatrics Society*, **47**, 1145–8.

Crawford, M.J., Turnbull, G. & Wessely, S. (1998) Deliberate self-harm assessment by accident and emergency staff – an intervention study. *Journal of Accident & Emergency Medicine*, **15** (1), 18–22.

Dalton, J.A., Carlson, J., Blau, W., Lindley, C., Greer, S.M., & Youngblood, R. (2001) Documentation of pain assessment and treatment: how are we doing? *Pain Management Nursing*, **2** (2), 54–64.

Davidson, L. & Lucas, J. (1995) Multi-professional education in the undergraduate health professions curriculum: observations from Adelaide, Linköping and Salford. *Journal of Interprofessional Care*, **9** (2), 163–76.

D'Avray, L., Cooper, S. & Hutchinson, L. (2004) *Interprofessional Education for Health and Social Care: Developing IPE in Practice*. King's College London, London.

Dechant, K., Marsick, V.J. & Kasl, E. (1993) Towards a model of team learning. *Studies in Continuing Education*, **15** (1), 1–14.

Department of Health and Social Security (1974) *Report of the Committee of Enquiry into the Care and Supervision Provided in Relation to Maria Colwell*. HMSO, London.

Department of Health (1998) *A Review of Continuing Professional Development in General Practice*. Department of Health, London.

Department of Health (1999) *Reducing Health Inequalities: an Action Report. Our Healthier Nation*. Department of Health, London.

Department of Health (2000) *A Health Service of all the Talents: Developing the NHS Workforce. Consultation Document on the Review of Workforce Planning*. Department of Health, London.

Department of Health (2001a) *Learning from Bristol: the Report of the Public Inquiry into Children's Heart Surgery at the Bristol Royal Infirmary 1984–1995*. HMSO, London.

Department of Health (2001b) *The National Service Framework for Older People*. Department of Health, London.

DePoy, E., Wood, C. & Miller, M. (1997) Educating rural allied health professionals: an interdisciplinary effort. *Journal of Allied Health*, **26** (3), 127–32.

Dickinson, C. (2003) *Interprofessional Education for Community Mental Health: Changing Attitudes and Developing Skills*. Ph.D. thesis. University of Durham.

Dombeck, M.T. (1989) Learning through symbol, myth and ritual. *Journal of Religion and Health* **28** (2), 152–62.

Dombeck, M.T. (1997) Professional personhood: training, territoriality and tolerance. *Journal of Interprofessional Care*, **11**, 9–21.

Dombeck, M.T. & Olsan, T.H. (2002) Ethics and managed care. *Journal of Interprofessional Care*, **16** (3), 221–34.

Dood, R. & Hinshelwood, E. (2002) *WHO monitoring project on Poverty Reduction Strategies (PRSPs)*. World Health Organization, Geneva.

d'Ivernois J.-F. & Vodoratski, V. (1988) *Multi-professional Education for Health Personnel in the European Region*. World Health Organization, Copenhagen.

Doyle, M., Earnshaw, P. & Galloway, A. (2003) Developing, delivering and evaluating interprofessional clinical risk training in mental health services. *Psychiatric Bulletin*, **27** (2), 73–6.

Drinka, T.J.K., Miller, T.F. & Goodman, B.M. (1996) Characterising motivational styles of professionals who work on interdisciplinary healthcare teams. *Journal of Interprofessional Care*, **10** (1), 51–61.

Eagly, A.H. & Chaiken, S. (1993) *The Psychology of Attitudes*. Harcourt Brace Jovanovich College Publishers, Fort Worth.

Elkjaer, B. (1999) In search of social learning theory. In: *Organisational Learning and the Learning Organisation* (eds M. Easterby-Smith, J. Burgoyne & L. Araujo), pp. 75–91. Sage, London.

Ellemers, N., Spears, R. & Doose, J. (1999) *Social Identity*. Blackwell Science, Oxford.

Engestrom, Y. (1999a) *Expansive Learning at Work: Toward an Activity-theoretical Reconceptualisation*, CLWR 7th Annual International Conference on Post-compulsory Education and Training.

Engestrom, Y. (1999b) *Expansive Visibilisation of Work: an Activity-theoretical Perspective*. Kluwer Academic Publishers, the Netherlands. *Computer Supported Cooperative Work*, **8** 63–93.

Engestrom, Y., Engestrom, R. & Vahaaho, T. (1999) When the center does not hold: the importance of knotworking. In: *Activity Theory and Social Practice* (eds S. Chaklin, M. Hedegaard & U.J. Jensen) Chapter eighteen, pp. 1–25. Aarhus University Press, Aarhus.

Engel, G.L. (1977) The need for a new medical model: a challenge for biomedicine. *Science*, **196** (4286), 129–36.

Eraut, M. (1994) *Developing Professional Knowledge and Competence*. The Falmer Press, London.

European Health Committee (1993) *Multi-professional Education for Health Personnel: the 1990/1992 Coordinated Medical Research Programme*. CDSP (93) 10 European Health Committee, Council of Europe, Brussels.

Evans, J., Lambert, T. & Goldacre, M. (2002) GP recruitment and retention: a qualitative analysis of doctors' comments about training for and working in general practice. *Occasional Paper of Royal College of General Practitioners*, **83**, iii–33.

Evetts, J. (1999) Professionalisation and professionalism: issues for interprofessional care. *Journal of Interprofessional Care*, **13** (2), 119–28.

Fairclough, N. (1992) *Discourse and Social Change*. Polity Press, Cambridge.

Falconer, J.A., Roth, E.J., Sutin, J.A., Strasser, D.C. & Chang, R.W. (1993) The critical path method in stroke rehabilitation: lessons from an experiment in cost containment and outcome improvement. *Quality Review Bulletin*, **19** (1), 8–16.

Fallsberg, M.B. & Hammar, M. (2000) Strategies and focus at an integrated, interprofessional training ward. *Journal of Interprofessional Care*, **14** (4) 337–50.

Fallsberg, M.B. & Wijma, K. (1999) Student attitudes towards the goals of an interprofessional training ward. *Medical Teacher*, **21** (6), 576–81.

Farrell, M., Ryan, S. & Langrick, B. (2001) Breaking bad news within a paediatric setting: an evaluation report of a collaborative education workshop to support health professionals. *Journal of Advanced Nursing*, **36** (6) 765–75.

Feazel, J.T. (1990) Interdisciplinary team training in geriatrics programs: a historical perspective on team development and implementation, reflecting attitudinal change towards team training and team delivery of health. In: *Interdisciplinary Health Care Teams: Proceedings of the Twelfth Annual Conference*. (ed. J.N. Snyder) pp. 18–23. Held in Indianapolis. Division of Allied Health Sciences, Indiana University School of Medicine, Indiana University Medical Center, Indiana Polis, Indiana.

Finset, A., Krogstad, J.M., Hansen, H., *et al.* (1995) Team development and memory training in traumatic brain injury rehabilitation: two birds with one stone. *Brain Injury*, **9** (5), 495–507.

Foldevi, M., Sommansson, G. & Trell, E. (1994) Problem-based medical education in general practice: experience from Linköping, Sweden. *Journal of Royal College of General Practitioners*, **44**, 473–6.

Foucault, M. (1972) *The Archeology of Knowledge*. Tavistock, London.

Foy, R., Tidy, N. & Hollis, S. (2002) Interprofessional learning in primary care: lessons from an action-learning programme. *British Journal of Clinical Governance*, **7** (1), 40–44.

Freeth, D., Hammick, M., Koppel, I., Reeves, S. & Barr, H. (2002) *A Critical Review of Evaluations of Interprofessional Education*. Learning and Support Network; Centre for Health Sciences and Practice, London.

Freeth, D., Hammick, M., Reeves, S. Koppel, I. & Barr, H. (2005) *Effective Interprofessional Education: Development, Delivery and Evaluation*. Blackwell Publishing, Oxford.

Freeth, D. & Nicol, M. (1998) Learning clinical skills: an interprofessional approach. *Nurse Education Today*, **18** (6), 455–61.

Freidson, E. (1970) *Professional Dominance: the Social Structure of Medical Care* Aldine Publishing Company, New York.

Freidson, E. (1994) *Professionalism Reborn: Theory, Prophecy and Policy*. Polity, London.

Garratt, B. (1990) *Creating a Learning Organisation: a Guide to Leadership, Learning and Development*. Director Books, London.

Gazarian, M., Henry, R.L., Wales, S.R., *et al.* (2001) Evaluating the effectiveness of evidence-based guidelines for the use of spacer devices in children with acute asthma. *Medical Journal of Australia*, **174** (8), 394–7.

Gelmon, S.B., Holland, B.A., Shinnamon, A.F. & Morris, B.A. (1998) Community-based education and service: the HPSISN experience. *Journal of Interprofessional Care*, **12** (3), 257–72.

Gentry, M., Iceton, J. & Milne, D. (2001) Managing challenging behaviour in the community: methods and results of interactive staff training. *Health & Social Care in the Community*, **9** (3), 143–50.

Gibbon, B., Watkins, C., Barer, D., *et al.* (2002) Can staff attitudes to teamworking in stroke care be improved? *Journal of Advanced Nursing*, **40** (1), 105–111.

Gilbert, J., Camp, R., Cole, C., Bruce, C., Fielding, D. & Stanton, S. (2000) Preparing students for interprofessional teamwork in health care. *Journal of Interprofessional Care*, **14**, 223–35.

Goble, R. (2003) Multiprofessional education: global perspectives. In: *Interprofessional Education: from Policy to Practice in Health and Social Care* (ed. A. Leathard) pp. 324–35. Brunner-Routledge, Hove.

Goffman, E. (1963) *The Presentation of Self in Everyday Life*. Penguin, London.

Gorman, H. & Postle, K. (2003) *Transforming Community Care: a Distorted Vision?* Venture Press, Birmingham.

Greiner, A.C. & Knebel, E. (eds) (2003) *Health Professions Education; a Bridge to Quality*. The National Academy Press, Washington, DC.

Guest, C., Smith, L., Bradshaw, M. & Hardcastle, W. (2002) Facilitating interprofessional learning for medical and nursing students in clinical practice. *Learning in Health and Social Care;*, **1**, 132–8.

Gunn, S., Hanisch, P. & Wood, D. (1995) CQI action team: responding to the detoxification patient. *Joint Commission Journal on Quality Improvement*, **21** (10), 531–40.

Hammersley, M. (1997) Educational research and teaching: a response to David Hargreaves' TTA lecture. *British Educational Research Journal*, **23** (2), 141–61.

Hammick, M. (1998) Interprofessional education: concept, theory and application. *Journal of Interprofessional Care*, **12**, 323–32.

Hargreaves, D. (1996) *Teaching as a Research-based Profession: Possibilities and Prospects. Teacher Training Agency Annual Lecture 1996*. Teacher Training Agency, London.

Hart, E. & Fletcher, J. (1999) Learning how to change: a selective analysis of literature and experience of how teams learn and organisations change. *Journal of Interprofessional Care*, **13** (1), 53–63.

Hayward, K.S., Powell, L.T. & McRoberts, J. (1996) Changes in student perceptions of interdisciplinary practice in the rural setting. *Journal of Allied Health*, **25** (4), 315–27.

Headrick, L.A., Knapp, M., Neuhauser, D., *et al.* (1996) Working from upstream to improve health care: the IHI interdisciplinary professional education collaborative. *Joint Commission Journal on Quality Improvement*, **22** (3), 149–64.

Health Canada (2003) First Minister's Accord on Health Care Renewal (http://www.hc-sc.gc.ca/english/hca 2003/accord.html).

Heckman, M., Ajdari, S.Y., Esquivel, M., *et al.* (1998) Quality improvement principles in practice: the reduction of umbilical cord blood errors in the labor and delivery suite. *Journal of Nursing Care Quality*, **12** (3), 47–54.

Hermida, J. & Robalino, M.E. (2002) Increasing compliance with maternal and child care quality standards in Ecuador. *International Journal for Quality in Health Care*, **14** (Suppl 1), 25–34.

Hewison, A. & Sim, J. (1998) Managing interprofessional working: using codes of ethics as an ethical foundation. *Journal of Interprofessional Care*, **12** (3), 309–321.

Hewstone, M. & Brown, R. (1986) Contact is not enough: an intergroup perspective on the 'contact hypothesis'. In: *Contact and Conflict in Intergroup Encounters* (eds M. Hewstone & R. Brown), pp. 1–44. Blackwell Publishers, Oxford.

Holman, C. & Jackson, S. (2001) A team education project: an evaluation of a collaborative education and practice development in a continuing care unit for older people. *Nurse Education Today*, **2**, 97–103.

Horbar, J.D., Rogowski, J., Plsek, P.E., *et al.* (2001) Collaborative quality improvement for neonatal intensive care. NIC/Q Project Investigators of the Vermont Oxford Network. *Pediatrics*, **107** (1), 14–22.

Hornby, S. & Atkins, J. (2000) *Collaborative Care: Interprofessional, Inter-agency and Interpersonal.* 2nd edn. Blackwell Science, Oxford.

Howkins, E. & Allison, A. (1997) Shared learning for primary health care teams: a success story. *Nurse Education Today*, **17**, 225–31.

Hughes, D. (1988) When nurse knows best: some aspects of nurse/doctor interaction in a casualty department. *Sociology of Health and Illness*, **16**, 184–202.

Hughes, L.A. & Lucas, J. (1997) An evaluation of problem-based learning in the multi-professional education curriculum for the health professions. *Journal of Interprofessional Care*, **11** (1), 77–88.

Hugman, R. (1991) *Power in the Caring Professions.* Macmillan, London.

Hunt, G. & van der Arend, A. (2002) Treatment, custody, support: an exploratory qualitative dialogue to map the ethics of inter-agency cooperation in hospital emergency departments in the UK and the Netherlands. *Journal of Interprofessional Care*, **16** (3), 211–20.

Hunter, D. (1994) From tribalism to corporatism: the managerial challenge to medical dominance. In: *Challenging Medicine* (eds J. Gabe, D. Kelleher & G. Williams). Routledge, London.

Hyer, K. (1998) The John A. Hartford Foundation Geriatric Interdisciplinary Team Training Program. In: *Geriatric Interdisciplinary Team Training* (eds E.L. Siegler, K. Hyer, T. Fulmer & M. Mezey) pp. 3–12. Springer Publishing Company, New York.

Il'enkov, E.V. (1977) *Dialectic Logic: Essays in its History and Theory.* Progress, Moscow.

Ingersoll, G.L. & Schmitt, M. (2004) Interdisciplinary collaboration, team functioning and patient safety. In: *Keeping Patients Safe, Transforming the Work Environment* (ed. Ann Page), pp. 341–82. Institute of Medicine, National Academy Press, Washington D.C.

Institute of Medicine Committee on Quality of Health Care in America (2001) *Crossing the Quality Chasm : a New Health System for the Twenty-first Century.* National Academy Press, Washington D.C.

Irvine, R. Kerridge, I. McPhee, J. & Freeman, S. (2002) Interprofessionalism and ethics: consensus or clash of culture? *Journal of Interprofessional Care*, **16** (3), 199–210.

Itano, J.K., Williams, J., Deaton, M.D. & Oishi, N. (1991) Impact of a student interdisciplinary oncology team project. *Journal of Cancer Education*, **6** (4), 219–26.

Jackson, N. & Burton, J. (2003) Theory and practice of work-based learning and why work-based learning in the new NHS. In: *Work-based Learning in Primary Care* (eds J. Burton & N. Jackson) pp. 13–24. Radcliffe Medical Press, Oxford.

Jackson, S. & Bircher, R. (2002) Transforming a run-down general practice into a leading edge primary care organisation with the help of the EFQM excellence model. *International Journal of Health Care Quality Assurance*, **6** (7), 255–67.

Jaques, D. & Higgins, P. (1986) *Training for Teamwork. The Report of the Thamesmead Interdisciplinary Project.* Oxford Polytechnic, Oxford.

Jarvis, P., Holford, J. & Griffin, C. (2003) *The Theory and Practice of Learning.* 2nd edn. Routledge Farmer, London.

Jenkins, G.C. & White, J. (1994) Action learning, a tool to improve interprofessional collaboration and promote change. Counsellors, general practitioners and the primary care team. *Journal of Interprofessional Care*, **8** (3), 265–73.

John Hartford Foundation (2004). Good teams just don't happen. http://wwwgitt.org (accessed 6 September 2004).

Johnson, T. (1972) *Professions and Power*. MacMillan, London.

Jones, M. & Salmon, D. (2001) The practitioner as policy analyst: a study of student reflections of an interprofessional course in higher education. *Journal of Interprofessional Care*, **15** (1), 67–77.

Jones, R.V.H. (1986) *Working Together – Learning Together. Occasional Paper 33*. Royal College of General Practitioners, London.

Jones, R.V.H. (1998) *Multidisciplinary Learning. CONCAH Workshops: Development of a Programme*. No. 4. CONCAH Publications, Sunninwell Village.

Karmi, G. (1993) Equity and health of ethnic minorities. *Quality in Health Care*, **2**, 100–103.

Kennard, J. (2002) Illuminating the relationship between shared learning and the workplace. *Medical Teacher*. **24** (4), 379–84.

Ker, J. S., Mole, L. & Bradley, P. (2003) Early introduction of interprofessional learning: a simulated ward environment. *Medical Teacher*, **37**, 248–55.

Ketola, E., Sipila, R., Makela, M. & Klockars, M. (2000) Quality improvement programme for cardiovascular disease: risk factor recording in primary care. *Quality in Health Care*, **9** (3), 175–80.

Kirkpatrick, D.L. (1967) Evaluation of training. In: *Training and Development Handbook* (eds R. Craig & L. Bittel), pp. 87–112. McGraw-Hill, New York.

Knowles, M.S. (1975) *Self-directed Learning: a Guide for Learners and Teachers*. Follett, Chicago.

Kogan, M., Henkel, M., Joss, R. & Spink, M. (1991) *Evaluation of Total Quality Management Projects in the National Health Service: First Interim Report to the Department of Health*. Centre for the Evaluation of Public Policy and Practice, Brunel University, London.

Kohn, L.T., Corrigan, J.M. & Donaldson, M.S. (2000) *To Err is Human: Building a Safer Health System*. Institute of Medicine, National Academy Press, Washington, DC.

Kolb, D. (1984) *Experiential Learning: Experiences as the Source of Learning and Development*. Prentice Hall, New Jersey.

Koppel, I. (2003) Autonomy eroded? Changing discourses in the education of health and community care professionals. Unpublished Ph.D. thesis, Institute of Education, University of London.

Krause, E.A. (1996) *Death of the Guilds: Professions, States and the Advance of Capitalism. 1930 to the Present*. Yale University Press, New Haven, Conn.

Kristjanson, L., Dudgeon, D., Nelson, F., Henteleff, P. & Balneaves, L. (1997) Evaluation of an interdisciplinary training program in palliative care: addressing the needs of rural and northern communities. *Journal of Palliative Care*, **13** (3), 5–12.

Lacey, P. (1998) Interdisciplinary training for staff working with people with profound and multiple learning disabilities. *Journal of Interprofessional Care*, **12** (1), 43–52.

Lacey, P. (2001) *Support Partnerships: Collaboration in Action*. David Fulton Publishers, London.

Lalonde, B., Uldall, K. K., Huba, G.J., *et al.* (2002) Impact of HIV/AIDS education on health care provider practice: results from nine grantees of the Special Projects of National Significance Program. *Evaluation & the Health Professions*, **25** (3), 302–320.

Larivaara, P. & Taanila, A. (2004) Towards interprofessional family oriented teamwork in primary services: the evaluation of an education programme. *Journal of Interprofessional Care*, **18** (2), 153–64.

Larson, M.S. (1977) *The Rise of Professionalism: a Sociological Analysis*. University of California Press, Berkley, Calif.

Lave, J. & Wenger, E. (1991) *Situated Learning: Legitimate Peripheral Participation*. Cambridge University Press, Cambridge.

Lawson, H. & Briar-Lawson, K. (1997) *Connecting the Dots: Integrating School Reform, School-linked Services, Parent Involvement and Community Schools*. The Danforth Foundation and The Institute for Educational Renewal at Miami University, Oxford, Ohio.

Lazarus, J. Maguire, P. Meservy, R. Lawrence, G. Ngobeni, F. & September, V. (1998) South African community partnerships: towards a model for interdisciplinary health personnel education. *Journal of Interprofessional Care*, **12** (3), 279–288.

Leathard, A. (1994) Interprofessional developments in Britain. In: *Going Interprofessional: Working Together for Health and Welfare* (ed. A. Leathard), Chapter one, pp. 3–37. Routledge, London.

Lennox, A.S., Bain, N., Taylor, R.J., McKie, L., Donnan, P.T. & Groves, J. (1998) Stages of change training for opportunistic smoking intervention by the primary health care team: part I: randomised controlled trial of the effect of training on patient smoking outcomes and health professional behaviour as recalled by patients. *Health Education Journal*, **14** (2), 140–49.

Lewin, K. (1952) *Field Theory in Social Science*. Harper and Row, New York.

Lia-Hoagberg, B., Nelson, P. & Chase, R.A. (1997) An interdisciplinary health team training program for school staff in Minnesota. *Journal of School Health*, **67**, (3), 94–7.

Lillie-Blanton, M. & Hudman, J. (2001) Untangling the web: race/ethnicity, immigration, and the nation's health. (Editorial) *American Journal of Public Health*, **91** (11), 1736–8.

Long, S. (1996) Primary health care team workshop: team members' perspectives. *Journal of Advanced Nursing*, **23** (5), 935–41.

Lucas, J. (1997) *The Politics and Economics of Multi-professional Education*. University of Bradford, Bradford.

Luecht, R., Madson, M., Taugher, M. & Petterson, J. (1990) Assessing perceptions: design and validation of an interdisciplinary education perception scale. *Journal of Allied Health*, **19**, 181–91.

McCallum, J. (1993) De-constructing family care policy for the elderly: a note. *Journal of Aging and Social Policy*, **15** (1–2), 1–5.

Macdonald, K.M. (1995) *The Sociology of the Professions*. Sage, London.

McGruder Watkins, J. & Mohr, B. (2001) *Appreciative Inquiry: Change at the Speed of Imagination*. Jossey Bass, San Francisco.

Mackay, L., Soothill, K. & Webb, C. (1995) Troubled times: the context for interprofessional collaboration. In: *Interprofessional Relations in Health Care* (eds K. Soothill, L. Mackay, & C. Webb), pp. 5–10. Edward Arnold, London.

McKinlay, J. & Arches, J. (1985) Towards the proletarianisation of physicians. *International Journal of Health Services*, **2** (15), 161–95.

McMurray, J. E., Cohen, M., Angus, G., *et al.* (2002) Women in medicine: a four-nation comparison. *Journal of American Medical Women's Association*. **57** (4), 185–90.

Madsen, M.K., Gresch, A.M., Petterson, B.J. & Taugher, M.P. (1988) An interdisciplinary clinic for neurogenically impaired adults: a pilot project for educating students. *Journal of Allied Health*, **17** (2), 135–41.

Mann, K.V., Viscount, P.W., Cogdon, A., Davidson, K., Langille, D.B. & Maccara, M.E. (1996) Multidisciplinary learning in continuing professional education: the Heart Health Nova Scotia experience. *Journal of Continuing Education in the Health Professions*, **16**, 50–60.

Marris, P. (1986) *Loss and Change*. Rev. edn. Routledge & Kegan Paul, London.

Magrab, P. Evans, P. & Hurrell, P. (1997) Integrated services for children and youth at risk: an international study of multidisciplinary training. *Journal of Interprofessional Care*, **11** (1), 99–108.

Meads, G. & Ashcroft, J. with Barr, H., Scott, R. and Wild, A. (2005) *The Case for Interprofessional Collaboration*. Blackwell Publishing, Oxford.

Meerabeau, L. & Page, S. (1999) I'm sorry if I panicked you: nurses' accounts of teamwork in cardiopulmonary resuscitation. *Journal of Interprofessional Care*. **13** (1), 29–40.

Melia, K. (1987) *Learning and Working*. Tavistock Publications, London.

Menzies, I.E.P. (1970) *The Functioning of Social Systems as a Defence Against Anxiety*. Tavistock Institute of Human Relations, London.

Miller, C., Freeman, M. & Ross, N. (2001) *Interprofessional Practice in Health and Social Care: Challenging the Shared Learning Agenda*. Arnold, London.

Milne, D.L., Keegan, D., Westerman, C. & Dudley, M. (2000) Systematic process and outcome evaluation of brief staff training in psychosocial interventions for severe mental illness. *Journal of Behavior Therapy and Experimental Psychiatry*, **31** (2), 87–101.

Mires, G., Williams, F., Harden, R. & Howie, P. (2001) The benefits of a multi-professional education programme can be sustained. *Medical Teacher*, **23** (3), 300–304.

Mohr, C., Phillips, A., Curran, J. & Rymill, A. (2002) Inter-agency training in dual disability. *Australasian Psychiatry*, **10** (4), 356–64.

Morey, J. C., Simon, R., Jay, G.D., *et al.* (2002) Error reduction and performance improvement in the emergency department through formal teamwork training: evaluation results of the MedTeams project. *Health Services Research*, **37** (6), 1553–81.

Morgan, G. (1997) *Images of Organisation*. 2nd edn. Sage, London.

Morison, S., Boohan, M., Jenkins, J. & Moutray, M. (2003) Facilitating undergraduate interprofessional learning in health care: comparing classroom and clinical learning for nursing and medical students. *Learning in Health and Social Care*, **2**, 92–104.

Nash, A. & Hoy, A. (1993) Terminal care in the community – an evaluation of residential workshops for general practitioner/district nurse teams. *Palliative Medicine*, **7** (1), 5–17.

National Health Service (2004) *Expert Patient Programme* http://www.expertpatients. nhs.uk/what.shtml (accessed 18 November 2004).

Oakland, J. (1993) *Total Quality Management*. 2nd edn. Butterworth-Heinemann, Oxford.

Oandasan, I, D'Amour, D., Zwarenstein, M., *et al.* (2004) *Interdisciplinary Education For Collaborative Patient-centred Practice*. University of Toronto, Toronto.

Obholzer, A. (1994) Managing social anxieties in public sector organisations. In: *The Unconscious at Work: Individual and Organizational Stress in the Human Services* (eds. A. Obholzer & V. Zagier Roberts), pp. 169–78. Routledge, London.

Onyett, S. (2003) *Teamworking in Mental Health*. Palgrove, Basingstoke.

Oppenheim, A.N. (1992) *Questionnaire Design, Interviewing and Attitude Measurements*. 2nd edn. Pinter, London.

Overdyk, F.J., Harvey, S.C., Fishman, R.L. & Shippey, F. (1998), Successful strategies for improving operating room efficiency at academic institutions. *Anesthesia & Analgesia*, **86**, (4), 896–906.

Øvretveit, J. (1997) How to describe interprofessional working. In: *Interprofessional Working for Health and Social Care* (eds J. Øvretveit, P. Mathias & T. Thompson), pp. 9–33. MacMillan, London.

Parsell, G., Spalding, R. & Bligh, J. (1998) Shared goals, shared learning: evaluation of a multi-professional course for undergraduate students. *Medical Education*, **32** (3), 304–311.

Peck, E., Towell, D. & Gulliver, P. (2001) The meaning of 'culture' in health and social care: a case study of the combined trust in Somerset. *Journal of Interprofessional Care*, **15** (4), 319–28.

Perkins, J. & Tryssenaar, J. (1994) Making interdisciplinary education effective for rehabilitation students. *Journal of Allied Health*, **23** (3), 133–41.

Pezzin, L.E. & Kasper, J.D. (2002) Medicaid enrolment among elderly Medicare beneficiaries: individual determinants, effects of state policy and impact on service use. *Health Services Research*, **37** (4), 827–47.

Pietroni, P.C. (1991) Stereotypes or archetypes? A study of perceptions amongst health care students. *Journal of Social Work Practice*, **5** 61–9.

Pietroni, P.C. (1992) Towards reflective practice – languages of health and social care. *Journal of Interprofessional Care*, **6** (1), 7–16.

Pilon, C.S., Leathley, M., London, R., *et al.* (1997) Practice guideline for arterial blood gas measurement in the intensive care unit decreases numbers and increases appropriateness of tests. *Critical Care Medicine.* **25** (8), 1308–13.

Pirrie, A., Wilson, V., Harden, R. & Elsegood, J. (1998) AMEE Guide No. 12: Multi-professional education: part II. promoting cohesive practice in health care. *Medical Teacher*, **20**, 409–16.

Pirrie, A., Hamilton, S. & Wilson, V. (1999) Multidisciplinary education: some issues and concerns. *Educational Research*, **41** (3), 301–14.

Ponzer, S., Hylin, U., Kusoffsky, A., Lonka, K., Mattiasson, A.-C. & Nordström, G. (2004) Interprofessional training in the context of clinical practice: goals and students' perceptions on clinical education wards. *Medical Education*, **38**, 727–36.

Porter, S. (1995) *Nursing's Relationship with Medicine*. Avebury, Aldershot.

President's Advisory Commission on Consumer Protection and Quality in the Health Care Industry (1998) *Quality First: Better Health Care for all Americans: Final Report to the President of the United States*. US Government Printing Office, Washington, DC.

Price, J., Ekleberry, A., Grover, A., *et al.* (1999) Evaluation of clinical practice guidelines on outcome of infection in patients in the surgical intensive care unit. *Critical Care Medicine*, **27** (10), 2118–24.

Quality Assurance Agency (2004) *A Draft Statement of Common Purpose for Subject Benchmarks for Health and Social Care Professions: Consultation*. The Quality Assurance Agency for Higher Education, Bristol.

Queen Mary University of London (2004) Medicine for Graduates. http://www.mds.qmul.ac.uk/courses/gep.shtml (accessed 19 July 2004).

Reason, P. (1994) *Participation in Human Inquiry*. Sage, London.

Reeves, S. (2000) Community-based interprofessional education for medical, nursing and dental students. *Health and Social Care in the Community*, **8** (4), 269–76.

Reeves, S. (2001) A review of the effects of interprofessional education on staff involved in the care of adults with mental health problems. *Journal of Psychiatric and Mental Health Nursing*, **8**, 533–42.

Reeves, S. (2005) Developing and delivering practice-based interprofessional education: successes and challenges. Unpublished Ph.D. thesis. City University, London.

Reeves, S. & Freeth, D. (2002) The London training ward: an innovative interprofessional learning initiative. *Journal of Interprofessional Care*, **16** (1), 41–52.

Reeves, S., Koppel, I., Barr, H., Freeth, D., & Hammick, M. (2002) Twelve tips for undertaking a systematic review. *Medical Teacher*, **24**, 358–63.

Reeves, S. & Lewin, S. (2004) Interprofessional collaboration in the hospital: strategies and meanings. *Journal of Health Service Research Policy*, **9** (4), 218–25.

Richardson, B. & Cooper, N. (2003) Developing a virtual interdisciplinary research community in higher education. *Journal of Interprofessional Care*, **17**, 173–82.

Roberts, C., Howe, A., Winterburn, S. & Fox, N. (2000) Not so easy as it sounds: a qualitative study of a shared learning project between medical and nursing undergraduate students. *Medical Teacher*, **22** (4), 386–7.

Rost, K., Nutting, P.A., Smith, J. & Werner, J.J. (2000) Designing and implementing a primary care intervention trial to improve the quality and outcome of care for major depression. *General Hospital Psychiatry*, **22** (2), 66–77.

Rowley, D. & Welsh, H. (1994) *Passport: Forging Creative Partnerships in Community Care*. Scottish Council for Voluntary Organisations, Edinburgh.

Royal College of Physicians of London (1995) *Setting Priorities in the NHS. A Framework for Decision-making*. The Royal College of Physicians of London, London.

Rubenstein, L.V., Parker, L.E., Meredith, L.S., *et al*. (2002) Understanding team-based quality improvement for depression in primary care. *Health Services Research*, **37** (4), 1009–1029.

Sasou, K. & Reason, J. (1999) Team errors: definition and taxonomy. *Reliability Engineering and System Safety*, **65**, 1–9.

Scally, G. & Donaldson, L.J. (1998) The NHS's 50th anniversary. Clinical governance and the drive for quality improvement in the new NHS in England. *British Medical Journal*, **317** (7150), 61–5.

Schön, D.A. (1983) *The Reflective Practitioner: How Professionals Think in Action*. Basic Books, New York.

Schön, D.A. (1987) *Educating the Reflective Practitioner*. Jossey-Bass, San Francisco.

Schön, D.A., (1991) Introduction. In: *The Reflective Turn: Case Studies in and on Educational Practice* (ed. D.A. Schön) pp. 1–12. Teachers College Press, Teachers College, Columbia University, New York.

Schreiber, M.A., Holcomb, J.B., Conaway, C.W., Campbell, K.D., Wall, M., & Mattox, K.L. (2002) Military trauma training performed in a civilian trauma center. *Journal of Surgical Research*, **104** (1), 8–14.

Seifer, S. & Kauper-Brown, J. (2004) Community-based participatory research 1. *Journal of Interprofessional Care*, **18** (4), 345–6.

Senge, P.M. (1990) *The Fifth Discipline: the Art and Practice of the Learning Organisation*. 1st edn. Doubleday/Currency, New York, NY.

Shafer, M. A., Tebb, K. P., Pantell, R. H., *et al*. (2002) Effect of a clinical practice improvement intervention on chlamydial screening among adolescent girls. *Journal of American Medical Association*, **288** (22), 2846–52.

Shakespeare, H., Tucker, W. & Northover, J. (1989) *Report of a National Survey on Interprofessional Education in Primary Health Care*. NHS Executive Personnel Development Division, London.

Shakespeare, R. (1997) *Multi-professional Education and Training*. King's Fund, London.

Sheffield Combined Universities Interprofessional Learning Unit (2004) *Interprofessional Capability Framework: a Working Document*. University of Sheffield and Sheffield Hallam University, Sheffield.

Sicher, P., Lewis, O., Sargeant, J., *et al*. (2000) Developing child abuse prevention, identification, and treatment systems in Eastern Europe. *Journal of the American Academy of Child & Adolescent Psychiatry*, **39**(5, May), 660–67.

Siegler, E.L., Hyer, K., Fulmer, T. & Mezey, M. (eds) (1998) *Geriatric Interdisciplinary Team Training*. Springer Publishing Company, New York.

Sinclair, S. (1997) *Making Doctors: an Institutional Apprenticeship*. Berg, Oxford.

Slack, M.K., Cummings, D.M., Borrego, M.E., Fuller, K. & Cook, S. (2002) Strategies used by interdisciplinary rural health training programs to assure community responsiveness and recruit practitioners. *Journal of Interprofessional Care*, (2), 129–38.

Solberg, L.I., Kottke, T.E., & Brekke, M.L. (1998) Will primary care clinics organise themselves to improve the delivery of preventive services? A randomised controlled trial. *Preventive Medicine*, **27** (4), 623–31.

Spears, R., Oakes, P., Ellemers, N. & Haslam, A. (1997) *The Social Psychology of Stereotyping and Group Life*. Blackwell Publishers, Oxford.

Spratley, J. (1989) *Disease Prevention and Health Promotion in Primary Health Care*. Health Education Authority, London.

Spratley, J. & Pietroni, M. (1994) *Creative Collaboration: Interprofessional Learning Priorities in Primary Health and Community Care*. Marylebone Centre Trust, London.

Stanford, R. & Yelloly, M. with Loughlin, B., Rolph, K., Talbot, M. & Trowell, J. (1994) *Shared Learning in Child Protection*. English National Board for Nursing, Midwifery and Health Visiting, London.

Stanford University School of Medicine (2004) Patient Education. http://patienteducation.stanford.edu (accessed 18 November 2004).

Stein, J. & Brown, H. (1995) 'All in this together'. an evaluation of joint training on the abuse of adults with learning disabilities. *Health & Social Care in the Community*, **3** (4), 205–14.

Stokes, J. (1994) The unconscious at work in groups and teams: contributions from the work of Wilfred Bion. In: *The Unconscious at Work* (eds A. Obholzer & V. Zagier Roberts), pp. 19–27. Routledge, London.

Stone, J., Haas, B., Harmer-Beem, M. & Baker, D. (2004) Utilisation of research methodology in designing and developing an interdisciplinary course in ethics. *Journal of Interprofessional Care*, **18** (1), 57–62.

Storrie, J. (1992) Mastering interprofessionalism – an enquiry into development of Master's programmes with an interprofessional focus. *Journal of Interprofessional Care*, **6**, 253–9.

Strasser, R. (1995) Innovative interactive multidisciplinary workshops. *Australian Journal of Rural Health*, **3**, 56–61.

Strauss, A. (1978) *Negotiations: Varieties, Contexts, Processes and Social Order*. Jossey-Bass, San Francisco.

Sullivan, T.J. (ed.) (1998) *Collaboration: a Health Care Imperative*. McGraw-Hill, New York.

Svensson, R. (1996) The interplay between doctors and nurses – a negotiated order perspective. *Sociology of Health and Illness*, **18**, 379–98.

Swieringa, J. & Wierdsma, A. (1992) *Becoming a Learning Organisation: Beyond the Learning Curve*. Addison-Wesley, Wokingham.

Szasz, G. (1969) Interprofessional education in the health sciences. *Millbank Memorial Fund Quarterly*. **47**, 449–75.

Tajfel, H. & Turner, J.C. (1986) The social identity theory of inter-group behavior. In: *Psychology of Intergroup Relations* (eds S. Worchel & L. W. Austin), pp. 7–24. Nelson Hall, Chicago.

Taylor, J., Blue, I. & Misan, G. (2001) Approach to sustainable primary health care service delivery for rural and remote South Australia. *Australian Journal of Rural Health*, **9** (6), 304–310.

Tepper, M.S. (1997) Providing comprehensive sexual health care in spinal cord injury rehabilitation: implementation and evaluation of a new curriculum for health care professionals. *Sexuality & Disability*, **15** (3), 131–65.

Thompson, C., Kinmonth, A., Stevens, L., *et al.* (2000) Effects of a clinical-practice guideline and practice-based education on detection and outcome of depression in primary care: Hampshire Depression Project randomised controlled trial. *Lancet*, **355** (9199), 185–91.

Tope, R. (1996) *Integrated Interdisciplinary Learning Between Health and Social Care Professions: a Feasibility Study*. Avebury, Aldershot.

Townes, C. Petit, B. & Young, B. (1995) Implementing total quality management in an academic surgery setting: lessons learned. *Swiss Surgery*, **1** (1), 15–23.

Treadwell, M.J., Franck, L.S. & Vichinsky, E. (2002) Using quality improvement strategies to enhance pediatric pain assessment. *International Journal for Quality in Health Care*, **14** (1), 39–47.

Trowell, J. (1994) Working together in child protection: some issues for multidisciplinary training from a psychodynamic perspective. In: *Learning and Teaching in Social Work* (eds M. Yelloly & M. Henkel), pp. 189–200. Jessica Kingsley, London.

Tucker, S., Strange, C., Cordeaux. C., Moules, T. & Torrance, N. (1999) Developing an interdisciplinary framework for the education and training of those working with children and young people. *Journal of Interprofessional Care*, **13** (3), 261–70.

Tuckman, B.W. (1965) Developmental sequence in small groups. *Psychological Bulletin*, **63**, 384–99.

Tuckman, B.W. & Jensen, M.A.C. (1977) Stages of small group development. *Group and Organisational Studies*, (2), 419–27.

Turner, J. (1999) Some current issues in research on social identity and self-categorisation theories. In: *Social Identity* (eds N. Ellemers, R. Spears & B. Doosjie), pp. 6–64. Blackwell Publishers, Oxford.

Turner, P., Sheldon, F., Coles, C., *et al.* (2000) Listening to and learning from the family carer's story: an innovative approach in interprofessional education. *Journal of Interprofessional Care*, (4), 387–95.

United Kingdom Central Council for Nursing, Midwifery and Health Visiting (2001) *Identification of Common Principles in Health Related Professional Codes/Standards – Discussion Paper*. United Kingdom Central Council for Nursing, Midwifery and Health Visiting, London.

United Nations (1948) *Universal Declaration of Human Rights, GA, res. 217A (III), UN Doc A/ 810 at 71 (1948)*. United Nations, New York.

Universities of Southampton and Portsmouth (2004) Common learning. http://www.commonlearning.net (accessed 6 September 2004).

University of Westminster (2004) Interplan. http://www.wmin.ac.uk/sih/page-86 (and 212 and 217) (accessed 3 November 2004).

University of York (2004) personal communication.

Usher, R. & Bryant, I. (1989) *Adult Education as Theory, Practice and Resarch*. Routledge, London.

Van Dijk, T.A., (1997) The Study of Discourse. In: *Discourses as Structure and Process* (ed. T.A. van Dijk), pp. 1–34. Sage, London.

van Staa, A., Visser, A. & van Der, Z. (2000) Caring for caregivers: experiences and evaluation of interventions for a palliative care team. *Patient Education & Counseling*, **41** (1), 93–105.

von Bertalanffy, L. (1971) *General Systems Theory*. The Penguin Press, London, Allen Lane.

Vigotsky, L.S. (1978) *Mind in Society: the Development of Higher Psychological Processes.* Harvard University Press, Cambridge, Mass.

Vroman, K. & Kovacich, J. (2002) Computer-mediated interdisciplinary teams: theory and reality. *Journal of Interprofessional Care*, **16** (2), 159–170.

Wahlström, O. & Sandén, I. (1998) Multi-professional training ward at Linköping University: early experiences. *Education for Health*, **11** (2), 225–31.

Wahlström, O., Sandén, I. & Hammar, M. (1996) The student ward at the University Hospital, Faculty of Health Sciences, Linköping, Sweden. *European Nurse*, **1**, 262–8.

Wahlström, O., Sandén, I. & Hammar, M. (1997) Multi-professional education in the medical curriculum. *Medical Education*, **31** (6), 425–9.

Wakefield, A., Cooke, S. & Boggis, C. (2003) Learning together: use of simulated patients with nursing and medical students for breaking bad news. *International Journal of Palliative Nursing*, **9** (1), 32–8.

Walby, S., Greenwell, J., Mackay, L. & Soothill, K. (1994) *Medicine and Nursing: Professions in a Changing Health Service.* Sage, London.

Wall, A. (1995) Ethical and resource issues in health and social care. In: *Interprofessional Issues in Community and Primary Health Care* (eds. P. Owens, J. Carrier, & J. Horder), pp. 57–70. Macmillan, London.

Walsh, P.L., Garbs, C.A., Goodwin, M. & Wolff, E.M. (1995) An impact evaluation of a VA geriatric team development program. *Gerontology and Geriatrics Education*, **15**, 19–35.

Way, B., Stone, B., Schwager, M., Wagoner, D. & Bassman, R. (2002) Effectiveness of the New York State Office of Mental Health Core Curriculum: direct care staff training. *Psychiatric Rehabilitation Journal*, **25** (4), 398–402.

Wee, B. (1997) *Working Together and Learning Together: a Collaborative Project. Final Report.* Countess Mountbatten House and Moorgreen Hospital, Southampton.

West, M.A. (1996) Reflexivity and work group effectiveness: a conceptual integration. In: *Handbook of Work and Group Psychology* (ed. M. A. West) pp. 555–79. Wiley, Chichester.

West, M.A. & Pillinger, T. (1996) *Teambuilding in Primary Health Care: an Evaluation.* Health Education Authority, London.

West, M.A. & Poulton, B.C. (1993) Effective multidisciplinary teamwork in primary health care. *Journal of Advanced Nursing*, **18**, 918–25.

West, M.A. & Slater, J. (1996) *Teamworking in Primary Health Care: a Review of its Effectiveness.* Health Education Authority, London.

Whittington, C. (2003) A model of collaboration. In: *Collaboration in Social Work Practice* (eds J. Weinstein, C. Whittington & T. Leiba), Chapter two, pp. 39–62. Jessica Kingsley Publishers, London.

WHO (1973) *Training and Preparation of Teachers for Schools of Medicine and Allied Health Sciences.* Technical Report Series No. 521. World Health Organization Geneva.

WHO (1978a) *Personnel for Health Care: Case Studies of Educational Programmes.* Public Health Papers Vol. 1, No 70. World Health Organization, Geneva.

WHO (1978b) *Guidelines for Evaluating a Training Programme for Health Personnel.* World Health Organization, Geneva.

WHO (1988) *Learning Together to Work Together.* World Health Organization, Geneva.

WHO (1998) *Health for all in the Twenty-first Century.* World Health Organization, Geneva.

WHO (1999) *Poverty and Health*, World Health Organization, Geneva.

WHO (2000) *Millennium Development Goals (MDGs).* http://www.who.int/mdg/en/ (accessed 9 December 2004).

WHO (2003) *Social Mobilisation for Health Promotion*, WPRO Nonserial Publication edn, World Health Organization, Geneva.

Wickes, D. (1998) *Nurses and Doctors at Work: Rethinking Professional Boundaries.* Open University Press, Milton Keynes.

Wilcock, P.M. & Headrick, L.A. (2000) Interprofessional learning for the improvement of health care: why bother? (Editorial) *Journal of Interprofessional Care*, **14** (2), 111–7.

Wilcock, P., Campion-Smith, C. & Elston, S. (2003) *Practice Professional Development Planning: a Guide for Primary Care.* Radcliffe Medical, Abingdon.

Wilmot, S. (1995) Professional values and interprofessional dialogue. *Journal of Interprofessional Care*, **9** (3), 257–66.

Wistow, G., Knapp, M., Hardy, B. & Allen, C. (1994) Community care: markets and enabling. In: *Social Care in Mixed Economy* (eds G. Wistow *et al.*), pp. 14–30. Open University Press, Buckingham.

Zwarenstein, M., Atkins, J., Hammick, M., Barr, H., Koppel, I., & Reeves, S. (1999) Interprofessional education and systematic review: a new initiative in evaluation. *Journal of Interprofessional Care*, **13** (4), 417–24.

Zwarenstein, M., Reeves, S., Barr, H., Hammick, M., Koppel, I. & Atkins, J. (2001) *Interprofessional Education: Effects on Professional Practice and Health Care Outcomes* (Cochrane Review). In: The Cochrane Library, Issue 2. Update Software, Oxford.

SCHOOL OF HEALTH & SOCIAL CARE
Library
- 8 AUG 2008
Arrowe Park Site
UNIVERSITY OF CHESTER

Index